JUST A BIT MUCH

Overachieving, People-Pleasing, and Going to Therapy (to Say I Did)

MARIAH SCRIVENS

Published by Sprinkle Toast Press: www.sprinkletoast.com

To request permissions, contact the author at
mariah@mariahscrivens.com

For speaking opportunities and coaching inquiries,
visit www.mariahscrivens.com

Paperback ISBN: 9781-997775256
Hardcover ISBN: 9781997775249
EPUB: 9781997775232

Cover design by **Mariah Scrivens**
Author brand photography by **Alana Winchester Photography**

First edition, September 2025

ADHD memoir; late ADHD diagnosis; late diagnosed ADHD in women; burnout memoir for women; motherhood and mental health memoir; funny memoir about burnout; women entrepreneurs; women in business memoir; friendship breakup memoir; teacher burnout memoir; people pleasing memoir; perfectionism memoir; overachiever burnout memoir; millennial women nonfiction

— From the Readers —

Just a Few Love Notes

"Raw, honest, and deeply relatable... **you'll feel seen in these pages.** Reading it feels like catching up with an old friend. It's comforting, binge-worthy and impossible to put down."

Mandy Lee, Business Coach and Teacher Author

"As someone who has wrestled with a lifelong inner critic, burnout, and complicated friendships... *Just a Bit Much* is **achingly funny, raw, and honest**. It's the kind of book that makes you feel less alone in the mess, and more hopeful about what comes after."

Amy Hanneke, Copywriter and SEO Expert

"*Just a Bit Much* is a heartfelt memoir that explores the journey of self-discovery amidst life's chaos... With authentic humour and honesty, Mariah shares her struggles with overachievement, identity, and reinvention. It's **a powerful read.**"

Ellie Laliberté, Award Winning Author of
Letters From You to You and Self-Awareness Coach

"I couldn't stop reading! It's real. It's relatable... **the book I didn't know I needed.** Thank you for showing that life is more than what we see online."

Kaitlyn Reid, Core French Teacher, Mentor and Curriculum Creator

"Mariah's energy is infectious and inspiring... *Just a Bit Much* made me laugh, but mostly **it made me feel seen**... You won't want to put it down."

Jamie, Spring Fling founder and "Boring Business" Coach

"As a formerly undiagnosed ADHD girly, reading Mariah's words felt like someone finally put words to what I've carried my whole life... She reminds us there's nothing 'wrong' with us, that we're not broken, and that we can move forward with compassion. **This book is a gift.**"

Jessie Burke-Trebell, Elevate Learning Co-Founder

1995

*To every young girl who was
undiagnosed and overwhelmed.*

You're not too much.

— From the Author —

Just a Quick Note

Writing a book is hard.

It was a lot more time in therapy processing my "core wounds" and a lot less cute Starbucks dates than I anticipated. While I wrote, the stories I shared changed and the people I shared about flowed. I started to feel pressure – how could I include every single person who impacted my life? It was hard to accept that I simply couldn't. It was also hard to accept that ending a book doesn't mean ending the story. So yes, there is a tidy ending to this memoir, but that doesn't mean my life is tidy. I'm still learning, making mistakes and showing up every day trying my best. That's life after writing a book – that's life in general.

Some names and identifying details have been changed in consideration for those included in this work of personal nonfiction – a collection of raw thoughts, memories, and reflections. I've done my best to be as honest and accurate as possible, while also writing with care. It's not meant to villainize anyone or paint a version of history that flatters me – just to tell the truth of how it felt.

There are always two stories. This one's mine.

Please refer to the back of the book for a full list of content and trigger warnings.

You know you love me,

xoxo

Gossip Girl / Mariah Scrivens

Ps. Gift giving is my (very expensive) love language. So, I gotcha something to make you love me.

Kidding. Sort of. I *did get* something - the e-book version of this book - but it's definitely *not* a bribe. Okay? Cool. Scan this and I'll send it to you:

PPs. In the great words of icon and legend Lizzie McGuire, "You rock. Don't ever change."

— Contents —
Just a Few Chapters

1	Google History: What's it called when	1
2	Roaming Charges	3
3	Teacher's Pet	14
4	"I thought you were better than this"	20
5	Google History: Why do I	30
6	No Skulls	32
7	Holding On	47
8	Google History: Why am I	55
9	The Moment I Knew	57
10	Unedited: Email Chain	62
11	High Highs, Low Lows	68
12	Google History: How do I stop	78
13	*Thriving*	80
14	Coconut	93
15	"I think you should kiss me"	100
16	Core Wounds	110
17	The Blue Couch	121
18	Google History: How come I	128
19	"Is she in love with you or something?"	130
20	Google History: Why does he	138
21	Unedited: Instagram Isolation	139

22 Coconut Shrimp ⋯⋯⋯⋯⋯⋯⋯⋯⋯⋯⋯⋯ 141

23 Mirror, Mirror ⋯⋯⋯⋯⋯⋯⋯⋯⋯⋯⋯⋯ 145

24 The Accident ⋯⋯⋯⋯⋯⋯⋯⋯⋯⋯⋯⋯⋯ 149

25 Taken ⋯⋯⋯⋯⋯⋯⋯⋯⋯⋯⋯⋯⋯⋯⋯⋯ 159

26 Unedited: FOB Speech ⋯⋯⋯⋯⋯⋯⋯⋯ 166

27 Blocked ⋯⋯⋯⋯⋯⋯⋯⋯⋯⋯⋯⋯⋯⋯⋯ 169

28 Unedited: The Cringiest Email ⋯⋯⋯⋯ 179

29 Nothing to lose. ⋯⋯⋯⋯⋯⋯⋯⋯⋯⋯⋯ 181

30 I love you, I'm sorry. ⋯⋯⋯⋯⋯⋯⋯⋯⋯ 185

31 Unedited: Trauma Dump ⋯⋯⋯⋯⋯⋯⋯ 194

32 Baby Boy ⋯⋯⋯⋯⋯⋯⋯⋯⋯⋯⋯⋯⋯⋯ 199

33 Google History: I'm scared I ⋯⋯⋯⋯⋯ 207

34 Go Get your Daughter ⋯⋯⋯⋯⋯⋯⋯⋯ 209

35 Not a Coach ⋯⋯⋯⋯⋯⋯⋯⋯⋯⋯⋯⋯⋯ 219

36 Unedited: Jealous of Teachergram? ⋯⋯ 228

37 Unedited: Intention vs. Impact ⋯⋯⋯⋯ 231

38 Rebrand ⋯⋯⋯⋯⋯⋯⋯⋯⋯⋯⋯⋯⋯⋯ 239

39 Unedited: Public Breakdown ⋯⋯⋯⋯⋯ 246

40 Get Home Now ⋯⋯⋯⋯⋯⋯⋯⋯⋯⋯⋯ 249

41 Unedited: The Goodbye Post ⋯⋯⋯⋯⋯ 254

42 Justin and Selena ⋯⋯⋯⋯⋯⋯⋯⋯⋯⋯ 257

43 Orange Power Suit ⋯⋯⋯⋯⋯⋯⋯⋯⋯⋯ 268

44 Google History: is ADHD ⋯⋯⋯⋯⋯⋯ 270

45 Permission Slip ⋯⋯⋯⋯⋯⋯⋯⋯⋯⋯⋯ 272

46 You're Not a Bad Person ⋯⋯⋯⋯⋯⋯⋯ 279

Epilogue 282

Appendix A 287

Appendix B 289

Thank You 291

Thank You (Again) 293

About the Author 294

Coaching Amy

— Foreword —

By Amy Maan

Founder of 123 Petits Pas Inc.

When Mariah told me she was writing a book, I knew it would be honest...that's just who Mariah is. But as a friend watching her bring these pages to life, I also saw how deeply healing it was. Not just for her to write, but for anyone reading. If you're a woman navigating business, motherhood, or identity, you'll find yourself in these pages.

This isn't a highlight reel. It's not a memoir with neat edges or perfect takeaways. It's raw, real, and unfiltered in the way that only someone who has lived through the breaking and rebuilding can write. And it's a gift to every woman who's ever felt like they were "too much" or not enough — or somehow both at once.

We met in teacher's college. Mariah was a big presence, and I remember admiring how naturally she took up space in a room. She came across so positive, ambitious, and completely unafraid to lead with passion. I wasn't the loud one – I never have been – but Mariah's energy never felt overpowering. It felt like permission. Her voice made room for others.

Back then, we were two high-capacity women trying to check all the right boxes. We overachieved, overextended, and did our best to be what we thought we had to be – especially as women in helping professions. Life eventually pulled us in different directions, but when we reconnected years later, something clicked instantly. We had both changed careers, become mothers, started businesses – but more than that, we had both walked through hard things that forced us to reimagine who we were becoming.

Mariah is the kind of friend who makes you an action plan when you're stuck. As a cheerleader, she's unmatched. And as a business coach? She goes all in. She's the one who'll help you get loud when you need to – even if you're someone like me, who's naturally more of a listener. That balance, that fire and steadiness, is part of what makes her so powerful to learn from.

I'm honoured to be part of Mariah's story. Our friendship holds a quiet kind of strength that I'll always be thankful for. We've supported each other through shifting relationships and the kind of emails that remind you that some people forget there's a real human behind every small business. We're two women juggling a lot: building something meaningful while trying to stay present for our kids. That pull between ambition and motherhood is something so many of us carry quietly. This book doesn't just name these experiences, it takes your hand and walks alongside you through them.

Just a Bit Much doesn't try to tie life up with a bow. It's nonlinear, full of real grief, real joy, and real growth. You'll find yourself in it – especially if you're someone who's ever had to rebuild in silence, or pick yourself up while still trying to be "fine."

Mariah didn't become someone new. She became more herself. And in doing that, she gives the rest of us permission to stop performing and start belonging – to ourselves, first.

Keep reading. You're in for something real.

Amy Maan

JUST
A BIT
MUCH

Apparently picking an inspiring quote that sets the tone for the book is recommended by 9/10 dentists. Something that the reader will resonate with and establish a little author kinship.

"I cry a lot but I am so productive. *It's an art.*"

TAYLOR SWIFT
I CAN DO IT WITH A BROKEN HEART

– CHAPTER 1 –

Google History:
What's it called when

> Q What's it called when I forget my keys but remember every dumb thing I've said since 2004?

Negative Self-Talk

Negative self-talk refers to the internal dialogue that focuses on self-criticism, doubt, and perceived failures. In individuals with ADHD, this pattern can be amplified by a lifetime of feedback that highlights mistakes, forgetfulness, or inconsistency. Over time, these messages can become internalized, leading to an "inner critic" that anticipates failure, downplays success, and interprets neutral situations as personal shortcomings. This internal narrative can significantly impact self-esteem, decision-making, and emotional regulation.[1,2]

Q What's it called when you sit on your bed after a shower in your towel, scrolling your phone?

Executive Dysfunction

A neurological symptom common in ADHD and other conditions, executive dysfunction refers to difficulties with initiating, organizing, sequencing, and completing tasks. It can affect planning, time management, working memory, and the ability to shift between tasks. Individuals may know what needs to be done and even want to do it, yet experience a mental block that prevents action.[3-5]

the day of the call

– CHAPTER 2 –

Roaming Charges

The text hit like a slap. I was in Arizona, sweating through my swimsuit, and sabotaging my entire career before it even started.

I knew I shouldn't have left. I knew this was going to happen. My inner mean girl was having a field day.

Inner mean girl: Well. That's what you get. You're selfish.

She was ruthless. She was me... but also, not. Confusing, but bear with me. Listen, I knew she wasn't real (or even right), but damn she was loud. And it was hard to ignore "loud." My inner mean girl got her unwavering confidence from years of girl drama, passive-aggressive eye rolls, and being called rude or way too sensitive.

She had an arsenal of zingers, all lifted from the comments people probably don't remember making like, "You always do this."

To me, they felt like a Sims Plumbob that exposed all my faults for everyone to see...and judge. And yeah, I had to Google what the green floating diamond above the Sims are called for this book. Are you already learning things from me? Look at us go.

Okay back to *her*.

She hadn't always been so overbearing, but back then her voice was everywhere. Look, I know it's early to be introducing a whole fictional frenemy. But trust me, she sticks around. And if you *can't* relate to this fictional frenemy in your brain? I'm jealous. Truly. But if you're reading this, I'm willing to bet you have an inner mean girl too. Your own worst critic. The voice in your head that tells you you're too fat, too old, too dumb, too slow, too late... too much (see what I did there?).

So yeah, my inner mean girl is going to show up time and time again in this book because that's how she shows up in my brain. Welcome. She's a bitch. We hate her.

Okay, back to the story about how I got a phone call that made me question all my life choices up to that point. I looked down at my phone in disbelief. The weight of it suddenly felt more like a brick than an iPhone. The same SMS came through every time I turned it off airplane mode:

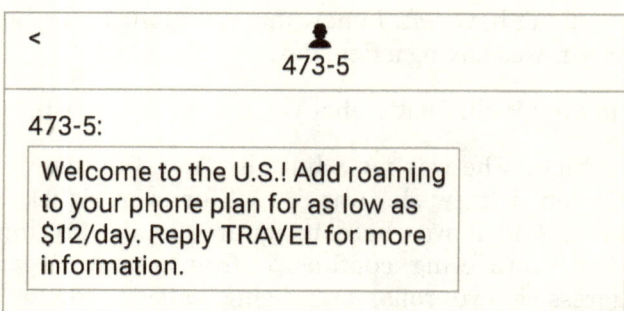

Racking up daily roaming charges just so I could be rejected from miles away. Loved that for me.

I pressed my forehead against the windowpane, felt the warm glass, and got distracted for a moment. Even the glass was warm there. I hadn't felt cold since stepping out of the air-conditioned plane a few days earlier.

That short, long-distance conversation left me ridiculously sweaty, and my chest was tight. Butterflies pounded in my stomach. Apparently their wings were made of concrete. I just wanted to jump in the pool and cool off. Instead, I tapped the blue and white envelope in the top left corner of my screen and wrote a frantic, but hopefully still professionally coded, email to the union.

New Message

August 29, 2016

To: Union Rep
From: Mariah S

Subject: Interview process

To whom it may concern,

I was called and offered an interview for an LTO this morning. Due to the information provided in the job postings that there would be no interviews for French or English jobs I booked a trip to Arizona. I am currently in the United States and unable to attend the interview tomorrow. I was told Skype interviews aren't permitted but I am hoping that an exception can be made as I am very interested in this position and believe I am an excellent match for it.

Thank you,

Mariah S
EIN: 5193875

To summarize: I got rejected and responded with a 12-paragraph thesis reeking of desperation.

I sat on the bed in silence, the muscles in my calves firing – clench, release, clench, release – as if I could burn off the static in my head through my legs if I just squeezed fast enough. Why had I decided to take a vacation? Why hadn't I waited at home for that call? I knew I should have stayed home. I'd told my mom it was a bad idea.

Ding

Ding

Two new emails hit my inbox and I scanned the previews quickly so I could either avoid them for four to six business days (bad news) or open them right away (good news).

^ Unread	
Union Rep	**Re: Interview Process** - Hi Mariah, we have fo..
Jess	**Interview tomorrow** - Hi, we are set to meet to..

Omg. omg. Omg. omg. Okay. Ah. Be cool.

I had an interview for a full-time teaching position. The news felt too big to keep inside: I had to tell everyone. Nothing ever seemed real until I told as many people as possible. Buzzing, I typed a quick message to my parents and brother and tapped the arrow. Satisfied by the *whoosh*, I swiped back to my inbox, but my hands started shaking, the initial excitement suddenly replaced by fear.

What chance did I have after being the girl who had called the union?

Inner mean girl: Literally zero, narc.

I found the staff directory, scanned the list and felt my stomach lurch. My thoughts got jumbled – wait, what?

Vice-Principal: Stephanie Bianchi.

Stephanie was a family friend. Like, "learned to drive stick in her car" family friend. My dad was best friends with her husband. She was the very person I had asked about canceling my vacation in case I got an interview, and her response was why I booked myself on the flight to visit my friend.

"You can't put your life on hold because you might get an interview. If they want you, they'll make it work."

Okay, calling the union? Minus one point. Knowing the VP? Plus five.

Things were starting to look a little better for me. I exhaled slowly. Maybe all *wasn't* lost.

I spent the day prepping for the interview and trying to pick out a presentable outfit to wear from my suitcase of vacation clothes. I was nervous, excited, and wanted to skip ahead so I could just get the whole thing over with.

That night, I lay in the unfamiliar bed, ceiling fan spinning circles above me, unable to sleep. I glanced at the clock: 2am. Another hour had passed. I wiggled each finger as I counted – eight hours to go. I sucked at sleeping in new places on a good night, let alone with a life-altering interview looming over me. I couldn't get my brain to shut up. At 4am, I gave up and opened *Bumble*, a dating app, on my phone.

I hated online dating. It was so boring to have the same conversation over and over with strangers who I'd never end up with anyways. But, as much as I hated it, I hated the idea of dying alone even more. Online dating was my best bet.

Talking to guys at the gym? Terrifying. Lingering eye contact at run club? Not working. Getting introduced by someone? Yeah, right. All my friends were already dating, and all their friends were already dating, too.

I swiped through the profiles as they popped up, eyebrows furrowing – there were certainly a lot more guys in cowboy hats than I remembered from my last swipe-a-thon. I paused on one profile and noticed the distance away from me was in miles. Oh. Duh. It was showing me guys near me. In Arizona.

I shut down the app and went back to counting backwards from 100.

No way I'd move for a guy.

*° +*₀ °*

I walked up the long path to the front door of the brick building and noticed the blue paint was starting to chip off. As I peered through the double-paned glass window in the middle of the door, I rang the doorbell of the school and tried to keep up with my racing thoughts.

What would my classroom be like? Which teachers would I eat lunch with? What would I wear on the first day of school? Would there be a cute, single guy teaching Grade Four, just waiting for a girl like me to magically show up down the hall so he could sweep me off my feet?

Inner mean girl: I can't.

Click

The door unlocked and I pulled it toward me, coming face-to-face with a tiny woman who was marching briskly on the spot. She was standing in the hallway, arms and legs pumping up and down, waiting for me.

"Hi. Are you Mariah? I'm Jess. Don't mind me. I need to get 10,000 steps by the end of the day."

What in the alternate universe was going on here? Okay, be cool. I forced a smile and followed her into the room directly beside the main entrance. She was still marching on the spot as I looked around.

The room, presumably her office, was small, tidy, and stuffed. Opposite the door was a big window overlooking the front entrance and kitty-corner to that was a floor-to-ceiling bookshelf. Every inch of the window ledge and shelf was filled with books and memorabilia shoved wherever it could fit. It was like a 90's Hallmark showroom for the "world's best teacher" line.

I perched on the little black couch in front of the window, trying not to knock the plants and cards behind me, and smoothed my shirt down, tucking my hair behind my ear and alternating between crossing and uncrossing my legs. I crossed them again. I needed to stop. Stop fidgeting. Stop thinking about sweating. Stop looking at the embroidered pillow across the room that said something about coffee and tiny humans.

Jess was talking a mile a minute, and I tried to zero in on everything she was saying instead of playing I Spy. She told me about the school, my new role, and what to expect during the first few days. I was getting a little overwhelmed when Stephanie walked in. Her big smile helped, and I felt my body settle, just a little.

Her smile comforted me and I pushed down the mean girl thoughts that were trying to creep in about her being the only reason I had gotten this job.

No. I crushed the interview. I was good. I deserved this job. And yeah, Stephanie knew me, but that was just a bonus. Right?

A few minutes later, Jess finished telling me about bell times and Stephanie walked with me down the long hallway. She turned right, then left, then another left. Or was it right? Maybe a right first, then the left? I had a horrible sense of direction, and knew I was going to have a hard time remembering all the different rooms I'd be teaching in.

As expected, I *was* teaching kindergarten half the day. The other half had me bouncing forty minutes here and an hour there, teaching French to all grade levels, booking it from one end of the H-shaped building to the other and hoping I wasn't headed in the wrong direction while trying not to cry when the Grade Six class refused to speak French, again.

Jess's step counter would have *loved* my schedule.

Eventually, I figured out the floorplan of the school, and I was only moderately embarrassed when I burst into the room a minute or two late for those first few weeks. FYI, there was indeed one guy who taught at the school. But don't get excited – he was older than my dad and married. Teaching, especially in elementary school, was a "woman's world" after all.

In teacher's college, I could count the number of guys in my cohort on one, maaaaybe two hands.

One of those guys – let's call him Dante – and I had been dating for a few months mid-semester but our relationship was a secret (his idea) to avoid "making it weird" in our small class setting.

Narrator: She hated it.

I didn't understand why it would be weird. And even if it was, why did it matter? Was he embarrassed by me? Unsure?

I spent a lot of time analyzing how he acted around me in class compared to how he was when it was just us. How he texted me in private versus how he spoke to me in public. Things weren't adding up, but I was determined to roll with it, convinced he'd come around when the stress of our practicum assignments were over.

Shockingly (to no one reading this) we ended up breaking up a few weeks before the end of the year and when I saw him at graduation it was a total disaster.

Allow me to paint you a picture.

I looked great, if I do say so myself. My dress was midnight blue, my hair was curled (at least for the moment), and I was trying to convince myself I didn't care about seeing *him*. My parents couldn't make it to my graduation ceremony, so my arms were linked with my best friends and co-workers, Katie and Seb, an anchor on each side, ready to head out the door.

"Okay. Let's go. It'll be great. Whatever. Who the fuck cares if I see him. Not me."

Narrator: She cared. And was louder than she realized.

My mom's eyebrows shot up.

"Mariah! Don't swear. You need to calm down."

I barely registered my mom's disapproval, too wrapped up in myself to feel the guilt that would normally accompany a slip up like that.

Half there, I hugged her goodbye and hopped into Seb's car, forever shotgun when he was the driver.

We cruised along, passing the community centre where we worked and the bars we went afterwards, while Katie and Seb tried to distract me. When that didn't work, they switched to reassurance. What were the chances I'd even see him anyway? There were like 700 people graduating. Maybe I'd see him across the room, but I looked fine as hell. He should be so lucky to see me.

We parked underground, walked into the lobby of the NAC, shoes clicking on the shiny floors, and bam. There he was. Dante. So close that I almost walked right into him, his mom, and his little brother as we rounded the corner – 7000 people graduating, and I bumped into him *immediately*?

I didn't remember stuffing marshmallows in my mouth, but I must have, because I couldn't get a word out, and no other explanation makes sense because I didn't care, remember?

He barely looked at me as he passed and my vision started to tunnel. I felt a hand on the small of my back. Katie was gently guiding me to the bathroom. I was laughing nervously, eyes wide, as I ran my hands under the cold water. She soaked a paper towel in the stream from the sink next to me to press against the back of my neck, fanning me with the program we'd gotten at the doors. Best friend mode officially activated.

"You look amazing. He is the worst. You're doing great. Everything is fine. He sucks."

I cracked my neck once to each side, shook out my hands and rolled my shoulders back. Katie grabbed my hand and we walked back out to the lobby to find Seb, who handed me a water bottle. It tasted a little weird – metallic, maybe? I'd never liked metal water bottles. I didn't even realize it was white wine, snuck in for this very reason, until they mentioned it hours later.

They were back to distracting me, but it wasn't working as well as it had in the car. The tunnel got smaller and smaller, my vision creeping into total blackness. Without a word, Katie's hand was back on the small of my back, guiding me to the curb outside the reception area. I sat on the ground, shapewear shorts providing a semblance of modesty while I wrapped my arms around my knees. Katie and Seb stood in front of me like bodyguards, creating shade for me to sit in, and, honestly, looking pretty angelic with their backlit halos in the process.

Eventually, I was able to speak. The marshmallows were gone, but I had a brand new problem to deal with instead.

"Katie. My hands. I, I, I can't move them. What am I going to do? I can't go across the stage with lobster claws. How will I get my diploma? What will Michaëlle Jean think?"

I couldn't move my hands, clamped into C shapes, and yet my biggest concern at that moment was what the retiring Governor General would think of me, one of 70,000 students she'd congratulate on the stage that day.

Katie reached out to put her hands in mine. She asked me to squeeze them.

I couldn't. It was like the wires between my brain and my hands had been cut.

Minutes (hours?) later, my hands unclenched, my vision widened, and Katie talked me through what had just happened.

"You're okay, but I think you had a panic attack." Her voice was filled with empathy and concern, which somehow made the whole thing even funnier to me.

Not funny like *wow that's a good one*, but funny like *what in the actual fuck is going on right now.*

Me? Have a panic attack? No way. I had never had one before. And I didn't even care about seeing Dante, remember? We'd only dated for like four months anyway. There was literally no reasonable explanation for why seeing him would give me a panic attack. That was ridiculous. Not me. No, ma'am. I was probably just being dramatic again. Causing a scene for attention or something.

Narrator: It was, indeed, a panic attack.

An announcement came over the loudspeaker asking all graduates to head backstage. I was shaken up and trying to convince Katie and Seb we should just skip the whole thing and go get lunch when a friendly face smiled as he walked by me. He seemed to sense my hesitation to follow the crowd shuffling down the hall and backtracked until he was right in front of me.

"Hey! Want to walk down with me? I think we both have S last names."

He wasn't in my cohort, and we'd only talked a few times when our social circles overlapped, but his smile was warm and calm. His casual confidence made me feel more confident, and I felt myself nodding.

Thanks to the kindness of a pretty-much-stranger, I made it across the stage for graduation. But I regret to inform you that in the moment, for some reason unknown to humankind, I chose to strike a pose with my hands like cat ears on my head when they said I was graduating *magna cum laude...* right in front of Michaëlle Jean. This from the girl who'd been worried about lobster claws?

Now you're like, "Woah woah woah – this boy-crazy girl was essentially white knight rescued and didn't immediately profess her love for him? And what about Seb? Her alleged best friend?"

Touché.

I won't be able to sneak anything by you in this book, will I?

The guy who rescued me at graduation *may or may not* have ended up making out with me at a club (okay fine, and at my apartment) a few months later, but it didn't go anywhere because at the end of the day I'm just not a church-on-Sundays girl (sorry, Dad).

And as for Seb? Big yikes.

Let's just say Seb is a story for a later chapter.

my first classroom

- CHAPTER 3 -

Teacher's Pet

"Uh huh. Got it. Nope. Are you kidding me? No. Well she's right here now. So. I'm just going to tell her. No. I'm doing it. Well, that's fine. Yep. Okay. Bye."

Marching on the spot, as always, Jess had her office phone wedged between her shoulder and her ear, the black coil cord swinging aggressively as she stepped from right to left.

I looked at her curiously and she smiled.

"You're in."

I jumped up and squealed, and she joined in, filling in the details once our feet were firmly back on the ground. Since September, Jess had been trying to move me out of the temporary position I was in and into the shiny new kindergarten position the board created after a surge in enrollment.

A few weeks earlier, she told me I could have it and I lost my mind. I couldn't believe my luck – my dreams were coming true so much faster than I'd expected. But it was a short-lived excitement. Turns out, I couldn't have it, and it wasn't Jess' to give. The position was assigned to a more senior teacher. No matter what, the board followed seniority rules.

It just wasn't my turn.

But when that teacher called and turned down the contract just hours before "Meet the Teacher Night," Jess picked up the phone, demanded HR tell her the next three names on the list she was allowed to interview and – bam – there I was.

Maybe I was lucky after all.

She told them she wouldn't be interviewing and gave me the job, for real, on the spot.

Minutes later, I was on the tiny stage at the front of the school gymnasium, standing alongside the other teachers, in front of a crowd of parents. Jess stepped up to introduce me as the newest kindergarten teacher, and the teachers on stage clapped happily at the news, when she hesitated before saying my name, lowering her voice slightly to ask, "Are you going by Madame Stassen?"

"No, Mademoiselle Mariah."

"Oh good. I prefer when teachers go by their first name."

There was a shift on stage. From excitement about the announcement to rolling their eyes. The good girl in me – the one who was always a pleasure to have in class – was both silently cheering and flushing with embarrassment.

Inner mean girl: Teacher's pet, much?

Looking back, that's when the reputation started: the try-hard. The overachiever. The girl who clearly didn't have much of a life outside of laminating tabletop activities on the weekends.

The truth stings.

I *was* single, living in a small apartment with two cats, and spending all my time (and let's be real, all my money) planning new activities for my class – partly to keep them busy and prevent them from destroying the classroom, but also because I'd started posting ideas online... and cute setups made for better content.

Marissa, the short, firecracker teacher across the hall, was impossible to ignore. Her classroom was a Pinterest dream – twinkle lights, matching bins, and labelled *everything*. Somehow, her glossy hair was always down, never mid-meltdown messy bun.

She embodied the nature-based, Reggio-inspired aesthetic I was obsessed with. Marissa was a cold glass of lemonade in our chaotic little hallway. She didn't drink coffee (?!), loved teaching kindergarten (me too!), and we bonded instantly over our shared obsession with early childhood education.

One day, I blurted out, "Do you have a blog or something?" Her ideas were so good, I was convinced she must be sharing them somewhere.

She laughed and told me about her *Instagram* account. "You should start one too!" she added.

"I have one too!" I said way too fast.

We exchanged handles in the hallway, and I walked back into my chipped-blue classroom feeling like my love of teaching – and sharing it online – wasn't weird or cringey. From that day on, we were solid. Work wives. Confidantes. Both laser-focused on one very specific mission: get assigned as teaching partners.

Genuine partnership in kindergarten was the golden ticket. Rare, coveted, and worth searching for even when you kept unwrapping duds. Shared planning. Collaborative everything. Knowing glances in staff meetings. Post-work drinks. Willy freakin' Wonka.

And while we weren't formally assigned together yet, or teaching the same classes, Marissa *was* my teaching partner that first year.

She introduced me to math talks, loose parts play, and her impossibly perfect book bin system organized by season and theme. Her handwriting was beautiful, with teacher-perfect letters, and her zero-inhibition dance moves during "A Tooty Ta" made me want to be more relaxed. More playful. More... fun. As a first-year teacher, I was beyond grateful to have Marissa across the hall.

She couldn't help me figure out how to teach French to a group of kids who couldn't even sit through a three-line "Bonjour" song, let alone a whole lesson – but she was there.

She listened when I shut the door and cried during recess (like the time a wood block was hurled at my head by a troubled three-year-old).

She was there to strategize (and swear with me) when my classroom got wrecked, again, by another student who had "monsters in their head."

She helped me clean up the chocolate milk dumped on the carpet in anger (not by me, for the record) and worded report card comments for me that had to be honest *and* kind.

Those first few months were a blur of effort, exhaustion, and desperately trying not to blow my whole paycheck on supplies that would either break, vanish, or be destroyed within seconds. I was so stressed I was basically vibrating. Looking back, I don't know how I thought that pace was sustainable. But I was trained to be a teacher. Figuring it out was my only option.

Stephanie, in her role as VP, observed my classroom as part of my first-year evaluation. The review itself was great, but she could see I was struggling.

"Remember," she said gently, "you're a kindergarten teacher first. A French teacher second."

I nearly cried.

The relief was instant. But instead of letting myself sit in that comfort, I brushed it off and focused on the things I didn't score high enough on according to my own expectations.

I left the meeting and walked straight into Daphne's classroom to debrief. She was the bubbly, wide-eyed Grade Two teacher I'd bonded with in the new teacher program, and she was nervous about her own evaluation. That conversation with Daphne ended up being a turning point – but I had no idea at the time. We somehow got on the topic of TeachersPayTeachers, a site where educators sell classroom resources online and she mentioned a girl she knew who was making more money online than she was as a teacher in Ottawa.

My jaw dropped.

Someone our age was doubling her salary... by uploading PDFs to a website?

Sorry, what?

I had to be missing something.

Narrator: She was. But not for long.

The seed was planted.

I knew there were dozens (probably hundreds) of young French teachers in the same boat as me: tired, stressed, and just trying to make it through the day with a lesson plan that didn't make them want to cry. If I could help even a few of them by sharing my resources, why wouldn't I?

It made sense. I couldn't find anything that actually worked for my students, so I was building everything from scratch anyway. My kids struggled hard with big emotions, unprocessed trauma, and a serious lack of support – at school and at home. I was supposed to be teaching French, but it was hard enough keeping them regulated in *any* language, let alone one they didn't know.

So, I gave it a whirl:

1. Upload PDF
2. Add title

3. Write description

4. Set price

Easy enough. A couple of lines here, an arbitrary price there. I skimmed the rest of the page and skipped the optional fields. They weren't required – how important could they be?

Over the next few months, my store slowly filled with black-and-white PDFs patched together for my own classroom – random Google images, quick instructions, nothing fancy. Uploading a resource only took a few minutes, and even though I was only making a buck or two a week, those tiny sales were a thrill when the *cha-ching* notification buzzed on my phone.

Besides, I needed something to keep me busy over the upcoming Christmas break. Sitting alone in my apartment, with a New Year's Eve party looming on my calendar, was a recipe for disaster. The only thing worse than showing up (yet again) as the only single friend was the possibility I'd get so lonely I'd cave and call Jack – just so I wouldn't have to.

Inner mean girl: Over my dead body.

the infamous muffins

- CHAPTER 4 -

"I thought you were better than this"

His sigh filled the air — heavy and hot. Not in a sexy kind of way. In a there-is-no-way-this-will-go-well kind of way.

"I need to tell you something."

I'd spent the last few hours ignoring Jack, the *Tinder* date turned boyfriend after our very first date.

I thought back to my day at work: paper ripped, blocks thrown, furniture flipped. It had not been a good day. I wondered if I had taken it out on him. If I'd been too sensitive. Too reactive.

When I had gotten home from work that afternoon, I had collapsed into my bed, completely drained, waiting for his reply. I wanted him to *Uber* over to see me.

Correction: I wanted him to *want* to *Uber* over to see me.

Instead, he brushed by my recount of the day with a quick, "Aw sorry babe" and immediately changed gears. He wanted me to sign up for the 5:45pm barre class because I'd missed the 4:30 one. He knew the schedule, and which classes I was normally at.

"Come on, babe. You should go. I really want us to be a hot power couple. Besides, you'll feel better after."

Mmmm? What?

Maybe on a better day, this would've been encouraging. Supportive, even.

But it hadn't been a better day and I instantly saw red.

Wasn't I already hot? Not a ten, but a seven felt fair. An eight on a good day. Between the three barre classes I taught every weekend and the mandatory classes I took on top of that, I was working out almost every single day of the week. Heaven forbid I take one day off while I questioned my life choices about becoming a teacher.

I was so mad that I didn't reply. I had nothing to say. So, I let the little blue read receipts speak for me.

And then I pulled on my leggings and left for the 5:45 class like he wanted.

Gold star for me.

The only thing more annoying than Jack – a guy who barely left his apartment, didn't drive, and literally never worked out – telling me I should go work out so we could be a "hot power couple" was that he was right about one thing.

I *did* feel better after.

By the time I got home, where I'd left my phone "by accident", I wasn't mad anymore.

But then, I felt my stomach drop. While I was out, he'd been busy. *WhatsApp. Snapchat.* SMS. Calls. Voicemails. Messenger. *Instagram.* My phone was bleeding red notifications.

He called again and this time, I answered.

Nervous and confused, but fairly confident he'd be on his knees apologizing and telling me I was beautiful.

He didn't say sorry. Instead, he wanted to know why my phone said I was at my apartment when I said I was at the studio. Instead, he doubled down, insisting he only wanted what was best for me, for us, for our future and that working out was essential for that. Instead, he said he was so hurt that I'd been so inconsiderate and that he'd been so worried he felt sick.

This was bad. He was *so* mad at me.

"Jack, stop. Listen to me. I'm coming over. We need to do this in person."

I could feel the relationship slipping away. I wanted to drive over, talk face-to-face and just put the whole thing behind us.

"No."

"Why? I can be there in 20 minutes. Please."

"No, Mariah. Just no. You shouldn't be around me right now."

What did he mean? I was dead certain being around him was exactly what I *should* do.

I told him we needed to see each other's faces before things got out of hand. We needed to be together. He didn't waver but his tone shifted. Cold and distant, he said that he wasn't in a state to have visitors and I needed to accept his boundaries.

I wasn't sure I'd heard him correctly. The boundaries part stung, but the visitor line cut deep. Was he implying I would be a visitor? I was his fucking girlfriend. Not a random *visitor*.

I hung up.

Inner mean girl: Very mature.

Instantly, my phone rang, our first selfie lighting up the screen. I dropped my head back and stared at the ceiling, grumbling before I answered. Maybe *this* was the apology call. But again, he didn't say sorry. This time, his opening was the dramatic exhale that made the hairs on my arms stand up and the six words that would be forever burned into my brain:

"I need to tell you something."

My adrenaline spiked, all the benefits of that stupid workout evaporating as I snapped back into my baseline state of stress. My heart started racing, pounding so loudly that I wondered if he could hear it through the phone. I leaned against the doorframe between the kitchen and the hallway to steady myself, physically bracing for whatever was coming.

I loved that apartment on Second Avenue – the bright windows, the vintage Barbie prints, the bright blue couch. Every inch of it felt like me. But at that moment, it was like an empty room.

The only things around me were the phone in my hand, the doorframe at my shoulder, and the voice in my head whispering, *run*.

Somehow, before he uttered another word, I knew what he was going to say. Deep down, I just... knew.

Years later, in therapy, I'd learn about hypervigilance – the constant scanning of the people around me, clocking every micro-shift in tone or energy, trying to anticipate whatever might come next to avoid as much conflict as possible and protect myself from hurt.

But at that moment, it didn't feel like vigilance. It felt like stupidity.

My mind flipped through all the red flags I'd ignored over the last two months of our relationship, each memory seeming to unlock another warning sign that I had shrugged off and considered fine. Normal, even.

Like the time I picked him up from work and drove silently down Vanier Parkway while he told me about the new hire who embarrassed him by jumping into his conversation with a customer. He proudly recalled pulling her aside, chewing her out in the back room, and making sure she understood the "pecking order."

Or the time he opened a savings account to start putting money aside for a ring, sending me screenshots of the balance and telling me he couldn't wait to lock me down and the quiet, inevitability I couldn't shake from the back of my mind: we'll get married, but we'll *definitely* get divorced.

And the countless times he told me about his fantasies involving me and other guys, and how much he enjoyed feeling jealous – bookended by endless references to his "psycho ex."

I ignored it all. Every single sign.

His charm, his height, his love... it all easily erased the less-than-ideal traits from the false reality I was living in. Anytime I started to get concerned, I told myself I was overreacting. Being too picky. I always found something to complain about, didn't I?

Instead of listening to my gut, I judged myself for never being happy and that I couldn't just enjoy having a boyfriend who cared about me so much that he kept my *Snapchat* location on at all times so he'd always know where I was.

My knees gave out.

*° + ⚓

I was on the floor, cross-legged in the hallway, trying to stop the room from spinning.

He kept talking, and the room moved faster around me.

"I don't want to tell you this. I thought you'd never find out. You're making me do this. I don't want to. It's going to ruin everything. It doesn't need to be like this. I know you're going to break up with me when I tell you, and I can't lose you. I love you."

How much do you really know someone after two months?

Finally, I interrupted. "Jack. Just say it."

"It's my psycho ex. I told you she would do anything to make me miserable. To keep you away from me. She told me to tell you, but I needed time. You have to be smart enough to see the real me."

I waited for the bomb I knew was coming. His stories about her had never added up. But they were about to.

"We had a fight. It was months ago. She *trapped* me, Mariah. She *set me up*. She picked a fight with me right in front of her laptop on purpose. She recorded the whole thing – crazy bitch."

I knew it.

He pressed on. "I don't remember what it was about, but she just kept badgering me for like ten minutes. She wouldn't stop talking. She was doing it on purpose. Pushing every single button. I don't know what happened. I don't remember."

He didn't remember?

"She says she has footage of the whole thing. She just wouldn't shut up. If she had just stopped talking, this whole thing could have been avoided. If it even happened. She says I pushed her to the ground and just kept kicking her. She said she was screaming. Now she's pressing charges – which is bullshit, because it was all a trap. She did it on purpose."

My mind went blank. What was I supposed to say?

I could tell he wanted me to say I understood. He wanted me to comfort him. Reassure him. And I wanted to do what he wanted – I *always* wanted to do what people wanted. But I couldn't get a single sound to leave my mouth.

"Mariah, you have to believe me. This is her fault. She made me do it. *Fuck.* Say something. This is why I didn't want to tell you. I *knew* you'd leave me. I knew it. You're going to let her ruin this. I shouldn't have said anything. Why aren't you saying anything?"

Wait. Why *wasn't* I saying anything?

"I'm only telling you because I have to go to court eventually. I don't know when. I wanted you to know because yeah, I could go to jail – but my lawyer thinks I'll just get house arrest. So, when you think about it, that's fine. We can just hang out at my house and I'll have an ankle monitor, but so what? It'll probably be the best thing that ever happened to us. Just us. No distractions. Until it all blows over. And then we can get married."

What would I tell my parents about him never leaving his house?

Wait – did he say his lawyer?

How long had this been going on?

"I...I...have to go shower," I stammered.

The phone was heavy as I pulled it off my cheek. Sweat glued my skin to the glass, and it took me a few long seconds to hit the end call button. Before my finger found its way to the smudged surface, I heard him.

"Mariah. Stop. Stop it right now. Do *not* be like her. Do *not* ruin this."

I stayed on the floor, stuck, trying to figure out my next move.

I knew I should call him.

But I couldn't.

Fight? Flight?

Freeze.

Ten minutes. *Ten minutes.*

That's all it had taken for blackout rage to overcome him. To beat his girlfriend and not remember any of it.

To me, it didn't matter that she "provoked" him or "set him up" to be recorded like he claimed. I deeply believed that the fact she *knew* he would react that way – and that she could get it on camera – meant there was more to the story than he was admitting. She was brave enough to get proof. To go through with it. To put herself in that position.

It made me feel sick to my stomach.

He said he didn't remember. What else didn't he remember? How many incidents had there been before she hit record?

Jack called me again, but I barely registered the sound. Instead, I flipped my phone face down, crawled over to the couch and opened my laptop.

I found her on *Facebook*. It wasn't hard. Her profile was partially public, and I scrolled through status after status sharing links, resources, and stats about domestic violence. I read her raw thoughts. I devoured the comments of support.

There was no way in hell she was making this up – was there?

Was I really jumping ship because some girl I didn't know made claims about the guy I'd been dating and thought I'd marry?

Was it *really* that bad? Was it even his fault? How could his admission feel so small and yet so huge at the same time?

And why was my body *yelling* at me to run?

Loudly.

Flight over fight.

*° * °*

° +⋆ₒ °⋆

I didn't know then that Jack would stalk me online for months after our breakup.

I didn't know that the five minutes I set my personal, private *Instagram* account to public – just so I could use the "Top Nine" app that was trendy that year – he'd somehow know. That he'd go through dozens of posts on my feed, find a picture of muffins I'd captioned saying we'd broken up and I was safe, and send me a stream of messages about how I was ruining his life and threatening his career by posting this "defamatory lie with irreparable damage."

I didn't know I'd delete the caption after getting his messages, filled with fear and guilt about what I'd done.

I didn't know he'd make a fake *Tinder* account, swipe for weeks until he found me, and pretend to be someone else – flirting in eerily similar ways to Jack – only to eventually tell me he had a dream I should get back together with my ex, who was being framed. That the universe told him the reason we matched was to deliver that message.

I didn't know he'd copy every photo I'd set my *WhatsApp* display picture to, recreating my poses and even posing with a dog (despite being allergic) within hours of me changing mine.

I didn't know I'd get sucked back in by his charm, only to have him say we could never date because his friends and family would never forgive me for what I'd done.

I didn't know any of that yet.

All I knew was that, for the first time, I was grateful he didn't know how to drive. There was no way he could get to me in my bright little apartment with a buzzer system, unless he spent money he didn't have on a cab or took the hour-long bus ride he hated.

I felt safe. *Ish.*

And, I felt like a coward. His ex had been so brave when she ended their relationship. She had done so much. I reached for my phone and felt like I was letting her down.

<	👤 Jack	
		Mariah:
		I can't do this. I'm sorry
Jack:		
...		

Again, my phone lit up, his face still the background photo. I dropped it to the floor like it had bitten me and ran to the shower. I turned the knob all the way to the right and stepped in, leaving my leggings and sports bra in a sweaty heap on the bathmat.

The boiling water ran down my body, mixing with my tears and turning my skin red while I sat on the floor of the tub. I stared down the drain and tried not to throw up.

How could I have been so stupid?

I got out when the water ran cold, which felt like a lifetime later but never took more than twenty minutes. My phone was still on the floor outside the bathroom, face up.

Five missed calls and a text message:

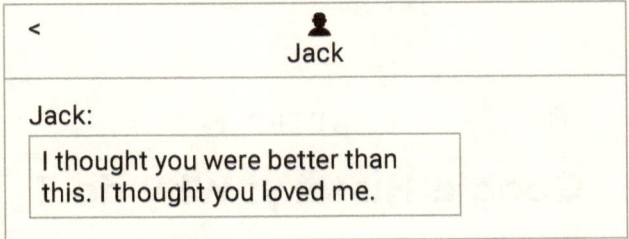

<	👤 Jack
Jack:	
I thought you were better than this. I thought you loved me.	

I did, didn't I?

I felt horrible.

NOSEY✦
✦ GIRLS
WANNA
KNOW ✦

- CHAPTER 5 -

Google History: Why do I

🔍 Why do I feel like running away all the time?

Sympathetic Hyperarousal

The sympathetic nervous system controls the body's "fight or flight" response. In individuals with ADHD, this system is often chronically activated – a state known as sympathetic hyperarousal. This heightened physiological state can cause increased heart rate, muscle tension, shallow breathing, and anxiety, even in non-threatening situations. It is linked to emotional dysregulation, sleep disturbances, and difficulty shifting into a calm, restorative state. Over time, chronic hyperarousal can contribute to burnout and other mental health challenges.[6]

Q Why do I always catch feelings so fast even when I know
it's dumb?

Limerence

A state of intense emotional and romantic infatuation,
characterized by intrusive thoughts, idealization, and a strong
desire for reciprocation. Limerence often involves heightened
sensitivity to perceived signs of interest or rejection and can be
accompanied by physiological arousal. It is distinct from love in
that it is often more obsessive, transient, and based on imagined
connection rather than shared experience. Limerence can be more
prevalent in individuals with ADHD due to intense waves of
hyperfocus and emotional regulation challenges.[7,8]

our dorm room

- CHAPTER 6 -

No Skulls

I started running because Marissa invited me along – and because I wanted to lose the twenty-ish pounds I was convinced stood between me and being hot. Trust me, I *wanted* to love it – free fitness, intense calorie burn, time with a friend, the outdoors. But running is *simply* the worst.

Oh, you noticed the switch to present tense there? That's on purpose. I just want to be crystal clear: running is still, to this day, the worst. The sheer amount of physical effort. The fact that I am not immediately good at it. The red face after. Pass.

But Marissa was officially my teaching partner now, our elaborate plans from the year before a huge success, and I really looked up to her. She was an avid runner and she encouraged me to stick with it, so I did. Motivated by weight loss and the distant dream of joining a run club (and maybe meeting someone who *wasn't* facing jail time), I kept it up.

And as much as I hated it, I was starting to get worried I'd soon lose the routines (and motivation) that kept me running and *somewhat* regulated. Okay honestly, this was just one thing on my list of growing anxieties about moving to suburbia.

Sure, I was excited – I had just bought my first house, for goodness' sake. I was freaking jazzed to stop paying overpriced rent in dingy apartments and start contributing to a mortgage in a sparkly new build. The day I'd stop sharing laundry machines with strangers couldn't come fast enough.

But, most of my friends didn't have cars. I had a lot of lonely 30-minute drives ahead of me if I wanted to stay connected – and I'd already seen how quickly distance had erased Chloe from the group.

Chloe and I had been friends for years, and our friendship was what I imagined having a sister would feel like. We were so similar that we really only had two modes: thick as thieves or completely at odds – and then always back to sharing clothes and secrets the next day without mentioning it at all.

Inner mean girl: Wow. A recipe for success. You two should definitely apply to be roommates.

We thought so too.

*° ⁺*ₒ °⁺*

Chloe and I didn't know each other that well when we realized we were both going to the University of Guelph. More nervous about the unknown than each other, we applied to be roommates and started spending more time together outside of work at the community centre.

Yep, the same community centre where I met Katie and Seb. Welcome to the intoxicating (and toxic) world of recreation.

Chloe was bubbly, loud, and unapologetic. And while we were both on a manhunt to find boyfriends who would become husbands who would become fathers, our approaches were very different. Chloe was who I might've been if I was a little less worried about what people thought and a lot more confident. Her big statement necklaces. Her sex jokes at staff training. Her refusal to hide hangovers. She didn't just command attention – the girl kept it. She didn't seem to care what anyone thought and she was undeniably the most popular girl in our circle, and in our work circle in general.

So when Chloe found the love of her life, John, and moved out of the downtown core, it was a punch to the gut that no one, other than me, from the group visited her. Like... ever. Nothing was ever said. Everyone still loved her, and was happy when she was around. But she fell from the ranks as quickly as she'd been idolized – because the drive was too far to make the trip out, or, I guess, to invite her in.

I did my best to make sure she got the memos about what was going on, and regularly spent 8-hour days at her house. I saw the hurt she was feeling. Was that going to happen to me?

Inside, Chloe was a people pleaser, struggling with depression, self-worth, and undiagnosed *something*. Inside, she was me.

That summer before university, Chloe and I got close, fast. As the only teen girls in our small, tight-knit group of coworkers, we bonded over missed references, older crushes, and sharing clothes at staff retreats. We were on top of the world that summer – uploading our student ID selfies side by side, texting pictures of the bedding we picked out at Bed Bath & Beyond.

But matching bedding wasn't enough. We grew apart by fall. Neither of us handled our first year away well: I was anxious and lonely. She was severely depressed. But I didn't know that back then, and neither did she. I just thought she was a really bad roommate – and she thought the same about me.

She left for the Christmas holidays and didn't return for the second semester.

Back in Ottawa for the summer, and both of us back at the community centre for summer camp, I handed her a Starbucks Frap. She looked up from her piles of papers, smiled, and said:

"So, we're good, right?"

I smiled back, wiping the condensation on my hand onto the back of my shorts.

"Duh."

Just like that. Completely at odds to thick as thieves, as per usual.

That year had been hard for both of us. Our falling out wasn't anyone's "fault." It was the byproduct of battles we were each fighting. We loved each other. We missed each other. At 19, holding overpriced drinks, we decided what really mattered.

*° +★₀⚡

Years later, sitting on the couch with Chloe's baby in my lap, I casually mentioned that I wanted to run the Disney half marathon someday.

Narrator: No, she doesn't suddenly like running. Yes, a half marathon is a questionable bucket list item.

Chloe immediately pulled out her phone to look it up. She backed out when she saw the price tag and remembered that running is, in fact, the worst but encouraged her husband, John, and I to register right then and there.

John and I trained together and ran side by side in matching mermaid skirts – me hitting a personal best, him pushing through a fever. That race didn't give me a love of running (running sucks), but it did give me hours with John. Watching John love Chloe – his patience, his loyalty, his ease – made something click for me. I still wasn't sure I'd ever find it – but at least I'd seen it. At least I knew what to look for.

If you had told me then that neither of them would be at my wedding, I never would have believed you.

But they weren't. And it's something we all regret, even now.

*° +*₀ °★*

It happens every year. Fifteen years of the same cycle, sneaking up so slowly I don't even realize it – until one spring day I catch myself happy again. Usually I'm driving, sun on my face, singing along when I feel it. The warmth in my chest, that sudden fullness of joy. Which, of course, means I hadn't been happy until that moment.

Seasonal depression, they call it. Winter in Ontario, I call it.

So, like clockwork, as the temperatures warmed up the spring of my runner era, so did my mood.

Everything was easier in nicer weather. The long commute. The nights on my balcony alone. Teaching.

Marissa and I spent most of our time outside with our classes, taking away the walls and volume concerns, and letting our students just breathe. Exist. Take up space and be loud. It was a welcome break from the seemingly constant ripping up of artwork, flipping of tables, and the need to call for admin support.

On the down-low, Marissa and I applied to move schools together – convinced that escaping the inner city for suburbia would finally give us a break from the violence in our classrooms.

The call came in on one of those perfect spring mornings while playing outside with my class: *I got the job*. Marissa's call was seconds later – she was in too. It felt like the stars were finally aligning... and in some ways, they really were.

I had a nice life, on paper. I was doing great, on paper.

I filled journals with mantras and gratitude lists, trying to convince myself it was enough: dream job, new house, solid pension, good friends, growing social media presence. But nothing I had compared to what I didn't.

So yeah, as much as I didn't want to make being stressed about being single my entire personality, it probably was.

Would I confront this head on and learn to accept that I am already enough? Absolutely not. You're hilarious. I did what I do best: ignored my feelings and dove headfirst into my business.

My "followers", (a word I hate, but it's quicker than 'the thousands of teachers who became a huge part of my life"), were surprisingly invested in my personal life, mainly because I let them be. I told them everything. Antibiotics, dollar store finds, TpT resources, smoothie recipes, annual teacher evaluations – nothing was off limits. They wanted to know, and I wanted to tell them.

I created; they consumed. The pressure I put on myself to stay interesting enough to earn their attention, and their sales, was intense. I knew I needed them way more than they needed me.

Just days after the call about my new job, I sparked up *Tinder* (again), told myself "Even if this date sucks, at least it'll make good content," and started swiping.

Now as my therapist, June (who I started seeing to help me process writing this book), loves to remind me, both things can be true.

Listen, I'm not trying to skew the past here. If anything, apparently I tend to be harder on myself than deserved (another thing June loves to point out). So, for the sake of total transparency, here's something you should know that I *promise* is not just me being overly self-critical: I was picky with a capital P on dating apps.

I knew it, and I was okay with it. If I was destined to meet someone online, they had better check every freakin' box. I swiped "no" way more than I swiped "yes," and I gave interactions almost no time before checking out.

And then I saw Blake.

° +★o °★*

Finally, a *Tinder* profile that didn't make me want to throw my phone in the Rideau Canal. Tall, bearded, athletic. The kind of cute that made you forget your standards. I swiped right, and boom – confetti.

We messaged back-and-forth and quickly set up a date for that Thursday night. I was *so* excited. I picked out a dress I'd never had the guts to wear – tight, orange and blue – and my confidence was up. So were my hopes.

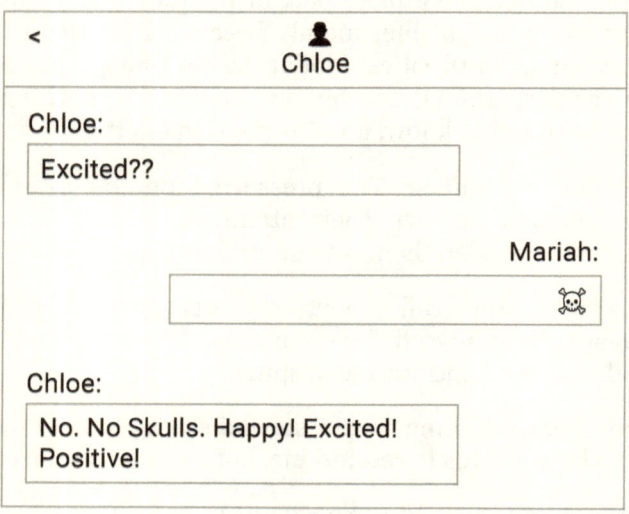

When I walked into the restaurant, Blake stood up to hug me and for the first time, ever, I was tiny. I'd always been self-conscious about my body and felt like someone had clicked the upper right corner of me and dragged my scale until it was bigger than everyone else. Proportionate and pretty, just... a little too big to belong.

At 6'6" I had to look up to see Blake's face – a complete first. Midsentence, he stood up and kissed me across the table. My cheeks flamed. My brain blanked.

Was this finally it?

I didn't want the date to end, and apparently neither did he. His text came through before I pulled out of my parking spot.

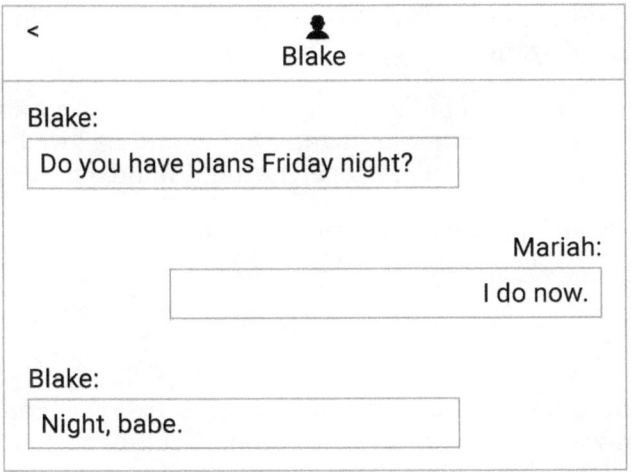

Blake:
Do you have plans Friday night?

Mariah:
I do now.

Blake:
Night, babe.

I think I almost passed out.

Chloe's string of question marks was my next priority. I always told her when I was going out and when I got home – you know, on account of murderers, etc.

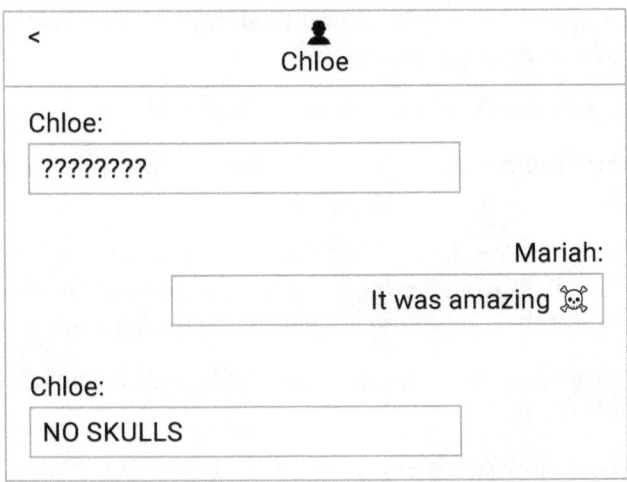

Chloe:
????????

Mariah:
It was amazing 💀

Chloe:
NO SKULLS

The next day, Blake and I messaged nonstop – flirting, spiraling, completely consumed. It was textbook lust, brand new to me, and deeply confusing. I was dying to see him again. To kiss him again. To feel that small again.

We spent the weekend hiding out in his one room apartment. Before we were done with dinner on night two, he said he loved me. I told him he didn't – but secretly, I hoped he did. I wanted to say it back.

Inner mean girl: Here we go again.

By the time I drove home, weaving around a tree that had fallen in the storm we hadn't noticed, I was already calling Chloe about my new boyfriend. I could feel her rolling her eyes through the phone when all she said back was, "Mariah."

Two could play that game.

"Chloe."

I pulled down the sun visor and turned left. Other than that one tree in the road, I never would have known how bad the weather had been. Then again, the weekend had been both the longest and short-est of my life, so maybe that tracked.

"Okay, let's just slow down a little here," she said.

Why did this always happen? Why didn't I ever get the reactions I wanted?

I didn't want rational. I didn't want devil's advocate. I wanted someone to yell, "I'm in!" after my slightly delulu proposition to just jump in the water—*it's fun and fine and probably aren't any sharks.*

I, for one, was already in the water. I didn't want warnings – I wanted their company.

So no, I didn't slow down and I didn't shut up about Blake either. We were hot, heavy, inseparable.

That summer was sweaty, sticky, and real-life purgatory – I had two months off work and was completely off routine. A heat wave hit Ottawa, then a tornado, and neither of us had AC. He moved out of his bachelor apartment and into a house with three other guys, a rental agreement set in place right before we met. The tension was building and three months in, the honeymoon phase was over.

His smoking was wearing on me – especially when he'd vanish midevent, like at a wedding, and come back reeking, only to disappear again minutes later. Packs on packs.

I didn't say anything.

I was becoming *his girl*.

The one who drank every weekend. Took sleeping pills to fall asleep beside him. Picked him up from work, watched him play softball, crashed with his roommates like we were back in undergrad.

I was reshaping myself just to stay in his life – but back then, I thought that was what I was meant to do. To me, every compromise I made was worth it... and working.

And don't get me wrong, when it was good, it was *good*.

After a typical night of drinking at *Bro House,* as they so affectionately dubbed it, we went out for breakfast at a retro diner. It was packed – hangovers, kids waiting for the $7 special, older couples on their second coffees.

After a short wait, the waitress led us up a steep, narrow staircase. I was right behind her when I reached the top, looked over her shoulder– and locked eyes with the guy sitting at the first table.

Jack.

Fight? Flight.

I turned to bolt, vision tunneling, words stuck in my throat. Tyler – Blake's best friend, now sort of mine – grabbed my elbow, steadying me so I wouldn't fall down the stairs. Exit plan foiled, I turned back around and stepped onto the vinyl floor. Oblivious, the waitress seated us inches from Jack and the woman he was with.

We sat – Blake, Tyler, Tyler's maybe-date, and me. I chose the seat directly behind Jack. Better to face my plate than face him.

By now everyone at the table was staring at me. Something was clearly off.

I blurted, "That's him. That's my ex."

Blake's body tensed. His arm slid across the back of my chair like a barricade. His leg bounced wildly. He rubbed his beard back-and-forth and gritted his teeth.

"I'm going to punch that guy."

Narrator: He definitely said something way less appropriate than that.

I felt the panic rising in me – and myself falling even harder for Blake.

Protected. Validated. Fought for.

It was everything I thought I shouldn't want as a modern, independent woman.

And yet, I was obsessed.

We got through breakfast. I don't remember much – just that Tyler gently told me to lower my voice, that I was safe, and that I hadn't realized I was being loud.

(*Graduation morning, anyone?*)

It turns out this is how my body does fight mode: Can't run? Get loud. Get noticed. Get help.

I spent the entire meal hyper-focused on Jack's way-too-close presence. I was scared, confused... and a little smug, because no matter what, I was there with an upgrade.

It was the rare but consuming moments like these when I felt certain Blake *was* the one and that he was my ticket to building the life I dreamed of.

*° +*ₒ °*

"You know, there's always adoption. You're intimidating, and there's more than one way to have a baby."

I was fifteen years old.

Standing on our deck, watching my mom hang laundry on the line. She clipped a shirt up one sleeve at a time, pulled the cord, squeaking the wheel, and made room for the next one. The clothes were heavy with water, barely moving in the summer breeze.

Focused on the laundry (and I'm sure a hundred other things), she was oblivious to the impact of her comment.

Hindsight is the gift of a fully developed frontal cortex and looking back I am sure she had meant to reassure me that my deepest fears didn't need to limit my outcomes. That there were other ways to get what I wanted. But I heard all my biggest fears being confirmed, not love behind her words.

Now, as a mom myself (oops, spoiler), I do.

That love had fueled her suggestion, alongside my dad, to stay with Jack. That maternal love came from her deep focus – her pressure – to make sure her children got what they wanted in life. She just couldn't always see the hurt it created in her attempts to protect.

Regardless of the intention – or the exact words – all I heard was that I was too much. That I would never find a man who could handle me. That no one would ever want to have a baby with me.

Blake and I stayed together, stuck in a toxic, co-dependent state of fighting and making up. Slowly, my willingness to be the version of me that fit his life faded, especially as I settled back into teaching in the fall.

Summer purgatory: gone.

I was at the new school, without Marissa. She was on maternity leave and without my partner-in-crime, I kept to myself for the most part. I avoided the staffroom and its cliques, but I have to admit – I did love introducing myself to my new coworkers and telling them about my life. Normally an interaction I totally dreaded, this time I finally had the answers that didn't make me feel like a total loser.

I'd met a lot of new people over the last four years and four schools I worked in, but one thing was consistent across the board: every single new colleague cared about learning the same five things within three minutes of meeting me:

1. My name
2. My previous school
3. How tall I was
4. If I lived nearby
5. If I was married

So now, for the first time, I could say my name was Mariah (yes, like Carey), I'd been teaching for two years at an inner city school (yeah, it was hard), I owned a house (thank you, I love it), I was six feet tall (yes, really), and no, but I had a boyfriend (yes, you can see a picture).

Moving to a suburban school hadn't changed everything like I'd hoped. There were still behaviour issues in my class, drama in the staffroom, and normal politics that frustrated me – but none of it consumed me like it had in previous years.

Maybe I'm just looking for excuses, but I'm tempted to give myself some credit here based on the dozens of messages I got from teachers across the country sharing similar classroom – and staffroom – experiences.

I was a trusted confidante to teachers I would never meet, and I tried my best to be there for them. I kept showing up online, as honestly as I could, so they knew they weren't alone. I reminded them, because I needed the reminder myself, that work was work. A job. And for the first time, I really believed it. It's not that I didn't care. I did, and my students loved me – so did my admin. But I also didn't beat myself up or put unrealistic pressure on myself to magically fix all the bro-

44

ken parts of education. I left job stress at the school doors, excited to go home, work on my business, and pick Blake up from work.

Now that I was working again, our pace slowed down as fast as it ramped up. I wanted more, but I couldn't ignore real life now that I was back in the classroom and back on a schedule. Besides, I needed to play it cool – Blake had started making offhanded comments about my "annoying assumption" that we'd be doing something every weekend.

In October, he tried to break up with me.

He said we fought too much and wanted different things. He closed the door gently behind him, and I sat on my stairs and sobbed.

This couldn't be happening.

I planned to leave his stuff on his doorstep. To not see him. To drop it off and go. But when I got to *Bro House*, every single bone in my body hurt, filled with hope he'd see my car and run out to say he was sorry and of course he was in love with me and this was all a huge mistake.

Why wasn't he looking out the window in devastation, hoping to see my car pull up at any moment?

I sat and waited.

Five minutes. Ten minutes.

Ever so briefly, my heartbreak turned into a familiar feeling: annoyance. This was ridiculous. I didn't want to break up and I had nothing more to lose. I was a desperate girl on an all-stakes mission.

I called his phone. No answer.

I rang the doorbell. No answer.

Eventually, he came to the door and let me in.

We sat on opposite corners of his bed silently. I watched, waiting for his eyes to clear back to white before starting the conversation, grateful that he, too, had taken the day off to mourn.

Narrator: He took the day off to smoke weed and play video games. He was a little sad, sure. But he was not "mourning."

He looked at his lap while he spoke, "I don't think I can give you what you want, Mariah."

I couldn't look up, either. I was ashamed of how desperate I felt to hold on to him.

"I only want you."

It took an hour, but I convinced him the breakup was a bad idea and that he was self-sabotaging, so we got back together.

Inner mean girl: Yikes.

After all, it had been a grueling 18 hours apart and we were meant to be together. It was the right choice.

I called my mom to let her know the good news, but her reaction surprised me.

"Are you sure? I'm not sure he's the best fit for you. Think about all the things you talked about with him yesterday. He smokes, he drinks too much, he doesn't know if he wants kids. He is nice, but I don't know, Mariah. I just want you to be sure."

I froze. Of course I was sure. He was the love of my life. We were going to get married. And what the fuck was this?

I thought back to the breakup with Jack and how my parents had taken that opportunity to remind me that people change. But *this* time, when nothing bad had actually happened, she questioned me. And there it was again: reaction disappointment.

I retaliated by bringing Blake on our family vacation to Cuba that Christmas.

the yellow purse

- CHAPTER 7 -

Holding On

I looked over at my mom and raised an eyebrow. I understood a little Spanish, but there's no way I got that right – right?

Her face confirmed my suspicions. The doctor would be giving me a needle. In my butt.

The doctor had just finished lecturing me – half in Spanish, half in stern stares – about how sick I was, how I'd better take every single pill she gave me and how I needed to get checked out the moment I landed in Canada.

I was mortified. I couldn't shake the feeling that I had really let her – this woman I had never met before – down.

Inner mean girl: This is why everyone says you're too sensitive.

A few hours earlier, I jolted out of bed and ran into the hotel bathroom to throw up. After cleaning my face, being careful not to get any of the tropical tap water in my mouth, I sat down to pee – and it *burned*.

TMI? Buckle up.

I looked down. Blood.

Not again. Not now.

I knew, immediately, that I had a UTI. How had I missed it? I usually caught them early – sometimes even cleared them up myself with over-the-counter meds before things got too bad. But, I'd been distracted all week long – tipsy, too. It was the second-last day of our family vacation in Cuba, and I paused before waking Blake up. It wasn't even 7am and he was struggling.

He didn't feel comfortable smoking in front of my parents, and honestly, I didn't feel comfortable with it either. After five days of only sneaking in two or three a day, the lack of nicotine was definitely affecting his normally peak form for my parents and friends. His confidence, outgoing personality, and commanding presence usually left a great impression.

I hesitantly shook his shoulder and whispered gently that I wanted to go to the hospital. Blake rolled over in bed, rubbing his eyes. "Are you serious? Why?"

I nodded and walked over to the safe, where I fumbled with the combination to our safe, trying to remember the code. I was terrible with numbers and growing more frustrated with each failed attempt. Finally, it clicked open. I pulled out my passport and cash.

I looked back over to the bed, and he was still lying there.

"I'm not taking you to a hospital in Cuba, Mariah. That is insane," Blake said while I rushed around the room, getting dressed, packing a water bottle, and trying to explain how sick I felt.

A note:

When I'm overwhelmed, I am *shockingly* bad at communicating. It's beyond frustrating to me, and everyone around me. Even if I know what I need (which I usually don't), and the person in front of me wants to help, the words just won't come out and I shut down and say, *"Never mind. It's fine. I'll figure it out."*

"So you're not coming with me?" I asked, irritated, as I stepped into my flip flops. Sand from yesterday's beach morning clung to the bottoms, and I slipped a little walking toward the door.

"No. This is ridiculous. I'm not encouraging you."

"Okay. Bye."

I held back my tears, disappointment filling my body, as I followed the empty paths across the resort to my parents' building, rehearsing my explanation for why Blake wasn't with me. I tried to remember their room number.

Why was I so bad with numbers? Between this and the safe, it had been a frustrating morning for my memory. I was good at math – I'd taken calculus and physics all through high school and actually liked math class. Moments like this made me feel like I was self-centred. Like I just didn't care enough to remember what people told me. Like it was an intentional choice.

I knocked on the door to what I hoped was their room.

No answer.

I shifted from foot to foot, weighing my options and chewing my nails.

If this wasn't their room, I'd be waking up a total stranger before 6am on their vacation. But if I didn't knock again, I'd have to figure out how to get to a hospital with barely passable Spanish while feeling worse by the minute.

I needed my mom.

I knocked again. The only sound in the otherwise silent building.

"Mom?"

Shuffling. Movement. Someone was getting out of bed on the other side of the door. That someone unlatched the chain lock, turned the knob, and shielded their eyes from the early morning light as the door cracked open.

"Mom, I need to go to the hospital. I have a UTI and there's blood in my pee already."

"Shoot. Okay, give me one minute." She scrambled to get dressed in the dark while filling my dad in on what was happening. He offered to come, but she told him to stay so my brother and sister-in-law wouldn't be confused when they woke up and we were all gone.

"I'm sorry, it's just – I don't speak Spanish that well. I need your help. I'm sorry," I stammered as we walked to the main lobby.

She looked at me like I had two heads. "Huh? Why would you say that? It's not your fault."

She acted like being inconvenienced was the last thing on her mind. I told her Blake was sick, so he couldn't come with us, and she nodded. I could tell she didn't believe me, but she didn't press.

An awkward conversation with the concierge, a light pink retro convertible ride, and a hesitant approach to what we hoped was a medical centre later, the doctor arrived, startled to see two tourists waiting for her. She handed me a little orange cup for a urine sample before we even got into the exam room.

I was sent to a bathroom around the corner – with no stall doors or light. I started to lose a little confidence in the experience at that point and had to count down from five, three times, to actually get myself to pee.

Fun fact: I've always had recurring nightmares about public washrooms – either impossible to get to (alligators, broken bridges, etc.) or with stall doors that offered no privacy because they were too short, too high off the ground, or missing altogether.

Narrator: One time, in Grade Three, the quietest girl in class accidentally opened the stall door on Mariah at school. Both girls were mortified and never talked about it again.

Here I was trying to pee in this weird, dark bathroom, without stall doors, in a foreign country, while my boyfriend was too annoyed to help me, and I didn't speak the language. Was *this* a dream?

I returned to the exam room and handed the doctor my sample. She gasped, clucked her tongue, and shook her head at me. I guess I'd forgotten to mention the part where I was peeing blood. A quick needle in the butt, a bottle of antibiotics so big they looked like they belonged to a horse, an unknown total on a bill I couldn't understand, and we were on our way back to the resort.

When I walked into the hotel room, Blake was sitting up in bed. He tossed his phone down and jumped up to give me a hug.

"I'm so sorry. I should've gone with you. I was so worried. I haven't been able to eat or do anything since you left. Does your mom hate me?"

Now, it was my turn to feel bad.

"I'm sorry I stormed out. I shouldn't have treated you like that."

Why was I always so reactive? These were exactly the kinds of things I knew would drive him to leave me.

He told me it was fine, that he loved me, and that we'd turn the day around.

This wasn't the first time I'd gotten sick traveling with Blake. A few months in, we took a quick getaway to Halifax. I got strep throat almost as soon as we landed – my third time that year – and ended up at a walk-in for antibiotics.

When we got back to the rental, my fever spiked – and so did the pain – so I quickly drifted into sleep. When I woke up, Blake was just returning from the store. Unable to drive, he'd walked all the way there to get the supplies and food he thought would cheer me up. I was so touched. I felt so safe.

The contrast to *this* illness was impossible to ignore.

My doubts about our relationship were getting stronger – but still, I ignored them. We'd been together for the better part of a year. I loved him. He was going to move in with me after his lease was up.

Fucking *Bro House*.

I was so over it. I blamed a lot of our problems on his living situation – the partying, the piles of cigarette butts out back, the lack of a single clean surface. I couldn't understand why he wanted to stay there. Why spend so much time talking about how much he'd *miss* it once he moved in with me.

Again, I pushed down my doubts and flat-out ignored all the signs that he wasn't ready. That he didn't want to grow up.

At least, not with me.

Instead of calling it for what it was and moving on, I doubled down by getting a puppy and inviting him to go with me to a conference in Toronto. He agreed, and we planned some fun activities to fill in the unscheduled time.

I was being scrappy – piecing together the life I wanted using puzzle pieces that didn't quite fit.

Ollie, an abandoned street puppy from the Bahamas, was essential to the vision I had of my life with Blake. The life I thought I'd have, that is.

Ollie became my world.

I felt horrible leaving him so soon after adopting him – worried his abandonment issues from a rough start would only get worse – but the timeline wasn't in my control. I debated cancelling my ticket to the teaching conference and staying home. But my mom encouraged me to go, reassuring me Ollie would be just fine staying with them.

"You need to have some fun," she said. "You're too stressed. Go, enjoy, try and just be a couple."

She was right. We were struggling, and the more people noticed, the harder it was to keep living in la la land. Besides, my parents were thrilled to take baby Ollie for the week and sent me updates the whole time I was away. He even walked up and down the stairs for the first time after watching Karma, our family dog, do it a few times. I was so relieved – until then, he'd been terrified of narrow spaces like hallways and stairwells, which made living in a three-story townhouse tricky. It was really going well.

Unlike my "romantic getaway" with Blake.

He was trying to quit smoking, and I was trying to be supportive. We spent most of the trip in sports bars, where he could focus on the TV instead of his cravings. I was trying to fill our awkward silences, and he was trying to make me feel appreciated. He surprised me with a yellow bag and the gesture was so out of character that for a brief moment, the thought passed through my mind that it was a farewell present. But, that was silly. We were in a rough patch. All couples experienced that.

Besides, I'd asked him so many times if we were okay – if he was okay – that he had insisted I stop bringing it up. He said the only thing bothering him was me constantly asking what was bothering him. So, it couldn't be that.

Before heading back to Ottawa, we went out for breakfast with my friend Rub. She was studying at the University of Toronto, and I was so excited to spend time with her, and Blake. It mattered to me that they got along.

Years earlier, I met Ruby at the community centre (told you it was consuming.) and like Chloe, she had red hair and a sense of humour that caught attention. Like Katie, she was friendly and popular. Like both of them, Ruby was a true girl's girl—loyal enough to flip like a damn switch if you asked her to. Ruby was, without a doubt, a cool girl. I felt old and frumpy around her, but never judged or out of place. Sure, she was a lot younger than me, even younger than my brother, but I often looked up to her.

We sat on metal chairs on the upper level of the restaurant she'd recommended and got caught up. The conversation flowed easily, but Blake was noticeably quiet. Some kind of sports thing was happening and pulling his attention to his phone. I was embarrassed – especially because it was obvious Ruby noticed. Why couldn't he pretend to care for just one hour? I spent every freakin' weekend with his friends and worked hard to make sure they loved me.

At the end of the meal, Blake's energy picked up and he swooped in with a confident grab of the bill, paying the whole thing. I quickly forgot all about the phone. All was forgiven by his chivalry and that smooth "no, no, I got this" moment.

Looking back, he was already halfway out the door but trying his best to stay in the room with me. I like to think he was hoping for a different outcome than the one that seemed to be an inevitability. I didn't need my inner mean girl to tell me that my gratitude at the bill payment was clearly me grasping at straws out of pure desperation that we were going to work out in the end.

I happily held on to anything.

I hugged Ruby goodbye – after taking a picture together, of course – and Blake and I climbed back into my tiny car to start the long drive home.

I still love that photo of us. But the bright yellow bag I'm holding ruins it, ever so slightly.

Because in the end, the purse *was* a parting gift.

- CHAPTER 8 -

Google History: Why am I

🔍 Why am I bad at mental math and estimating?

Dyscalculia

A specific learning difference that impacts numerical processing, dyscalculia affects the ability to understand, remember, and work with numbers. Symptoms may include difficulty reading clocks, estimating quantities, memorizing basic arithmetic facts, or performing calculations. It is sometimes referred to as "number dyslexia" and can occur alongside other neurodivergent traits. Approximately 11% of people with ADHD have dyscalculia.[9,10]

Object Permanence

In the context of ADHD, object permanence refers to the ability to maintain an emotional or mental connection to people or tasks that are not currently present or visible. Difficulties with relational object permanence may cause individuals to lose touch, not think about, or emotionally disconnect from someone when there is no active contact, despite still valuing the relationship.[11-13]

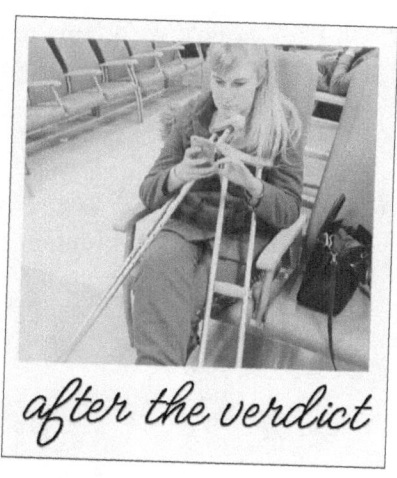

after the verdict

- CHAPTER 9 -

The Moment I Knew

Fear of rejection followed me everywhere. I replayed interactions for hours, wondering if I'd been misunderstood and ended friendships at the first sign of trouble to avoid being hurt. I rarely held on to a best friend title, and when I did I stressed about being replaced the entire time.

For a while, Katie and I *were* best friends. We met as dance instructors at – you guessed it – the community centre, and ended up trav-eling across Europe and South Africa together. Somewhere between those two trips and before having real jobs we found ourselves out for brunch on a cold Friday in January.

Katie was everything I wished I was. Stunning. Poised. British. And the kindest, most compassionate girl I'd ever met. Or ever *would* meet. She carried a level of empathy I could never imagine for myself, and simply being around her brought me peace. Most of all, she was the kind of friend you could talk to about anything. Conversation with her was always effortless and no matter how much time passed between hangouts, we always picked up where we left off – almost like we'd just paused a long-running conversation.

Narrator: That is still true today.

Less than half a block from where we'd finished our eggs, hugged goodbye and said "love you" over our shoulders, I found myself laughing – and sitting on a patch of ice.

I'd broken my ankle.

Instead of calling for help, I called my boss at the barre studio to apologize because I wouldn't be able to volunteer the next day. Then, I texted Katie:

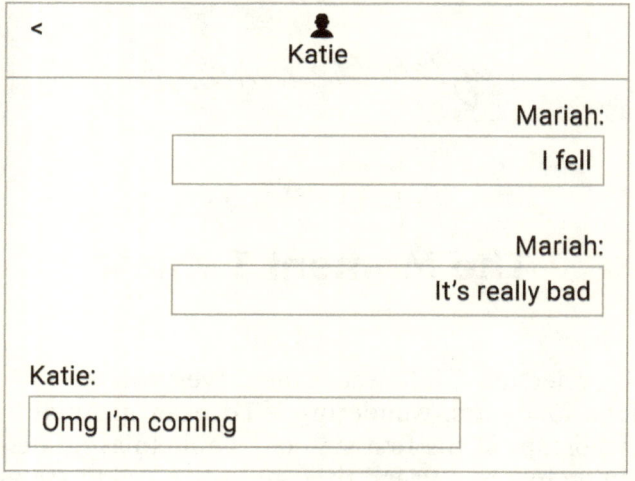

She came *running* down the street, eyes wide, coat flying behind her like a cape. I messaged my parents who, at first, thought I was joking. I wasn't. It really fucking hurt.

At the hospital, with a temporary cast snug around my leg, the shock started to wear off – and fear replaced the pain.

Fear of how I'd pay my bills.

Fear of how I'd get out in an emergency.

Fear of missing my training sessions.

Fear of needing surgery.

Fear of falling again.

Fear of being alone.

It was the most painful and scary experience of my life.

Until it wasn't.

*° *_*° °_**

The breakup destroyed me.

Together for almost a year and then just… done?

Blake, having tried this before, knew it wasn't going to be a simple 15-minute conversation and a goodbye kiss. This time, he came prepared – and with an ace up his sleeve, just in case.

For every concern Blake gave, I backpedaled shamelessly.

It was fine, I didn't need kids. Of course I would be happy travelling the world with him for years at a time. It was okay if he didn't move into my house. I loved partying every weekend.

I don't know if I was lying to myself, him, or both of us, but he wasn't buying it. And finally, after almost an hour of back-and-forth, he played his ace.

"Look. Mariah, I love you. And I didn't want to say this, but I don't know how else to make you understand…"

Make *me* understand? I was trying to make *him* understand.

"I just don't miss you when you're not around. I'm not *in* love with you."

I froze. Stomach clenched and silent – no rebuttal existed. He looked away, covering his face with his hands, "I'm sorry, I know that's so horrible to say. But, it's true. I barely even think about you when we aren't together."

He might have kept talking, but that was the last thing I ever heard him say.

The door clicked shut and he didn't look back.

I didn't want to talk to anyone, but I needed to *tell everyone*.

I had three minutes of functionality between the door closing and crawling to the shower to sob alongside *The Moment I Knew*. I texted my mom first, knowing she'd set off a chain reaction and spread the word throughout the family, and then Chloe.

Copy. Paste.

Two minutes left.

I wondered if there was anyone else I needed to loop in. Times like this – and making any kind of guest list – always amplified my lack of a group. Being close to individuals had been my norm for years, but it's not like I wanted to bring them together anyway. No freakin' way. I was way too anxious they'd realize they liked each other more than me.

One minute left.

I didn't wait for their replies. On autopilot, I found *Red*, the Taylor Swift album that held me in every heartbreak, and pressed play. My phone glowed on the bathmat, before timing out and leaving me in the black. Good. I couldn't bear to see myself in the mirror.

I gathered my last bit of strength and reached out to turn on the shower from my knees. The water hit the back of my head as I doubled over—hair hanging, tears streaming, clutching my stomach. Still clothed, I stumbled into the tub and curled up on the cold ceramic. The darkness and water swallowed me whole.

3-2-1

"You should've been there

Should've burst through the door

With that "Baby, I'm right here" smile"

- CHAPTER 10 -

Unedited: Email Chain

New Message
May 23, 2019 3:17 PM From: Chloe To: Mariah Subject: about last night
I think I need to address a few things from our conversation last night. I really don't like that I'm not doing this face to face, but there is too much on my mind to leave, and you haven't wanted to see me lately so I feel like I'm left with only this option.

First and foremost, I want to say that if you felt like I was belittling your break up, I'm sorry. This awful thing happened to you at a moment I couldn't really be there for you, so the best thing I thought I could do was just to get you up and moving forward instead of wallowing. You didn't accept any of my numerous offers to come see you, and didn't want to talk on the phone, so I'm honestly not sure what I could have done differently. I would have loved to come and sit with you and talk it through, you were the one who wouldn't let me come. I actually think that maybe what made you mad in the first place was that I was away the next week and not really there for you. I wish it had happened when I could have been more available, but that just wasn't the case.

I really didn't like that you were making me wait to be friendly again, and I've reached out several times since I've been home. It's ok to need some space and sort things out, but it's not ok to do that without communicating it to me. You can be mad at me; I'd just like to know what's going on. It felt like you were trying to punish me for being away when I should have been there.

That really leads me to my next point, which is that while you might think that my life is absolutely perfect because I'm married and a mom, I can assure you it's not. I have had a pretty trying month, and really could have used a friend in my corner, and someone to talk to. You are right that having John is very helpful and great, but I think you need to reconsider your idea that having a spouse means having support and help %100 of the time.

You are right that my marriage and child are things I am extremely grateful for, but it's not fair that that somehow makes my pain or difficulties less than yours because I have these 2 boxes checked off on my life list. I am very thankful for John and Hank, but the problems I am currently facing are not for you to diminish because of them.

The hardest part of our exchange last night for me to swallow was that how you minimized our fertility struggles by mentioning things that I want but don't have. While I can appreciate that fact that I'm lucky to have what I have, and that others would be happy with nothing more, the past 2 years of trying, along with all the medical procedures I have put my body through this past year, is not something I would wish on anyone. It has been hard on my physical and mental health, and my relationship with my husband. I know that it's hard to understand when you aren't in it, but I wish you might have a little more sympathy for my situation.

It was also really difficult for me to realize that you are seemingly just comparing our lives, instead of being happy with what each of us has. There are many things you have in your life that I wish I had – parents that are still together, a sibling and soon to be sister-in-law you genuinely love, and that love you, and very well paying job, just to name a few. I hope you get to accomplish all your goals, whatever they are, and I wish you felt that for me as well.

I'm going to end with some tough love, because that's what I do, but I really want to you read it and take it to heart.

YOU are enough. You do not need a husband or partner to finish the Mariah puzzle.

You are a successful, sought after kindergarten teacher.

A home owner.

A pet mom.

You have tons of friends.

You have a close, loving family.

You have pets who love you and rely on you.

You have interests and hobbies.

And you have lots of people who are here for you. Your definition of being alone is wrong, because you are not. Right now, you are actively keeping me out of your life, when all I've tried to do these last 6 weeks is make sure you feel loved. You have tons of supportive people around you who want to help. Just because you are not currently with someone does not mean you are starting at zero, you are much higher on the accomplishment score board than you give yourself credit for.

All this being said, I'm still really upset about how you treated me yesterday. I think I deserve better than how you spoke to me, and I think we still need to sit down and talk, if you want to. I don't like where we've left everything.

Chloe

Thursday, May 23, 2019
4:02 PM

From: Mariah
To: Chloe

Subject: Re: about last night

I would never belittle fertility problems and am sorry I made you feel that way. I cannot understand what you are going through but I acknowledge you are going through a difficult time right now mentally and physically and hope it resolves itself soon.

I am not angry that you were away that weekend. I am angry that your first reaction to the break up was, "oh well it's better to know now and if it wasn't working it's better it ended now". I am angry that you expected me to just move and go and see friends 24 hours after it happened. Regardless of your intention, to me this is completely undermining the relationship and pain I was experiencing. It was an unreasonable expectation that showed me you do not understand what it meant to me to lose him.

I am upset that before the break up you told your mom and me that we only ever talk about Blake and quite frankly it makes me not want to talk about the break up with you.

I am angry that other than the one time you offered to come over and see me, your offers were for me to come all the way to see you. I love Hank and John but this is not what I need right now. I have been trying to drive less because driving was giving me suicidal thoughts of crashing into poles. There is no need to be concerned about this or talk about it further. I have received help and worked through it.

I am angry because you continue to not seem to understand or value what I am going through and missing, nor can I expect you to as we are in very different positions in life. Comparing the fact that I have a well-paying job to having a partner in life is just ridiculous and hurtful to me. These things are nowhere near equal important.

I do not think a conversation would be a productive decision at this point as we are both very angry.

Mariah

me at rock bottom

- CHAPTER 11 -

High Highs, Low Lows

The emails ended, but the spiral didn't.

I told myself I *was* "getting help," like I claimed to Chloe, but what that really meant was letting Ollie sleep in my bed and putting myself on therapy waitlists I had no intention of following up on if they ever called me back. That was it. That was "getting help." And I thought it would be enough.

Even though, yeah, I wanted to die.

But, I mean, I was *fine*.

The only other person I told was Katie.

Inner mean girl: And no, she didn't learn from her mistakes. She used the same "drop a bomb" strategy that worked *so* well with Chloe.

Everything fell apart during Harper's out-of-town bachelorette party. Harper was marrying my brother and her girlfriends and I were headed to wine country for the weekend – AKA the weekend I hit rock bottom.

Oh did you think we were already there? Buckle up and cover your eyes because what comes next are the word-for-word messages I sent Katie that weekend in May 2019. And if you thought the email transcripts were bad then you're in for a treat because these are the ones that make me cringe to this day.

Katie

Katie:
Are you okay?

Mariah:
Nah

Katie:
Do you need me to call someone??

Mariah:
It's fine

Mariah:

I'm not going to do anything.
I have pets to think of

Mariah:

But do I fantasize about running
my car off the road everyday?

Mariah:

....yeah.

Katie:

I would be coming over right now
but I'm on my way to the airport.

Katie:

I love you so much and so do
so many people. This will pass.
You're so strong.

Mariah:

Thanks. I'm fine, don't worry.

I told you it was bad. And it was only about to get worse.

I'd met the girls at Harper's bachelorette a few times, but didn't *know them* know them. Still, I'd been looking forward to the weekend: a little escape, cute pictures, girl time – heck, maybe even a little fun.

The breakup was still fresh and I hoped getting out of town that was stained in Blake memories would help. Maybe, I could outrun the ghosts. I was haunted by heartbreak, and a pesky little memory that wouldn't stop surfacing every time I thought about my brother in a suit.

He couldn't have been older than twelve, sitting with me on the back deck, halfway through an ice cream sandwich when he said between bites, "I bet I'll get married before you."

When I tell you that hurt... damn. How could someone so young already have formed the opinion that I wouldn't ever get married? That I was too much for someone to commit to? That I'd be the older, un-wanted, spinster sister?

Narrator: You will notice that wasn't what he said at all.

I guess, maybe, you *could* say, I'd been holding on to Blake more out of fear of our relationship being my one chance at marriage than anything else. And I have to give him credit because he'd tried to get out of it, remember? It was me who got us back together and me who wouldn't let go.

Anyways.

My brother's prediction had come true. What if the others did too? Did I need to consider adoption, like mom said? Write an autobiography by age 20, like my graduating class voted? Be too intimidating, like dad joked? All these assumptions filled me with shame. Each one was proof everyone else already knew what I refused to admit: I was full of it. And unlovable.

Better sweep that one under the rug for a bit.

*° ⁺*₀⚡

Don't get me wrong, I was genuinely excited for my brother. He was marrying a girl he loved, and who he'd known almost his whole life.

They'd met in elementary school, sure, but the relationship didn't start until later, when they reconnected while working at, you guessed it, the community centre.

The community centre, with its giant green dome and tennis courts, was the heart of our neighbourhood. I learned tennis there, performed airbands, worked nine straight summers, and somehow went from idolizing the camp counselors to being one. It wasn't *just* a building. It was our landmark, our hangout, our second home.

It had a chokehold on the people who worked there. People stayed for years, even when it was clearly time to go. But we all saw what happened when Chloe left. She was out. No one wanted *that*.

Summer was synonymous with the community centre. Katie, Seb, Ruby, Harper, my brother – they were all there. Work all week. Volunteer after hours. Party every weekend. We'd walk to work together, visit each other mid-shift, then hit the pub at night.

Rinse. Repeat. All. Summer. Long.

It's where I grew up – where *a lot* of us grew up. And the bonds between us felt thick, comfortable and a little codependent.

Which brings us back to April 2019, 10:57am.

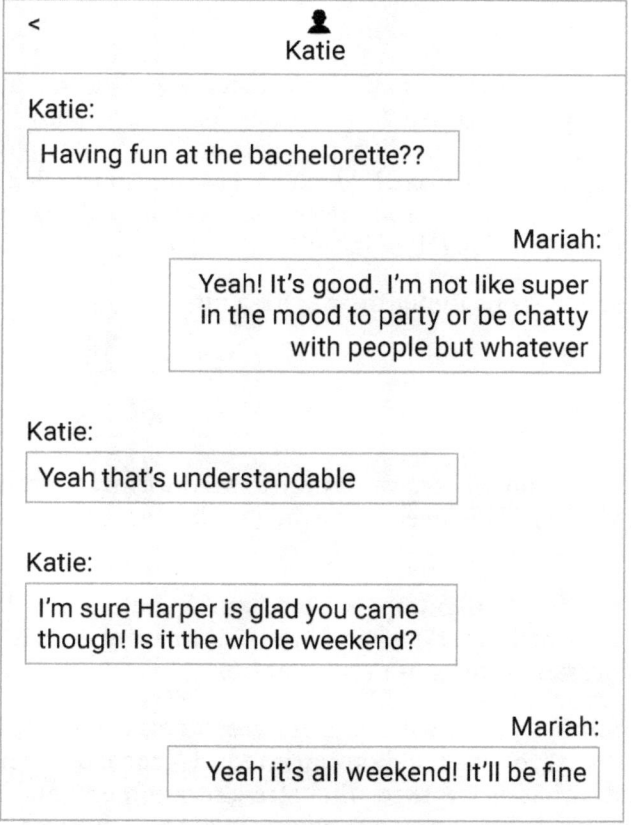

Katie:

Having fun at the bachelorette??

Mariah:

Yeah! It's good. I'm not like super in the mood to party or be chatty with people but whatever

Katie:

Yeah that's understandable

Katie:

I'm sure Harper is glad you came though! Is it the whole weekend?

Mariah:

Yeah it's all weekend! It'll be fine

Texts pinging from Katie in my pocket, the girls and I were off on a winery tour wearing unicorn headbands. And in my defense, it really *did* start out fine. A few hours later, we were back at the AirBnB and settling in for a night straight out of a high school slumber party: drinking games, boyfriend banter, sex talk, wedding plans.

In therapy, when I actually went years later, I learned about masking. June told me I was really good at it – which I'm pretty sure wasn't a compliment, but I took it as one. It's what you do when you hide your symptoms and behaviours so no one judges you. And it's completely exhausting.

Midparty, I fizzled out. Eyes glazed, energy gone, I mumbled something about being tired, climbed the stairs to the tiny single bed I'd be sleeping in, and shoved in my earplugs. I could still hear them laughing and singing downstairs as tears streamed down my cheeks, leaving little wet marks on a pillow that wasn't mine. Unfamiliar. Scratchy.

I had made a mistake. And I was done. Twelve hours after telling Katie I was "fine," I wasn't.

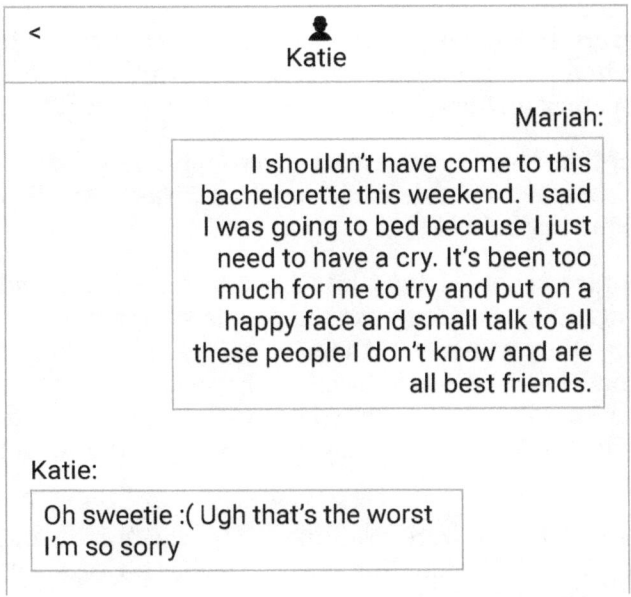

Lying in that bed, I knew I was in trouble – because after I messaged Katie, I did the unthinkable.

I copy-pasted the message and sent it to my mom.

*° *★ₒ ° ★ *

My mom has always done everything she could to give me the life she didn't have for herself.

> Her closet became my closet when I needed something fancy to wear.
>
> Her cookies were so perfect, I never even tried to bake anything.
>
> Her body issues became my body issues.

We talk every single day, if not once, then twice. But I didn't talk to her about *that* stuff until I was so broken down that all she could do was try and pick up the pieces, rather than help prevent the pain.

So the fact that I had a grand total of zero fucks left and was bearing my soul to her was an undeniable sign that I was at an all-time low... and desperate for help.

In elementary school, I'd get into little fights with friends – tiny, dumb things like who got to use the purple skipping rope – and end up walking the perimeter of the yard alone, silently willing one of them to come tell me I was allowed to play again. They always moved on. I never could. My stomach would twist into knots, and I started going home for lunch every day just to avoid the anxiety of not knowing where I stood.

In middle school, we were braiding each other's hair and passing notes one minute, then holding the art teacher hostage with intense roundtable discussions in her classroom during lunch about who hurt whose feelings. Days later, everyone else was back to normal. But I'd still be rehashing every word, wondering what I said wrong.

In high school, the boyfriend I adored cheated on me in a movie theatre with a girl from another school. I was crushed. But for some reason, everyone stayed friends with him. The message felt clear: *My pain was mine to carry - and unwarranted.*

Big things, small things. Burned into my brain. Over the years nearly every adult in my life rolled their eyes and labeled me highly sensitive. Those labels didn't just sting – they felt permanent. Decided. Unchangeable. They made me second guess everything I said, every-thing I did, everything I *was*.

Eventually, I came to the only logical conclusion:I was the common denominator.

I was the problem.

I tried *(and often failed)* to filter myself. Especially at school. I'd hold it all in, trying to be palatable and calm and good. Then I'd get home, and the floodgates would open. Tears, anger, shame...my mom bore the brunt of all of it once I burst through our front door.

As I approached the end of high school, it wasn't just my personality that felt like a problem. Suddenly, I hated my body. I started staring at myself sideways in mirrors, pulling at the skin on my stomach, fixated on whether I could see my ribs. Suddenly, I started sweating when I was nervous. Then I got nervous about sweating. Then I just... sweat. All the time. Suddenly, I started to dim myself because I didn't want anyone to *see* me. And I thought I was doing a good job.

But more on that later.

High highs and low lows were part of me – and not a part I felt good about.

And because I knew how exhausting my emotions were to other people, I started to do whatever I could to keep the tidal waves internal. So, it made sense that my "calm beach with occasional storms" exterior came across as impulsive when it came to big decisions. All of a sudden, I would announce something out of the blue that didn't seem to fit. Meanwhile, below the surface I'd been obsessively weighing my options, collecting evidence, and playing out every possible scenario in my mind for weeks.

A Totally Chill List of Snap Judgments That Were Secretly Overanalyzed to Death:

1. Midway through fourth year university, I unceremoniously announced I was going to Teacher's College while out for dinner with my parents.
   They were shocked – this wasn't the plan. I was supposed to become a vet.
   I was enrolled in Animal Biology, volunteering with horses, and had already taken the MCAT. I'd never once even spoken about becoming a teacher.
   But really I'd been weighing my options, and hating the science world for *months*.

2. I was really close friends with my manager at the community centre and spent most nights hanging out with her. Older and wiser, I see now that we weren't really that similar, and we were close out of convenience (and availability).
   But I wasn't mature enough to gracefully exit. Sometime after helping her decorate her first apartment and binge-watching three seasons of The Bachelor, I stopped putting effort into the relationship.
   Like him, I had been mentally collecting receipts: how her moods impacted my life, how I felt like I was always giving and never receiving.
   I don't even remember what spurred my decision to distance myself. I just know she was hurt when it ended. And I wasn't (even though I still feel guilty about it today.)

3. I cut off contact with members of my extended family at 19 years old after a two-minute Thanksgiving confrontation when my uncle pulled me aside, told me I was rude, and forbade me from speaking "like that" to his wife again.

The night before, fed up with my aunt's passive aggression, I had looked up from my book and blurted:

"If you want the door closed, just close it."

Years of biting my tongue had built up to that moment. Their treatment of my mom – sometimes subtle, sometimes not – had always bothered me. The toxic family culture.

That night just confirmed what I already knew: I was done pretending. Everyone else stayed in touch. I didn't. It's been 15 years, and I have no plans to release the grudge.

(*Narrator*: Her therapist has other plans.)

Some doors should stay closed (yep, I went there).

Yikes, eh? I told you this book wasn't about making me look good.

Speaking of not looking good: did you read the emails between Chloe and I in which I oh so maturely cut her off and never reached out again? I was fuming when our friendship ended. Fuming. Fu-ming. For months.

Looking back, I think I needed a distraction from the depression. Focusing on my anger toward her was almost a relief. I know that sounds terrible, but it was a more comfortable emotion to sit in than heartbreak. It felt more *productive*. At the very least, it felt more un-derstandable and much more controllable.

I didn't want to talk to her ever again... and was absolutely devastat-ed that we weren't.

So yeah. My personal life was fully unraveling, but at least I was thriving at work.

Narrator: She was absolutely <u>not</u> thriving at work.

- CHAPTER 12 -

Google History: How do I stop

> 🔍 How do I stop wanting to drive into a pole

Depressive Tendencies

Individuals with ADHD are at a higher risk of developing depression compared to the general population. Factors include chronic stress from managing symptoms, frequent experiences of criticism or misunderstanding, and challenges with self-esteem, emotional regulation, and life stability. The overlap of ADHD traits – such as rejection sensitivity, executive dysfunction, and difficulty maintaining routines – can make it harder to recover from low moods, increasing vulnerability to depressive episodes.[14,15]

Q How do I stop spiraling when someone takes too long
to reply?

Rejection Sensitivity

A heightened emotional response to perceived or actual rejection,
criticism, or disapproval. Often associated with ADHD and other
neurodivergent profiles, rejection sensitivity can trigger intense
feelings of shame, anger, anxiety, or withdrawal. Even minor or
ambiguous social cues may be interpreted as rejection, leading to
significant distress.[16-18]

post date goal setting

- CHAPTER 13 -

Thriving

So, just to recap: my personal life was in the toilet, but my professional life? *Thriving.*

If by *thriving at work* you mean spending the day after the breakup wearing sunglasses at my desk, crying while my team gently took over all my responsibilities, then yeah – I was thriving.

And if by *thriving* you mean doing a great job and getting compliments on my teaching, but crying from exhaustion in my car every afternoon and continuing to fantasize about driving into a pole, then yes, I was absolutely thriving.

Or if by *thriving* you mean having the lowest seniority in the school, getting surplussed (aka laid off in union lingo) the *same day* I got dumped, and needing to reapply for jobs across the entire school board to avoid being placed in a school I didn't want – then sure. Thriving.

No boyfriend. No job security. No air conditioning in my car.

It felt like I had an extremely short list of things going for me at this point.

The Extremely Short List:

1) My puppy, Ollie, and our morning adventures to the off-leash park. Watching him sprint in pure joy made the 15-minute scramble to leash him again worth it. Plus, we'd found a quiet time slot – just two other dogs, both non-threatening enough that Ollie wouldn't be scared or try to bite them. A win is a win.

2) My TpT store. I had just made my first "holy shit, I made that?" resource – a guide to teaching meditation *in French* to kindergarteners. I picked a special watercolour clipart collection from TpT to nail the exact vibe I wanted for the visuals. It was calm, soothing, and stood out from the usual bold-and-bubbly cartoon aesthetic most elementary resources used. And it was... taking off.

I was still making less than $50, but that was like $100 CAD, so every 11th of the month, when the payout hit my inbox, I felt like a millionaire.

Narrator: A millionaire with about $65.

I was slowly making big progress with this little online store – one of those "interests and hobbies" Chloe had so lovingly referred to in our breakup email. I was learning about thumbnails, preview files, product descriptions... mostly through obsessive competitor research and some budding online friendships in the niche.

Everything changed with that meditation product (see: Extremely Short List, item two).

*° +★o ⚡

I wasn't sure if anyone would actually like my meditation resource, but it was making a huge difference in my own classroom, and I knew it could help other teachers, too. I had finished it during my lunch break at school, planning to list it in my shop once I got home – after I walked Ollie.

I always rushed home to take him out. I dreaded running into other dogs, so I tried to walk him during the least popular times of day. We were working with a trainer on his reactivity, so I technically knew what to do when he got triggered, but I was so emotionally wrung out by the end of the day that managing his fears on top of mine felt like too much. Avoidance felt easier.

Inner mean girl: Bet a better owner would've prioritized his training.

Ollie was a rescue dog. A beautiful, floppy-eared mix of Australian shepherd, collie, and husky (I think). He had the goofiest grin and the fluffiest tail and could outrun anyone, anywhere. He was bouncy and happy and made strangers smile.

He was also terrified of basically everything. He refused to walk down hallways or go in his crate. He cowered on windy days and cringed passing garbage cans. He barked at anyone passing the house and lunged at other dogs. He ignored treats, freaked out in the car, and had intense separation anxiety.

But, he was my baby. And honestly, at this point, my reason for staying alive.

Most days, I was *fine*. And then the drive home would hit. Every day, that same stretch of dirt road. The same intrusive thought. But every time, I told myself: *I can't. Ollie's waiting for me.*

A familiar numbness would settle in as I finished my commute. Tears in the corners of my eyes. Hands clenched on the wheel. But then I'd walk through the front door. And for a few minutes, as Ollie bounced and wagged and greeted me like I was his whole world, I forgot how sad I was. Those few minutes were my escape.

*° +★o★

After our walk (we didn't see any other dogs that day thank goodness) we crashed on the couch and I sparked up my laptop. Click, click, click: new product live. I snapped a picture of my screen, posted it to my *Instagram* stories, and closed the lid.

A few minutes later, my phone buzzed: cha-ching.

A little smile crept onto my face when I saw it: someone had already bought my meditation guide.

Cha-ching. Another one.

That month, for the first time ever, my store passed the $100 mark. The total kept climbing until I could hardly believe it. By the end of the month, my dashboard showed a number that felt life-changing: $203.76.

I screamed into my pillow and paid off my credit card.

In July, I released what felt like another legacy piece – a full-year writing and drawing package with illustrated word banks – and brought in $303.

I texted my mom and bought a Keurig.

From that point on, I was all in. Every spare moment and ounce of energy I had that summer went into creating new products, fixing up old ones, and sharing everything on *Instagram*.

In August, thanks in large part to the site-wide back-to-school sale, I made $2,205.

And after that, I never dipped below four figures a month again. It felt like I had joined a secret club – the unspoken, elite circle of French sellers who were actually making money online. Friends from *Instagram* started asking for help with their own stores. And in turn,

I started looking for mentorship from someone further ahead – like, *way* further ahead.

Enter: Audrey.

*° + ⭐ₒ °⭐

Audrey was queen bee of the online French kindergarten seller community. She was the go-to for tens of thousands of teachers all across Canada.

When my store started picking up momentum, I came onto her radar. A story tag here, a collaborative post there. Before I knew it, we were virtual friends. She was generous with what she knew, and I loved talking about it. We messaged daily about teaching, products, and life, eventually moving from *Instagram* to texting...like real friends.

She was a little older than me, married, with a daughter and a doodle. They lived in a tiny East Coast town. She painted a picture of a romantic, seaside life filled with yoga, nightly beach walks, and a classroom where the biggest issue was someone blurting during circle time.

Audrey was my first real mentor, and I trusted just about everything she said. She was living the life I wanted and was happy to help me get there.

My business started growing fast.

With her in my ear, I registered my business, started an email list, and bought my own domain (even though the $15 charge stressed me out.) She was light-years ahead of me, but my name was starting to come up in the same conversations as hers.

Shortly after I moved into my townhouse, Audrey asked me to host the waiting room for her first masterclass. I was honoured, excited, and happy to help. She was really nervous, and after everything she'd already done for me, it felt like the least I could do.

My job was simple: let everyone into the Zoom room, greet them, and keep the energy up with light conversation until she went live. It was something her business coach recommended - *how freakin' cool that she had a business coach, eh?* I was game.

Unlike Audrey, I wasn't nervous. After all, I didn't have anything on the line and I had no idea what to expect. I made jokes with the teacher from the Northwest Territories, talked about polar bears with a girl in Manitoba, and did my best to keep things fun. This was before online learning and virtual webinars were mainstream, by the way, and talking to my screen felt... different.

It was my first time being live online and I loved it. Talking in an empty room while bouncing around the chat was weirdly natural. A bunch of new people followed me afterward and even messaged to say they were glad they'd "met" me.

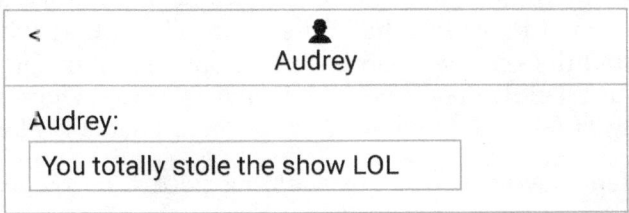

I didn't realize she'd been watching the waiting room. I laughed, but something in me twisted. Was that a compliment... or something she was clocking? Before I could clarify, she moved on, so I did too.

She never asked me to host again.

Audrey was direct and her texts took a little getting used to. I kept wondering if she was mad at me, but eventually figured out she was just... blunt. Logical. Ambitious. Competitive. She played hockey on weekends and was the breadwinner in her household. She was brilliant. I admired her.

So I ignored the pink flags. You know, the ones that aren't quite red but catch your eye briefly?

Inner mean girl: You're SO picky and judgmental.

She'd say she was a better mom when she spent less time with her kid. She made sharp comments about her husband and a newly postpartum friend – sometimes she just rubbed me the wrong way, but I never said anything about it. But her favourite topic by far was her "twin flame."

We were listening to a podcast about auras (Audrey was getting into "woo") and when the twin flames episode dropped, she was convinced hers was her ex. He was married now, but they still talked – sometimes intimately. She told me they connected in dreams and would pop up in her life after "astral meetings."

It was... triggering. I've always been sensitive about people not taking marriage seriously, but I told myself to cool it. She called herself a guy's girl and said she'd always struggled with female friendships so she was glad we'd connected – and I was, too.

Audrey really wanted me to move to Nova Scotia and it wasn't long before I wanted that too. I had fallen hard for Halifax when Blake and I visited the summer before. The chipped paint on the rainbow houses. The friendly people who said good morning. The seafood my mom always told me I hated but I'd discovered I actually liked.

I associated moving with a fresh dating pool – at 28 years old I wasn't getting any younger. Plus Audrey was there. So I'd have new dating a friend *and* a business mentor built in.

Attending my little brother's wedding a few months after the Blake breakup was tough, but I kept it together. In fact, I would award myself MVP. Setting up decor and drink stations, entertaining guests – I was in major big sister mode and crushing it.

Narrator: Can confirm... Unlike the bachelorette party where zero "keeping it together" occurred.

Probably (definitely) too soon, I updated my dating profile with a picture from the afterparty. My dad's bright orange Crocs, oversized teacher sweatshirt, double-fisting full bottles of wine. I was going for an *"IDGAF, this is me"* vibe. Maybe if I led with over-honesty, I could avoid the performance of online dating.

And with that, I jumped back in with a strict set of self-imposed rules, which I told myself were just strong, healthy boundaries.

Mariah's New First Date Requirements:

- Dates must be Monday-Thursday
- Dates may last to a maximum of 90 minutes and end by 9pm
- Dates must be set within 48 hours of matching online

Being a 'pleasure to have in class' had trained me to mask really, really well. My dates would drag into three or four hours and always end with an attempted kiss. Meanwhile, I'd usually decided if it was a *yes* or a *no* within the first 15 minutes.

Narrator: It was always a *no*.

Setting rules gave me a sense of control over the most uncontrollable part of my life: falling in love. I hadn't dated at all since Blake, and it felt like I was *supposed* to try again. To "get back on the horse" as they say. I really wanted a horse. Not that my tiny front yard would have an acceptable pasture for a palomino, but a girl can dream. Okay wait this analogy got away from me. The "horse" is dating. Back to that.

It's safe to say I had almost no patience for shenanigans at this point. Teaching was sucking the life out of me. Between classroom evacuations, strike threats, four-year-olds throwing furniture, and my monthly bouts of strep throat, I was barely holding it together.

Inner mean girl: Literally no one is under any illusion you were holding it together in any capacity and it's embarrassing how much you suck at being an adult.

My mom started to notice.

"You work too much. It's not healthy. All you do is go to work and come home and work more. You're young and fun. Go out with your friends!"

I knew she was right. But those heavy thoughts had already started creeping in. It felt like my brain was a glass of cloudy water. Every intrusive thought filled it up until it spilled over, making a mess I couldn't clean up.

It's still like this.

Sometimes, I let it overflow and I get lost, dissociating in my overwhelm. My husband (oops, another spoiler) calls it "that thing where I lose you."

The only things that bring me back are hard resets: sleep or a shower. My go-to escapes.

I have different tools now, thanks to June, but back then I'd often trick myself out of the impending overflow. I'd get up, get dressed, and post a selfie. Then I'd invent a reason to leave the house — even if it was just groceries.

At the time I had about 3,000 followers on *Instagram*. Not massive, but damn they were loyal. They checked in when I was sick. Noticed if I stopped posting. Bought my products the second I shared them. Some even came to a kindergarten meetup I hosted with themed snacks and discussion prompts. (Obviously.)

No one made me share so much online. In fact, people told me not to. But I couldn't stop. I loved feeling like people cared – and some of them really did (love you!). My honesty stood out. I didn't pretend my classroom was Pinterest-perfect. I wasn't preaching fully immersive French driven by the interest of the child. That might have been the dream. But my reality? Not a chance. I talked about reusing supplies, reading the same five books over and over, and going outside as often as humanly possible. I was upbeat and had good ideas, but I was in the trenches with them, and I never pretended otherwise.

In early December, I shared a "date night outfit" selfie and got a dozen DMs hyping me up. That night, I sat across from a hot firefighter at Jack Astor's. The music was loud. The vibe was fine. The candy ribbon on my unicorn cocktail was the highlight.

He was nice. But I knew: he wasn't it. So, I checked the time. One hour, fifteen minutes. That was my cue. I felt bad. I could tell he was having a good time; meanwhile I was already plotting my escape.

"So, my dog's been alone all day. I should get home to take him out."

Total lie. Ollie had already had his long walk. But he was my best excuse. Who gets mad at a dog?

When the bill came, I jumped in and paid for both of us. It was my thing – no expectations, no awkward goodnight. Just a clean exit.

Narrator: Finding "the one" was getting expensive.

Alone in my car, I exhaled, only realizing how tense I was when my shoulders lowered a full inch as I clicked the seatbelt into its slot.

I already had a message from him, asking to see me again. I let him down easy – told him I was busy and said I'd reach out when my schedule opened up.

Narrator: Her schedule would never open up.

Then I called Audrey.

"Well of course it sucked," she said. "Your dream guy is in Halifax."

Maybe she was right.

When I got home, I stared at the squares I'd just strung above my desk – my new "vision board." Audrey had voice-noted me on my drive home about manifesting. Write your goals. Look at them every day. That's how you make them come true.

I wasn't sold, but I was down to try.

I made mine in PowerPoint (still resisting this new site called *Canva*) and sat back, scratching Ollie's head, as I read them out loud.

- 3 weeks in Nova Scotia
- Upgrade laptop
- 6-figures by 2023
- Be open to love

Okay so, some of them were glorified just to-do list items. But, others were big. I was proud of myself for admitting them. For writing down that I wanted to move. That I wanted to fall in love. That maybe, just maybe, I didn't need to pretend I was fine on my own.

Inner mean girl: Yeah, no one was buying that.

Winter break was coming up, and I was ready to crush it. I was in a 5-day business challenge, had collabs to boost my email list, and a possible webinar with Scholar's Choice in the works. I needed the time away from the classroom and I couldn't wait to dive into business stuff all day, every day.

I was used to working on my business in stolen moments – in the paper room at lunch, tucked away in a corner of the library, late nights with a laptop and Dragon's Den. The two full weeks ahead of me felt like heaven and the first week was everything I dreamed of: a blur of spreadsheets, product mockups, and reality TV.

Christmas landed smack dab in the middle of my work sprint, and for the first time, I was hosting. This was a *big* deal. I decorated the whole main floor, made a full breakfast for my family and had the perfect Christmas playlist in the background. I wanted to give my mom a break after thirty years of Christmas pressure, and I wanted to prove that I could do it.

My parents and brother came over in matching pajamas and the whole morning was simple and perfect.

By the afternoon, everyone trickled out. My brother went to his inlaws and my parents went home to their cats (and to give Karma a break from Ollie's relentless energy). I shut the door behind them and looked at the narrow section of wall by the entrance. Just a foot or two wide and unimpressive to most. But it meant something to me.

Exactly two years earlier, we'd visited this house while it was under construction. The drywall wasn't up yet, so my mom and I hid a tiny porcelain rabbit inside that wall – one I'd had since childhood. I wanted something old and grounding tucked into the brand new. Something special and maybe even a little lucky. I imagined someone finding it one day, and wondering what it meant.

I put my hand on the wall, emotions prickling up, chastising myself for being so silly before turning to walk up the stairs. Ollie was already asleep on the couch, passed out after the morning's hustle and bustle that was so different from our normal routine.

The house was quiet. Too quiet. It felt vacuum-sealed. All the warmth from the morning was gone. I was very much alone. Again. Now what?

Tired of *Tinder*, I opened *Bumble* and swiped a few times. I felt myself getting hopeful.

Maybe today's the day. Maybe I don't need to move. Maybe 2020 is my year. Christmas miracles are a thing, right?

Swipe.

Swipe.

Swipe.

Then the screen went yellow.

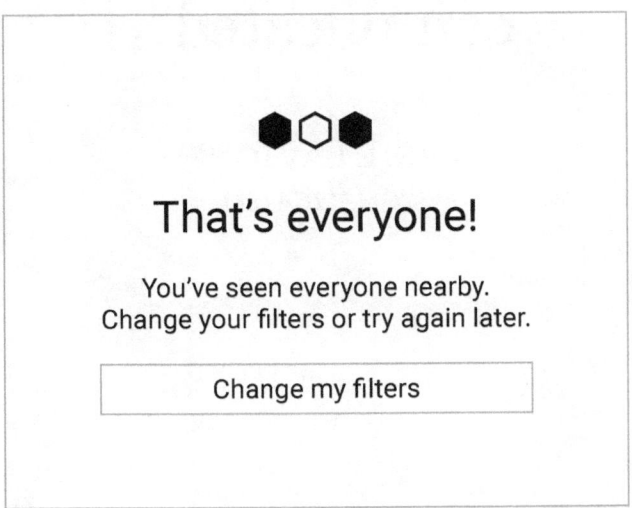

That's everyone!

You've seen everyone nearby.
Change your filters or try again later.

Change my filters

Merry Fucking Christmas.

"Why'd you have to go and make things so complicated"

AVRIL LAVIGNE
COMPLICATED

the hexagon table

- CHAPTER 14 -

Coconut

Seven minutes.

I sat on the low, hexagonal table, and stared out the door of my classroom. Coat zipped. Boots on. Fully packed and ready to bolt. I waited out the mandatory fifteen-minute buffer between student and teacher departure.

My routine was to arrive at work really early and then leave immediately after school. I was so mentally fried by 3pm that there was no point sticking around and pretending to be productive – even if I felt judged as the first car out of the parking lot. But it was the last day before March break and I wasn't leaving to go home and crash on the couch in exhaustion.

My watch buzzed with an incoming text message:

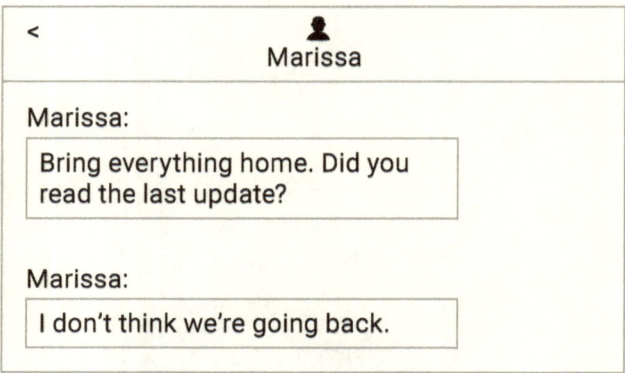

<	👤 Marissa

Marissa:

> Bring everything home. Did you read the last update?

Marissa:

> I don't think we're going back.

Marissa didn't know this, but I'd started taking my stuff home a few days earlier. Not because of some alleged illness I couldn't comprehend sweeping the world (???), but because I was crossing my fingers that my doctor would write me a note for a temporary stress leave.

The day before, I hit my all-time low as a classroom teacher and booked an appointment with my family doctor.

Standing in the hallway outside my classroom, twenty-seven tiny faces stared up at me from the cold, tiled floor where they sat, crosslegged, waiting. I was pacing, trying to calm myself down enough to read the story I had grabbed on my way out of the room. One of the stories now stacked beside me on the table.

On the other side of the glass door, I could see two of my students climbing the window ledge, pushing over shelves, and throwing chairs. They were ripping books, dumping basket after basket of toys, and yanking the blinds.

In an instant, they'd gone from screaming in anger and hurting their classmates to laughing about their destruction. The moment we evacuated the others from what was supposed to be their safe learning space, the chaos had given them what they wanted: space, attention, and a release valve for feelings too big to hold.

It was a cry for help. I knew that. Logically, I knew that.

But it still hurt.

The vice principal was making his way down the long hallway toward us. Admin had given us a walkie-talkie to call them when this happened, so no matter where they were, they could come and offer support. It happened *that* frequently. Contractually, I wasn't allowed to do anything. I simply had to get the rest of the class out of the way and wait for the students to either calm down or be handled by some-one in a different union than me.

It was completely fucking with my mind.

How was it reasonable to let the needs of two overrule the needs of twenty-seven? How was it okay that none of the other parents were even allowed to know what their own child was experiencing every single day at school?

I, teacher's pet, no longer shared the board's opinion. How could I, when it felt like we weren't even on the same team? I understood their position, and in theory, I agreed. But logic went out the window when those tiny faces stared up at me – confused, scared, and hurting.

As the VP approached, I could see the smile on his face. Ever positive. Ever understanding. Honestly, refreshing and rare in the admin world. It was his turn to come down to the Brown Bears class and try to calm the dynamic duo – super freakin' cute, and super freakin' challenging. I tried so hard to connect with them, to see the good, to focus on restorative justice and natural consequences. But I couldn't stop the frustration and exhaustion from taking over any rational part of my brain.

I was stuck in the "why is this happening again, why doesn't anyone do anything, why are there zero consequences" stage that every teacher, especially in kindergarten, has found herself in.

These tiny humans were in control. With policies and procedures ironclad in the education space, there was nothing anyone could do about it. There would be no consequence. No call home or time in the office. No missed recess or time out. They'd barely contribute to cleaning up their mess.

On the one hand, I got it. They were so young, and this was clearly a cry for help. They needed better tools and more support. But on the other hand – the hand that felt so heavy and limiting – it felt like nothing would ever change. Because once things escalated, our protocol was to remove everyone else from the danger zone (aka their learning environment), wait it out, clean it up, and have it all happen again the next day.

My anxiety was so intense it seemed to hit the roof of my car and suffocate me during my morning commute. I'd fallen into a pattern of bribing myself to show up with a drive-through double double and sour-cream glazed donut.

The sight of the Vice Principal's friendly face as he approached put me over the edge. I burst into tears. Right there, in front of my entire class. I wanted to stop. I was filled with shame that I couldn't be stronger for them. I wanted to show them they were safe with me – that I would protect them, always.

The tears slipped down my cheeks, picturing my lunch break picking up toys, rearranging furniture, trying to tape together ripped artwork like nothing had happened. My brain was buzzing with frustra-tion. I had trained to be a teacher. I specialized in early childhood education. I was damn good at it – but I wasn't even teaching anymore. Not really. My days were spent putting out fires and trying to keep everyone safe.

It felt like there was no room left in my body to hold the stress, so it leaked out the only way it could.

He didn't judge me. He didn't flinch. He told me to take a walk in the parking lot, to take whatever time I needed, and to come back when I was ready. I appreciated it. I really did. And I took him up on it. But I knew I needed more than a five-minute walk.

I called my doctor and booked an appointment for the following week to talk about what my options were. I hoped, even with her mega-boomer "you're not depressed, you just need to exercise" stance, that she'd see how much I was struggling and give me the note I needed to take some time off.

After work that day, I walked into the union office. I was co-chair of the board-wide professional development day and planned workshops and speakers for 20,000 teachers. It was going to be *incredi-ble*– I even arranged for Audrey to fly in to host a workshop. People were stoked.

Just over a month from the event, the committee met regularly.

Even though my day had hit an all-time low, I walked in with a smile on my face and pep in my step. New environment. New focus. But when I walked through the doors that day, the mood felt... off. Quiet. I took my seat at the long boardroom table, swiveling the high-backed leather chair to face the group. I scanned their faces, trying to figure out what had changed.

Half smiles. Furrowed brows. Something was up.

The union president started talking and I struggled to make sense of what she was saying but my brain felt like it was flickering in and out of the present, a scratched CD skipping between tracks. I didn't watch the news and I didn't know what *flatten the curve* meant. I was still trying to flatten my freakin' lesson plan into something manageable.

"We should cancel the event. We want to be ahead of the optics and be seen as proactive and supportive."

"Agreed. And we don't want to be responsible for anyone getting sick."

Marissa's *Snapchat*: "Enough groceries for four weeks."

"We need to give people time to rearrange their schedules. It's better to cancel now and wish we hadn't than wait any closer to the date."

The radio: "Breaking news. OCDSB and OCSB have officially extended March Break from one to two weeks."

"Did everyone stock up on toilet paper?"

Finally, I interrupted, "Wait, sorry – are we talking about that virus? Is that a real thing?"

Five faces turned toward me, their expressions immediately softening into parental concern. I suddenly felt ten years old, not ten years younger. Yes, it was real. Yes, it was serious. Yes, I needed to get gro-ceries on the way home and prepare to be alone for a while. Yes, this was only going to get worse.

I called my mom and dad with shaking hands the second I got to my car. "Did you guys know about this Covid thing? I just left the meeting and everyone's freaking out, telling me I need to prepare for weeks at home. What is going on?"

They were calm. My mom put me on speaker so they could both talk at once. My dad confirmed there was a virus, that it was serious, but made it clear I didn't need to panic. They agreed I should stop at the grocery store on the way home – and while I was at it, hit the pet store to make sure Ollie had enough food, too. They said the time at home would help stop the spread, and we'd be back to normal in a few weeks. Still, I was back in that place. That dissociated, watching-myself-from-above place. "Self-isolating" for the next two weeks felt weirdly dramatic. So final.

I wandered through the store on autopilot. The lines were longer than usual, and the energy felt off. I grabbed more than my usual weekly haul, focused on things that would last, and passed by shelves that had been completely cleared of toilet paper. I didn't need any, but the sight rattled me. How long did people think we'd be home? Why did they need so much toilet paper?

It added to the confusion. All of it did.

*° *_{*o} °_**

The next day at school was a blur. The Prime Minister told us we needed "two weeks to flatten the curve," but the message from Marissa was what actually made it real. Unlike me, she knew things, and I trusted her judgment over everything. I still wasn't really *worried* – just confused. Was I happy to have extra time off? Nervous about why that was even happening? I was all over the place.

I picked up the handmade doll treehouse my uncle built for me. Then I looked around at the hundreds of dollars of supplies I'd collected over the years.

Was any of it worth making multiple trips to the car? I just wanted out.

Four minutes left. An announcement came over the intercom: bring Chromebooks home "just in case."

Three minutes left. Fuck it.

Excitement. Fear. Relief. Sadness. It all hit at once, crowding my chest. My body couldn't decide if it wanted to collapse, celebrate, or scream. I called goodbye to my co-teacher across the hall and walked out. My watch buzzed:

I'd never been so happy to see the coconut emoji in my life.

the day everything changed

- CHAPTER 15 -

"I think you should kiss me"

So, I may or may not have led us down a *slight* path of diversion. Sorry. Love you. I'll tell you everything now, pinky promise.

By the time the world shut down in 2020 thanks to the worldwide panini, I did, in fact, have a Dave in my life. It started on Christmas Day a few months earlier.

Remember when I told you I had been swiping on *Bumble* after my family left, feeling all the feelings, and praying for a Christmas miracle – only to get the digital slap of "you've run out of matches" and then *Bumble* tried to soften the blow by asking if I wanted to reassess my criteria?

Well. I did.

I clicked the button, thinking, "What the heck, I have nothing to lose," and reviewed my preferences.

Height: 6'2. Okay, fine. I could lower that to 6'1.

Education: Postgraduate. Okay, fine. We could get rid of that too. I'm down with a handyman anyway.

Nothing else really felt negotiable. He needed to want kids, like dogs, and be a non-smoker, for example. Two edits would have to do. I hit save and refreshed my account. The little yellow hive in the middle of the white screen finished loading, and a new profile popped up.

Dave | 28 | 7.4 km away

I tapped his face, and his picture filled my screen. There was something about him I couldn't quite put my finger on. I read through his profile to see what preferences had kept him hidden before.

Sure enough: he was 6'1 and hadn't finished his degree.

I kept reading. He was in the Air Force. About to be posted to Halifax. Looking for something serious.

I flashed back to high school conversations when the girls all swore they could *never* date someone in the military. Too hard. Too unstable. Too many moves. Too many goodbyes. I was the exception.

I always thought I'd crush it as a military wife. Who doesn't love a man in uniform? And I *loved* alone time. Deployments? Romanticized. Solo parenting? I'd babysat groups of them – overnight! How hard could it be?

Narrator: Very. Very hard.

And Halifax? That was already on my vision board. I'd planned to spend three weeks there that summer, testing out a "fake move" before deciding if I'd go for real. Honestly, what were the chances?

I had never seen a guy mention a move in his *Bumble* profile before. And here this guy was, name-dropping the very city that was hanging alongside my other goals on the fairy light strung list above my desk.

Oh, what the heck. I swiped right. The screen turned yellow, again.

On *Bumble*, the girl has to send the first message – and you only have 24 hours before the match disappears. Unlike the other apps, *Bumble* made me feel like I had a little more control, a little more safety, and honestly, a little more accountability to actually *talk* to people.

So I messaged him:

Mariah
Hey! Merry Christmas

Dave
Hey, Merry Christmas. How are you?

Mariah
I'm good, thanks! You?

Dave
I'm good - do you want to go out tomorrow?

Mariah
Yeah, sure!

And that was it. I picked the time, he picked the place. We didn't message again until an hour before we had planned to meet.

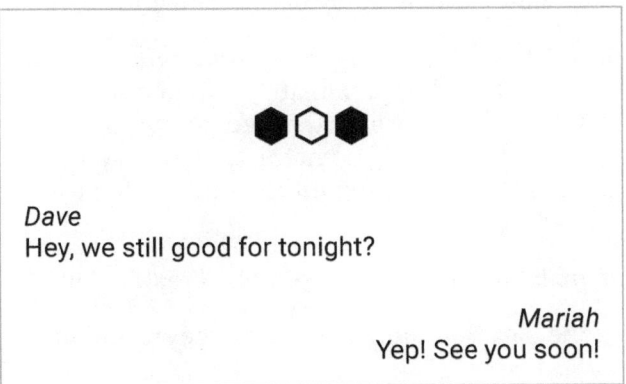

Dave
Hey, we still good for tonight?

Mariah
Yep! See you soon!

It was the least back-and-forth I'd ever had on an app. I *loved* it.

I was so tired of the same basic conversations and constantly pressuring myself to be just the right mix of witty, flirty, interesting, and smart – while still being approachable. Not at all intimidating.

While I was getting ready, I decided to try out the magnetic eyelashes I'd gotten in my Christmas stocking. The people were *pumped* to hear my review, so I filmed myself attempting to put them on (I give myself a 7/10) and shared it on my *Instagram* stories. Normally, I'd tell them if I was going on a date. But for some reason, I didn't say where I was headed that night – just that I was going out and being young and fun.

To balance out the over-the-top lashes, I kept the rest of my outfit simple: jeans and a black top. It was one of my favourites, and it opened in the back to show off one of my tattoos.

Bet you didn't think I was a tattoo girly.

Narrator: She had the most basic tattoos you could imagine. The word *love* in her grandmother's handwriting on her left wrist, a tiny elephant on her right forearm, and what was supposed to be an ampersand – but looked more like a capital E – in the middle of her back. She hated that one and tried to save it by adding flowers later. Don't ask what it means. It's dumb.

I went through phases where I loved showing off my tattoos, and others when I pretty much forgot I even had them. But it felt like a good omen to show the one on my back that night.

When I got it, I was deep in my *everything-will-work-out-how-it's-meant-to* phase. It lasted approximately two and a half seconds. The ampersand (aka this: &) was supposed to symbolize that there's always an "and." Always something else, something better, something meant to be, waiting on the other side of whatever hard thing is hap-pening right now.

Inner mean girl: We tried to warn you. So. Freakin. Dumb.

Still, I liked the idea that tonight could be the start of my "and."

I finished posting my lash review to my stories and checked the time on my lock screen. There was a new notification from the Weather Network:

Warning: severe winter storm watch in effect.

Meh. It would be fine. I wouldn't be out that late anyway. I had a strict one-and-a-half-hour rule, remember?

As I drove to the pub – about ten minutes from my place – the snow started to fall. It was piling up faster than I expected, and I felt my SUV, a recent upgrade from my tiny hatchback, slide a little as I came to a stop at the corner. Okay. I'd just drive slower. No biggie.

A little later than I intended, but still early, I pulled into the tiny parking lot, a thick layer of snow already covering the ground. I couldn't see the painted lines and it looked like the snow was turning into rain. I made my best guess at where to park, pulled in, and stepped out – immediately regretting the completely non-waterproof booties I'd chosen and my even more impractical jacket.

I tugged open the heavy wood doors and stepped into the vestibule (yes, I had to look that word up – it's the little space between the outer and inner doors) peering through the glass at the final barrier between me and this date with Dave. A man I'd exchanged a grand total of thirteen words with. Who, might I add, didn't even exist in my universe 36 hours ago.

The pub was small, with just enough space for two rows of tables across its width. I figured it could hold maybe 50 people, but I was terrible at estimating. It could've been 30. Or 70. Dyscalculia, remember?

I was early, but I somehow knew he'd be there. Sure enough, there he was waiting for me at a high-top table. Dave saw me through the glass, pushed his stool back, and stood up to greet me.

Should I hug him? I was a hugger. Was he? Was that why he stood up?

My stomach tightened, the familiar ripple of anxiety starting low and crawling up toward my throat. I walked over and opened my arms for a hug and the second he wrapped his arms around me, that pit in my stomach and heaviness in my chest evaporated.

My anxiety shifted. The tension in my stomach didn't disappear, but it instantly changed. Into butterflies...? Huh. That was definitely *not* standard first-date protocol.

We started talking. Or rather, *I* started talking. The butterflies flapped their way up into my throat, making me speed through stories, questions, and whatever other thoughts popped into my brain. I couldn't seem to stop.

Inner mean girl: Mariah. You are SO annoying. Stop talking so much. This is so awkward. He's going to get bored and never text you again. You're ruining everything.

I forced myself to pause, to ask *him* questions. I tried to give him room to steer the conversation. In my head, I was coaching myself – stay focused, keep the tangents to a minimum, don't interrupt, don't hijack the vibe.

This was nothing new. Most of my social interactions were an exercise in self-control. I spent so much energy trying not to blurt, not to dominate, not to be the *too much* girl. But Dave didn't seem to mind. He wanted me to talk. He asked questions and actually listened to the answers. He seemed to *enjoy* the way I spiraled into side stories and then somehow looped them back around.

We talked about everything – from nacho toppings to whether I'd ever homeschool my future kids. Why he joined the military. Some light family trauma. Casual first-date banter.

At one point, I got up to go to the bathroom, squeezing through the narrow space between tables and the bar. Once inside, I looked at myself in the mirror, instantly self-conscious.

Inner mean girl: Why did you wear those stupid lashes? It's so over the top and obviously fake. He's not into that kind of girl. And why are you sweating? You're so gross. At least you're wearing black. Maybe he can't tell.

I peeled the lashes off and splashed a bit of water on the back of my neck to cool down. My confidence slipped another notch as I adjusted my jeans. Pulled them higher. Fidgeted with my shirt. Tucked in? Not tucked in? I couldn't even remember how I walked in here.

Normally, I didn't care much about first impressions. My investment was low. But suddenly, I cared. A lot. I wished I'd dressed up a little more for the occasion. I took one last glance in the mirror and accepted that this was as good as it was going to get. Back at the table, Dave smiled as he slid his phone into his pocket. I sat down and, in true Mariah fashion, immediately blurted that I'd taken my eyelashes off because I felt like they were too much.

He chuckled and said he hadn't even noticed, then casually moved the conversation along. I glanced down at my watch and let out a small gasp. Assuming it was bad news, Dave asked if everything was okay.

"Uh... yeah, I guess so? I mean, no. I just – I broke a rule."

He tilted his head, confused. And I realized I was a 28-year-old woman talking about breaking rules like I was sneaking out after curfew. Which, to be fair, I kind of was.

"I have a first-date rule. Ninety minutes max. It's already been over two hours."

I thought back to the firefighter, the chiropractor, the guy with no job and a shower curtain that looked like a murder scene. On those dates, I'd spent most of the time sneaking glances at the clock, counting down the minutes until I could make my exit. But this time? I hadn't even checked the time in the bathroom when I took off my lashes.

"So... are you going to leave?" he asked slowly.

"I... I guess not?"

I tucked my watch back under my sleeve, and just like that, we kept talking – didn't miss a beat.

Another few hours passed (yep), and the pub started shifting from casual date night to crowded dance floor. The university students home for winter break trickled in, turning the cozy bar into a sweaty mess of flannel, crop tops, and cheap beer. Their very presence reminded us we were tired, and should probably go home.

Dave grabbed the bill, not even entertaining my default offer to split it. Before I knew it, we were slipping into our jackets and heading for the parking lot.

We stood in the middle of the snowy lot, close together, dragging out the goodbye. That classic "will he, won't he" buzz hung in the air, distracting me from whatever words were actually being said.

Kiss me. Just freakin' kiss me.

We talked for a few more minutes, my feet wet and freezing, my teeth starting to chatter thanks to my excellent outerwear choices. Hours had passed, and the snow was still falling. The flurries danced through the beams of the streetlights, making it feel like we were standing inside a real-life snow globe.

Eventually, the moment broke. It was time to go.

He asked for my number so we could talk off the app. We hugged again – our second hug – and turned toward our cars.

He didn't kiss me. I felt a jolt of awkwardness. *Maybe he didn't like me? It seemed like he did. Was I reading this wrong?*

Inner mean girl: lol

It got worse. We'd already said goodbye, but we were parked one car apart and awkwardly scraping thick layers of ice and snow off our windshields side by side. Five hours in the warm, cozy pub meant our poor cars had been left out in the cold to fend for themselves.

Finally, with my windshield clear and my hands frozen stiff, I plopped into the driver's seat. I sat on my fingers, letting my butt and the seat warmer double-team the job of thawing them out so I could drive home.

I replayed the night in my head, running through the conversations, the laughter, the look on his face when I left. The goodbye. The almost-kiss. And then, through the static in my brain, I heard Ruby's voice echo back to me, "Sometimes, you just gotta make the first move."

Ruby, like me, had been dating and putting in the effort. And like me, she'd been asserting herself more. When she told me she was tired of waiting around for guys to get the courage and had started asking them out herself I was so impressed.

That young girl in the grey prom dress, who needed me to fix the hair she hated after paying someone to do it but not speaking up, had grown up. Right in front of me.

What would Ruby do?

Told you I looked up to her. I opened the car door before I could talk myself out of it and walked around the snowy mound separating our cars. I tapped on his passenger side window and he rolled it down. I leaned my head in and blurted:

"I think you should kiss me."

He did. Without hesitating.

"Okay, bye for real," I said, pulling my head out of the window and running, carefully, back to the warmth of my waiting car. I texted Ruby to tell her I'd done it, and drove home. Giddy. Proud of myself.

Years later, after we were married (*oops, another spoiler*), Dave told me I ruined his plan. Apparently, he'd been sitting in his car having the same regrets. He was just about to reverse out of his spot to block me in and come to *my* window.

He *did* want to kiss me.

first day of grade seven

- CHAPTER 16 -

Core Wounds

"3, 2, 1, Happy New Year!"

Our screams echoed those on the TV from the New York City ball airing inside Rachel's tiny living room.

The noise only got louder as the room, crammed with about a dozen people, noticed Olivia kissing Austin. I was a little buzzed, partly from the wine (though I wasn't drinking much these days), but mostly from being in on the secret. I laughed and jumped up and down alongside the girls I'd known for over twenty years.

A few hours earlier, I'd gone over to Olivia's new downtown apartment so we could head to the party at Rachel's house together. It was reminiscent of our old pre-drinks, just with way less vodka-chugging and way more wine-sipping. We chatted while waiting for a couple other girls to arrive. It was just the two of us, and Olivia sat down across from me on the couch and said she wanted to talk to me about something.

I laughed nervously and took another sip.

My stomach tightened. My chest got heavy. That familiar feeling of anxiety crept its way up into my throat. I didn't want to go there. I didn't want to slip away. But it was too late.

I was underwater. I was in a tunnel. I was stuck in mud. I was everywhere and nowhere. I felt everything and nothing.

I couldn't think of anything except the last time we'd sat across from each other and she'd said those words, seventeen years earlier. I couldn't believe it was happening again. I couldn't believe I'd been so stupid. I thought I was being mature by showing up here early. The bigger person. I'd been proud of myself.

Inner mean girl: You're such a drama queen.

I tried to say something, but no words came out. I just sat there – eyes unfocused, face flushed. I was too busy trying to remember what breathing was supposed to feel like. Was it always this hard to fill my lungs? I could've sworn that I usually took longer inhales. It was like breathing into a space too tight to fully expand.

Certain I was doing a great job of looking cool, calm, and collected – while internally wondering if I was literally about to die – I nodded at her to continue. She took a big breath in.

Olivia and I used to be super close. Like, *I invited her – out of all my friends – to spend a week at my cottage with me the summer before Grade Seven* close. *Wearing matching horoscope baby tees* close.

Our friend group consisted of six girls: half of us had been together since kindergarten, and the other half joined when their school closed and their entire population got absorbed into ours for the sixth grade. We're going to call this group "The Core Group."

The Character Summaries You Didn't Ask For:

Rachel: Hilarious, outgoing, and loved by everyone, Rachel grew out of her "big ears" and mushroom cut and into a captivating teenager. She wasn't academically motivated, but every teacher adored her... and so did every parent (mine included. My mom basically wanted her to move in with us).

Jessica: Brilliant, well-spoken, destined for Harvard med school. The only one of us with divorced parents, and the only one on a sports team outside school. Her nails were always long, clicking on desks, and she could see right through your bullshit.

Marie: Blunt, brave, and self-assured. The middle child and a rare combo of smart, athletic, and social. She had the coveted loft bed with a Lego city so epic it belonged in a museum.

Sarah: Stunning, quiet, compassionate. Her parents let us draw in permanent markers on her bedroom walls (major cool points) and she shocked us by deferring nursing to travel the world solo at seventeen.

Hannah: Ahead of her time and unafraid to speak up. She got us to stop saying "that's so gay" long before it was cool to call that out. Her laugh was iconic, her rhythm nonexistent, and she was always game for anything.

Olivia: Head Girl, valedictorian, cheerleader, serial "bad-boy" dater. On paper, the classic popular girl, but without the mean streak. She followed every rule, was friends with everyone, and laughed off our constant (cringe) weight jokes.

A moment for the diet culture we were raised in. These "jokes" about Olivia's – again, totally normal – size were peak early-2000s girlhood. Think Samantha in *Sex and the City* treated like she had a shocking stomach, or Natalie in *Love Actually* called "the chubby girl" (huh??). Our jokes definitely weren't meant to be mean-spirited. But make no mistake: it was messed up.

By high school, The Core Group sat together every day in the cafeteria for lunch and spent every weekend in Hannah's basement. We were an established presence in the school – just as often seen as one unit as we were as individuals. Over time, subgroups emerged and flowed, but there was never an official hierarchy. In theory.

At sixteen, our priorities were bopping around town, exploring our independence, picking the perfect lyrics for our MSN statuses, and watching DVDs of *Friends* (even though I wasn't allowed – sorry, Mom). Back then, *geography* played a huge role in close-ness. I was one of the only girls to have a cellphone and social me-dia was only just picking up speed, so ease and access were major drivers of closeness.

This is a good point to start taking notes for the quiz.

I'm kidding.

Rachel, Jessica, and I were the Glebe girls. On the other side of the bridge in Old Ottawa South, Olivia, Sarah, and (eventually) Hannah lived about a 30-minute walk away. Marie – and Hannah before she moved – lived next to the high school, across another bridge, in a neighbourhood I never really knew the name of. Old Ottawa East, maybe? Our addresses definitely shaped some of the group dynamics – but there were other factors at play, too.

Hannah, Marie, and I carpooled to horseback riding every week.

Hannah, Marie, Sarah, and Olivia walked home from school together every day. Meanwhile, Rachel and I walked to and from school together, while Olivia, Sarah, Marie, and Hannah were altar girls at church on Sundays.

Jessica and I spent hours at the local bead shop making bracelets. Marie and Hannah grew up a few houses apart. Hannah and Olivia were deeply involved in school plays.

Sarah and I started running together after school.

Best friend status wasn't something we typically said out loud in the larger group – but everyone *knew.*

The Unofficial and Unauthorized High School Main Best Friends List:

- Hannah and Marie
- Sarah and Olivia
- Mariah and Rachel

The Unofficial and Unauthorized High School Subgroup List:

- Rachel and Olivia
- Sarah, Jessica, and Olivia
- Mariah, Marie, and Hannah
- Hannah, Olivia, and Sarah

You'll notice: Olivia was in *many* subgroups. Just... not any with me.

So when she said she wanted to talk to me on New Year's Eve, the little girl in me froze. That same girl – the one who always noticed where Olivia's name appeared, and where mine didn't – suddenly felt very, very small.

I've held this story close to my chest for what feels like my entire life, only really unpacking it in therapy when I sat down to write this section. It's probably one of the scariest things for me to share with you – not because it's dramatic or traumatic, but because I *know* it sounds trivial. And yet... it shaped the rest of my life.

June – sweet, sweet, doesn't-allow-me-to-stay-in-shame-spirals June – explained that this is a *core wound*. And me feeling *stupid* about holding onto something "so small" doesn't actually minimize the impact it had on me.

K. Rude.

I'm procrastinating telling you, can you tell? Here we go.

° +✭° °✭*

Olivia and I were sitting in the busy cafeteria, directly across from each other – the chatter of hundreds of students creating a strange sense of privacy that didn't make any logical sense in such a public space. We were a few seats away from the rest of The Core Group, and she was calm. Hands clasped on the dark table in front of her.

"My mom said we shouldn't be friends anymore."

I crossed and uncrossed my legs, hitting the bar that jutted out underneath the table and wincing – but whether it was from the sharp pain or the sentence itself, I wasn't sure. My face flushed.

Her mom (probably tired of hearing about our normal tween drama and distracted by making dinner) told Olivia to distance herself from me. That it wasn't worth it. That I was too dramatic, too emotional, and way too sensitive.

As an adult, I can appreciate that Olivia, fellow good girl and people-pleaser, was doing what she thought she was supposed to do. What she thought was best. Maybe even mature.

She probably practiced what to say. She probably thought I'd shrug, and we just wouldn't sit beside each other in French class anymore. I don't look back and think she was trying to be cruel. Or even that she was in the wrong. She, too, was just a twelve-year-old child, and I think it was hard for her to look me in the eye and say that. I think she probably did her best to say it nicely.

There's no way she could have known just how much that interaction was going to fuck me up.

Truthfully, I don't remember any specific issues or fights leading up to that moment – but I have no doubt they were there.

I know I was highly sensitive. I know I responded emotionally to what I perceived as judgment. I know I often felt on the outs – misunderstood, and like I cared more about my friends than they did about me. I know I sought validation in ways that annoyed people.

This wasn't the first time I'd heard a perception like Olivia's mom had shared with her. Marie's mom once called mine after too many playground blowups, saying the same. Even my own mom – who I pushed and triggered most of all – echoed it at times.

I felt so confused, always wishing I had "a friend like me." I couldn't put my finger on it, but I just felt different. Misunderstood. Alone. And those feelings only made me retreat further into my own world.

I wish I'd known those thoughts and feelings were my ADHD. That rejection sensitivity and lack of impulse control weren't proof I sucked, but part of how my brain worked. That my executive dysfunction made regulating emotions harder than it looked. But back then, no one knew. Instead of tools or support, I was handed brand after brand of birth control pills to "balance my hormones." The message was clear: my emotions were a problem to be solved, not supported.

Everything changed after that moment in the cafeteria.

Because though the group wasn't "divided," in that no one picked her side or stopped being my friend, the super shitty feeling of not being picked, or even just defended, consumed me. It hurt that no one said hey, that's not really nice. Or, I don't think you're a bad friend. Or that her mom was wrong.

Life continued. The Core Group stayed friends. There were still weekly sleepovers and nights out. We still sat together for lunch every day and were lumped together as a unit.

If anything, it was *me* who broke up the band. I changed, and so did my relationships within the group. I let myself drift away and become a welcome afterthought. A polite invitation. A "so nice to see you, it's been so long."

In therapy I've been sitting with the notion that they didn't pick me, *but they didn't pick her,* either.

June pointed out that at twelve years old, the bravery it took to continue to be both our friends and not pick a side was a big move in and of itself. It feels good to believe that. Most of the time, I do. Most of the time, I'm the adult in the room. But sometimes, I still feel like that twelve-year-old little girl.

*° +*ₒ °*⋆*

I've never given up on The Core Group. And they've never given up on me.

Our group chat still exists. Some relationships are stronger than others, but as far as I know, everyone in there would show up if someone needed them. It takes work for me to stay connected. To be open. To keep trying. Over the years, we've all acknowledged that it's not effortless. That we could all try harder. For me, that's easier said than done.

Still, I show up in person at least once or twice a year. I spend time in the chat when the messages catch me in a window I can reply in. I never regret being in their orbit.

A few months ago, I went to visit Rachel to meet her baby. Like Katie, she's one of those people that no matter how long it's been, it somehow feels like no time has passed.

While I was there, Rachel told me Olivia had brought up the cafeteria moment once or twice over the years. She said it gently, casually, while picking up toys and tidying the room. And then she said something that in almost 20 years, I'd never considered: Olivia regretted it.

Olivia told her she couldn't remember the cause either but that no matter what it *had* been about, the reaction hadn't made sense. That we were young and impressionable, and none of us understood how powerful our words could be.

I couldn't look at Rachel and distracted myself by playing with her daughter.

I felt the little girl inside me curl up, pulling her knees tighter to her chest, when Rachel added another observation I'd never considered. She said she noticed a change in me after that day. That my light dimmed. That I started censoring myself. She said the girl who used to be her best friend, make jokes, call her out, be fully herself was just gone.

A few weeks later, Marie was in town, and we were back at Rachel's – just days before Olivia's wedding. I brought it up, playing it off

117

with a joke about how, in therapy with June, we'd identified it as a "core wound" and how ridiculous it felt to still be hurt by something so small.

Marie, who I'd gotten close with again after we both became moms, walked over without hesitation. She hugged me and whispered, "I'm sorry."

I hadn't anticipated an apology. I changed the subject.

*° +★o ♣

Okay, it's been a minute since we started this chapter. Remember how I was on the couch and Olivia said she wanted to tell me something... and then I took you down about 37 pages of core wound trauma?

Showing up at this New Year's party was one of those attempts to find my footing in The Core Group again. I was pushing myself to attend – choosing this event over seeing my old coworkers from the community centre, my teaching friends, or even my running club buddies. And I was excited. Nervous, sure. But excited to spend the holiday with my oldest friends.

Plus, I was still riding the high of meeting Dave.

As I sat there, waiting for whatever bomb Olivia had to drop, my excitement for the night twisted into shame and regret. My stomach started hurting the way it did before most social gatherings. The way it did every day at lunch in sixth grade.

What was I thinking, coming here? Why did I put myself in this position?

Inner mean girl: I truly don't know why you thought she'd actually want to spend time alone with you.

I rubbed my hands along my thighs, the crushed velvet of the jumpsuit soothing my anxiety just a little. I started squeezing and releasing my toes while I waited.

"I know we've been bonding and connecting more lately about being the only single girls in the group," she said, "and you've been so supportive."

It was true. The Core Group was full of rock-solid relationships, which made our single girl dating life even more annoying – and more lonely. We'd been leaning on each other when feeling like a third, or seventh, wheel really sucked. I tried to anticipate what she'd say. Normally, I could tell how a conversation would end within the first breath.

"So, I wanted to tell you before everyone else that Austin and I have been dating for a while... and we're going to tell everyone tonight."

I couldn't have been more shocked. Not about them dating. I barely knew Austin and had zero strong feelings about them as a couple. I was shocked there *wasn't* a bomb. And even more so, that she had intentionally chosen to tell me first. That she had so intentionally considered my feelings.

After years of feeling left out, overlooked, or always the last to know, that short conversation with Olivia – just the two of us, across from each other, like that day in Grade Seven – felt huge.

I clapped my hands together in relief, masking it as excitement, and asked her to start from the beginning. To tell me *everything*. The plan was to reveal the big secret by kissing at the countdown, in front of everyone. I checked the time. Almost 9pm. I sucked at keeping secrets, but I could do it for three hours. That was fine. I was fine. It was kind of fun being in the know when I was usually the last to find out anything.

Waiting for midnight went by faster than expected. All it took were some early 2000s hits playing on the TV, flowing drinks, and a tipsy call with Dave to make it to the ball to drop.

At midnight, I was surrounded by couples kissing, but for once, I felt fine being the only girl without a date. Happy, even.

The phone call with Dave replayed in my mind. I'd spent about 30 minutes talking to him, sitting on the floor between Rachel's bed and the wall, when she and Hannah burst in, ready to confiscate the offending device that was pulling me away from the party. Full of laughs, they stumbled over and took my phone, launching into a light-hearted inquisition of Dave and his intentions with me.

I loved it.

After a few minutes, I got the phone back and Dave said he should go – I heard his buddies in the background telling him to get off the phone with his girlfriend and get back to the party.

"Girlfriend?" I asked.

"If you want," he replied steadily.

"So we're just boyfriend and girlfriend now?"

I was giddy.

"Guess so, girlfriend."

"Sounds good, boyfriend."

I hung up, announced the news, and it was my turn to be celebrated – jumping up and down with my oldest friends.

It felt like I was finally in the room.

I think I stopped dimming, just a little, at that moment.

the night he said it first

— CHAPTER 17 —

The Blue Couch

"Hey man, I approve!"

He yelled it after us as we climbed the steep hill from the waterfront bar to the main road in downtown Halifax. We'd spent the night out with Dave's friends, but this particular guy was the one Dave was closest to. I couldn't stop the huge smile from spreading across my face.

He approved! He liked me!

Without missing a beat, Dave looked over his shoulder and called back, "It wouldn't have mattered if you didn't," keeping his hand tight in mine as we kept walking. Okay, that was pretty freakin' cute. But still – his friend liking me was a huge win.

The wind picked up the higher we climbed, but I was so flushed from dancing that I barely noticed the cold.

Dave's one-bedroom apartment in downtown Halifax was surprisingly clean when I arrived the day before. Military guy – I guess that checked out. I could see why he loved it here. His place overlooked the harbour, and everything he needed was twenty minutes, max, on foot.

It was late February, just a couple of degrees above freezing, and this was my first time seeing him since our quick meetup in Toronto the month before. I'd rushed out of school the second the bell rang – screw the 15-minute buffer rule – to catch my flight. I'd never forget the look on his face when I stepped off the escalator and into his arms.

"Baggage check is this way," he said, motioning to the left.

"Oh, this is all I brought. I'm only here for two days," I replied, twisting slightly to show him the bag on my back.

I could tell he liked that.

"Awesome. I'm a carry-on only guy too."

Cue internal hair flip at how perfectly matched we were based on this one tiny and ultimately insignificant trait.

We held hands and walked out of the terminal, both of us a little nervous. We talked every day and definitely liked each other, but we hadn't spent much time in person. A few days over Christmas break, one night in Toronto, a stopover in Ottawa when he was moving from Borden to Halifax – and now, this weekend.

What if we didn't get along? What if we actually didn't like each other?

That first night, he made pizza and we spent the whole evening talking and laughing. All my nerves melted away. It was so easy being there. I didn't feel a lick of anxiety all weekend.

Well – other than worrying about Ollie, who was staying with my parents and now taking daily medication for his own anxiety.

We'd planned to spend the weekend doing nothing and everything. Just existing as a couple. Watching movies, ordering food, going for walks. It was cold, but the sun was shining, and we weren't in a rush to get anywhere. On Saturday, we walked to and from the downtown core, grabbing coffee (for me – possible red flag that he didn't drink any??) and wandering along the waterfront. All of these normalcies were such luxuries for us as a long-distance couple. We did our best to "date" from different provinces with virtual game nights and fancy FaceTime dinners, but none of it compared to actually being together.

These little strolls taught me one thing very quickly: Halifax was made for walking. The booties I was wearing were not. And since no one wants a play-by-play of my blister situation, let's get into the juicy stuff.

I'd never been in a long-distance relationship before, and I didn't know what to expect. But a big part of me felt it was the safest choice. I wouldn't be tempted to change my routines or my entire personality – his presence in my life would be specific and compartmentalized. I couldn't go so hard, so fast like I always did.

Narrator: She says, after becoming boyfriend and girlfriend in less than a week.

Most importantly, I was determined not to fall in love first. But *very* early on, it happened. Like... first week of January about a week after we met early on.

Narrator: You were saying?

I was setting up a fish tank I'd picked up off *Facebook* Marketplace for my classroom. Struggling to get the filter going, my phone was propped against the kitchen faucet while I leaned over the tank, trying to figure out why it wasn't turning on.

Dave was a few weeks into his final stretch of training learning to repair helicopters in the Air Force. He too had his phone propped up while we chatted, like we'd done every night since he left.

"Okay, it says here you need to start by taking off that back clip."

I looked up, stunned. He was helping me. *Unprompted.*

Dave had looked up the manual for the filter, downloaded the PDF, and was reading the troubleshooting guide out loud to me over the phone.

And suddenly, warmth. My cheeks flushed. My heart swelled with gratitude.

There was no judgment about my struggle to set up the tank. No annoyance that this was how I was spending our call. No excuse to get off the phone. Just... help. Because he *wanted* to help me. That was the first moment the words *I love you* popped into my brain. But I mentally calculated how long we'd been together (three weeks) and told myself I needed to calm down.

I tried not to think about it again.

We kept walking up the hill, laughing and chatting the whole way. Back at his apartment we immediately collapsed onto the blue couch.

"It's green," Dave teased.

I rolled my eyes. Our first "fight" was about the couch. Was it blue (yes) or green (no)? We both agree it was teal, but the colour family that teal belongs to remains hotly debated to this day.

I snuggled deeper into the cushions. I was tired, and content. I couldn't even remember the last time I'd gone out dancing. Earlier that night, Dave and I had met up with his friends at a taco place for drinks.

By the time the tacos were gone, we'd decided to walk around the main streets to find somewhere to dance. I was on a self-proclaimed mission to help them "wheel" and planning to be the best wing woman ever. Being the only girl in a group wasn't my normal anymore. But it had been, when I was best friends with Seb. Just in a *way* more toxic way.

The summer after I graduated from teacher's college, I spent most of my time with a subset of my community centre coworkers – "the bros." I was the only girl accepted as a regular in their tight bromance.

Let's be clear: I was not a "cool girl." I gave major golden retriever energy. Just happy to be there.

It was easy to relax around them. I was included in the jokes, but could also just sit back and enjoy their company. No pressure to perform. No one to impress. No judgment (except for my inability to drink like they did). Just a bunch of dudes being dudes – and me, fading comfortably into the background.

Seb was the most popular guy at work and by far the most codependent friend I'd ever had. Our houses were two blocks apart, and we saw each other every single day.

"Come fold laundry."

"Want to return this shirt with me?"

"Come sit in the yard."

"Can you help me clean out my room?"

Everyone assumed we were secretly dating, but we weren't.

Inner mean girl: You are delusional if you thought you had a chance.

Years later, while gathering receipts for this book, Katie cut me off mid story: "No, girl. No, no. He was *hardcore lovebombing you.* It was unreal. This was not in your head."

Maybe. But in 2014, "lovebombing" wasn't in my vocabulary – or even on my radar as what was happening. I was happy. Accepted and safe – the girl who was chosen.

Until I wasn't.

Seb started dating a girl he met on a night out. I was hurt – and our friendship was never the same. She didn't want her boyfriend to be best friends with another girl (I wouldn't either). So, suddenly, I was on the outs. That's when I couldn't hide from the truth anymore. I *hadn't* been chosen. I was filling a role until someone he *actually* wanted came along.

In Halifax with Dave, I felt the same kind of safety and closeness I'd felt back then – but this time, it wasn't convenient or conditional.

With Seb, I was picked when it was easy.

With Dave, I was chosen on purpose.

*° +*₀*

After tacos in Halifax, I realized Dave *might* be in love with me. We were in an almost empty bar, dancing like idiots, scream-singing, pulling out ridiculous moves just to make each other laugh.

Standing face-to-face, I was scream-singing *"I don't care! I love it!"* as Icona Pop blared over the speakers. Disco ball lights swirled above us. Dave put a hand to his ear and teased, "What? What's that? You love me?"

I rolled my eyes, did a spin, and yelled in his ear, "If you have something you wanna say, say it. I'm not saying it."

He laughed. "Not here."

What did that mean? Did he?

Inner mean girl: He isn't saying it because he doesn't.

An hour later, our buzz was fading and our energy was, too. We said goodbye to the guys, went our separate ways, got the shout of approval from his friend, and eventually collapsed onto his blue (not green) couch. I looked up at him, trying to play it cool while also tee-ing him up. Lights from the harbour glowing behind him. I asked, "Is there anything you want to tell me?"

"What? That I love you?" He smiled and looked away.

"Well. Do you?" I pressed.

He turned back to me, grinning. "I do."

I smiled back, snuggled in a little closer, and replied, "Oh, that's nice."

He rolled his eyes. I laughed. And *then* I said it.

"I love you, too."

— CHAPTER 18 —

Google History: How come I

🔍 How come I feel so awkward eating in front of people

Disordered Eating

ADHD is linked to a higher prevalence of disordered eating patterns, including restrictive eating, binge eating, and body image concerns. Difficulties with impulse control, emotional regulation, and interoceptive awareness (recognizing hunger and fullness cues) can contribute to irregular eating habits. Social anxiety, rejection sensitivity, and a history of self-consciousness may further intensify discomfort when eating in public or in front of others. These factors can combine to create complex, often hidden, relationships with food and body image.[19]

🔍 How come I won't go to bed even though I'm tired and not doing a good job anymore because I want to finish my website?

Hyperfixation

An intense and prolonged focus on a specific interest, activity, or topic, often to the exclusion of other responsibilities or needs. While hyperfixation can lead to high productivity or mastery in the chosen area, it can also result in neglect of basic self-care, disrupted routines, and difficulty shifting attention to other priorities. Common in ADHD, it differs from general interest in its immersive and consuming nature.[20-22]

first meeting

— CHAPTER 19 —

"Is she in love with you or something?"

I found a high-top table facing the departure gates and opened my bag. I pulled out my laptop and a bottle of Gravol rattled at the bottom of my bag.

It was time for me to go back to Ottawa. Well. Almost.

Dave dropped me off at the airport before heading into the base and I settled in at the Starbucks, five hours ahead of my short flight home. It had been totally worth it to book the later flight. I wanted to squeeze every last second out of the trip. Besides, Audrey always said she got her best work done at airports and car dealerships.

I picked up the bottle, surprised by how full it was, and carefully placed two tiny yellow pills into my pocket for the flight.

Normally, sleeping next to someone meant not sleeping at all. I was a notoriously light sleeper, and I had carefully rationed the pills to make sure I'd have enough for each night and the flight home. But I hadn't taken Gravol once all weekend. I'd fallen asleep easily every night, cuddled up next to Dave in the middle of his massive California King bed.

It was a sign.

Inner mean girl: There's no such thing as *signs*. You read into everything.

The first few times we'd spent the night together, I chalked it up to a fluke. But after we met up at that noisy hotel in Toronto – squeezing in a quick visit while we both happened to be there between my conference and his flight to Halifax mid January – I slept fine. Like, *actually* fine. Even with the noise. Even in a strange bed. Even with a man beside me. And that fluke started to feel a little less like luck, and a little more like home.

I pressed the button, and swayed side to side. The numbers lit up as the elevator slowly made its way up to the room number sprawled in permanent marker on my keycard.

One.

This was crazy. Scandalous honestly.

Two.

I'm in a different city, at a hotel, for less than twelve hours.

Three.

It's already 9pm and he said he needs to leave by 7am.

Four.

Okay. It's fine. I can just leave if I need to.

Five.

I barely know this guy.

Six.

We hadn't seen each other in weeks, and only once since making it official on New Years, but the second I stepped into the room, my nerves disappeared. I was instantly calm – and very tired. We decided to stay in.

We ordered fancy hot dogs and poutine, eating them in bed and trying not to drip ketchup and relish onto the white sheets. We watched cooking shows and got into all the conversations you're not supposed to have. Money. Politics. Religion. Gender roles. We agreed on some things and our values behind the others lined up. More importantly, we could talk through the things that we didn't agree on.

Soaking up every second we could together, we went to bed way too late (early?). Dave switched off the lights and I fell asleep.

Just like that.

The extra espresso shot in my Chai latte was hitting hard after a weekend of instant coffee, and I leaned into it – ready to bury my feelings under a mountain of productivity. I opened up PowerPoint and set out to finish and post a new product in my online store.

Saying goodbye that morning in Toronto had been hard. Leaving him after the weekend in Halifax was even harder.

We wouldn't see each other for another month, and I was already counting down the days. I couldn't wait to pick him up at the airport. To introduce him to my parents. To meet his. To just *be together* again and do normal things like watch TV and walk Ollie.

Distracted from my original attempt at a distraction, I texted my mom to ask how Ollie was doing.

I stared at the screen, anxiously waiting for her reply. Less than a year in, and Ollie was already on his second dog trainer. My mom was an incredible dog owner, and I wanted reassurance Ollie was fine, and that I wasn't totally fucking him up.

A wave of self-loathing hit. I decided to punish myself by replaying the memory I hated most: puppy school.

*° *⋆ₒ °⋆*

"Why didn't you walk out?" my mom fumed.

I sat in the car, crying into Ollie's fur, his tiny body shaking in my arms.

Why *hadn't* I walked out? I knew I'd never go back. But was I too late? Had I already done the damage?

When I first brought Ollie home, I signed up for puppy classes. He was the youngest in the group, the only rescue – and, obviously, the cutest. He was also the most fearful and reactive. I struggled to find a treat that could hold his focus when he was overstimulated. We weren't star students, but we were figuring it out. Until the day we practiced recall.

I was sitting alone, closest to the trainer's chair, trying to keep Ollie calm while other puppies ran across the room to their owners. It was the first time we'd been asked to *untether* their leashes one by one and he wouldn't stop barking.

I didn't know it then, but this kind of scenario is a known trigger – especially for rescues. A leashed dog watching other dogs run off leash is a recipe for panic. They can't flee, so all they have left is fight.

The trainer told me to stand with Ollie at the back of the room beside a closed door telling me, "Every time he barks, open the door, put him inside and close the door."

She demonstrated. It was pitch black. Ollie was afraid of the dark. Everyone was staring at us, their judgment (empathy?) making me feel hot and exposed and I didn't know what else to do. So I did what she said, simply because she told me to. Again. And again.

My throat tightened. My chest got heavy. That familiar tunnel vision crept in – the one that hijacks my ability to speak up, to walk out, to do *anything* but comply.

I have no idea how many times I shut him in that room – responding to his fear with more fear. Every time I opened the door, he barked. Every time he barked, she told me to be consistent. To do it again. That he would learn. Autopilot engaged.

When class ended, I scooped Ollie up, tears streaming down my cheeks onto his tiny body, and ran to my car without saying a word. I *knew* it was wrong. But I'd done it anyway. I called my mom, sobbing and full of shame. I was supposed to be his protector. His safe place.

I never went back. I couldn't.

My mom's reply came within a few seconds of me checking in on Ollie. He was doing well and her biggest complaint was that he barked a little when he heard the neighbours. I let myself hope that the work we were doing with a new, private trainer, was actually working.

Satisfied, I turned back to my computer, ready to finish up the product on my screen that I'd been putting off finishing for weeks. I couldn't focus on the screen. Couldn't get myself to upload it to TpT. I just kept having the same thought over and over: *I wish I could stay a bit longer.*

Narrator: Time for a dopamine hit. We will *not* be crying at the airport, ma'am.

I opened *Instagram* and posted a picture of my Starbucks setup and a sneak peek of the product I was definitely not procrastinating.

I still hadn't told my followers that I was dating anyone. But I felt like I would soon. Especially now that we'd dropped the L word. He was the first big part of my life I kept offline and I *liked* keeping Dave private. Safe. Sacred even. No opinions. No outside energy. I didn't want their approval (or disapproval, and for the first time, I didn't need it.

My weekend adventures had been carefully shared, and though some of my closest followers were starting to get suspicious, the majority assumed I had gone to Halifax to see Audrey. Two of their favourite kindergarten creators had finally met in person! We had a very public friendship, and the people were *invested* so visiting her was a reasonable assumption. And we *did* meet up.

But brunch hadn't gone quite how I expected and yes, gentle reader, it's time for me to tell you about it.

At first, I chalked it up to nerves – or the pressure of finally meeting someone I'd only known online.

Dave saw it differently.

Let me start by saying: for every intrusive, hypersensitive spiral I had, Dave was grounded in logic. Steady. Calm. Rational to a borderline annoying degree. Like okay, we get it – you're *emotionally regulated*.

He was also the least gossipy person I'd ever met. The man didn't have a mean thing to say about anyone and couldn't care less about other people's business. Again: slightly annoying.

Narrator: More like, mentally stabilizing.

So when we left brunch with Audrey, her husband, and her daughter... Dave's debrief on the walk back to his apartment caught me off guard.

"Well, that was uncomfortable," he said, glancing at me as we walked back toward his apartment.

"What? Why do you say that?" I was immediately on the defensive – my stupid blister hurt, and so did my feelings.

"Is she in love with you or something?"

I stopped walking. "What?"

"I don't know. Maybe I'm way off base, but that was weird. She was just staring at you the whole time. Barely said a word to me. It's like I wasn't even there. Honestly, it's like her husband and daughter weren't even there either. She only wanted to talk about herself – to you. Like she was pitching something. It was so weird."

I didn't know what to say. This was the first – and honestly, maybe the only – time I'd ever heard Dave say something overtly critical about someone. Normally, he either didn't care, didn't notice, or didn't think of it that way. But he had said something. Unprompted. That had to mean something... right?

I mean, yeah. I felt like something was off. But I told myself we were just nervous and adjusting to offline expectations. I was confident she wasn't in love with me – *that* part was way off – and I told him as much. But I didn't have anything else to say. I couldn't defend the brunch. It *had* been weird.

Before we met, I would've called Audrey one of my closest friends. We talked all day, every day. Her and Viv, another teacher creator in the online space, were the first people I told anything – *everything*. It was hard to imagine my life without our rock solid group chat pinging every few minutes.

Meeting her in person had felt different than I expected. Not *bad*, per se. Just... off. And I wondered if the person she presented online was different from who she really was. That thought made me feel guilty. I didn't want to be the kind of person who judged someone for how they showed up. Sure, I was an oversharer who had no boundaries and showed up as my honest-to-goodness-hot-mess self online. But, I didn't think my approach was particularly strategic or healthy and didn't expect it from others. Certainly not from an experienced business owner like her building a huge brand.

Still, I couldn't ignore it. I found myself replaying old conversations, looking for clues. Trying to make sense of it. I felt unsettled. Unsure.

What was I missing?

Inner mean girl: You're such a psycho. No wonder you don't have any friends. Look what you're doing to one of your so-called best friends. What do you think *she's* thinking about *you?*

In the group chat, it was like nothing had happened. We never acknowledged the weirdness of the in-person meetup – it just went back to business as usual. Daily messages. Constant tagging. Our usual banter.

I couldn't bring myself to share our brunch selfie for a few weeks. Nothing I captioned it felt genuine. But when I finally did, buried in a blog post about my Halifax weekend and boyfriend reveal, our online communities were delighted.

< aplayfulpurpose	
● primary 5 ● general 13 requests >	
👤	**TrilingualTingle** Finally photo evidence of your meeting! I was starting to think you made it up!
👤	**AaronF** My two favs!
👤	**SaraBug** looks like the best time ever!

Little did SaraBug know – it actually *was* the best time ever.

Just not for the reasons she thought.

— CHAPTER 20 —

Google History: Why does he

Q Why does he feel like "home"

Co-Regulation

Co-regulation is the process by which one person's nervous system helps stabilize another's emotional and physiological state. In safe, trusting relationships, a more emotionally regulated person can non-verbally communicate calm through tone, body language, breathing, and presence. This interaction can help someone experiencing heightened anxiety, stress, or dysregulation return to a steadier state. For individuals with ADHD – whose nervous systems may default to hyperarousal – consistent co-regulation from a trusted partner can reduce emotional reactivity and support long-term nervous system health.[15]

the grid photo

— CHAPTER 21 —

Unedited: Instagram Isolation

[Alt text: A woman with long blonde hair in a ponytail sits on a couch in a cozy living room, wearing a bright yellow sweater and black leggings. She smiles warmly at her brown dog, who is lying across her lap on a light blue quilt. The dog looks up at her lovingly. Behind them is a blue accent wall with framed art and a modern copper lamp.]

♡ 113   💬 20

March 16, 2020

aplayfulpurpose Something has been weighing heavy on my mind the last few days but I'm going to try to keep the tone positive while I share a perspective I haven't yet seen on social media.

Social distancing has been causing my anxiety to skyrocket and my tears to flow, resulting in countless phone calls to those who support and love me. I can't help but compare my situation to those who are home with families. I haven't had physical contact in 4 days and as someone who's love language is physical touch, this feels dehumanizing. I have had a few visits with people, but I imagine those will slow to a stop. I'm lucky and grateful that domestic travel is permitted and that Dave is due to arrive for a few days tomorrow.

Is it challenging to be home with the same people everyday? I'm sure that it is. I only know my challenge, which is that I'm supposed to be home alone for the foreseeable future.

Will it be two weeks? Will it be three months? The uncertain timeline seems daunting and overwhelming.

Video calls and texts are great, but for me they don't replace human connection. They help a little, and I'm thankful to live in a world with so much access to technology. I can't imagine being in this situation without the internet or my phone.

I also can't imagine being without my pets. They are truly part of my family. They bring me interaction, joy and a forced routine that I'm so grateful for.

So, let's be mindful and supportive and loving to those friends who wish for a family, a baby, a pet, a partner. Because in this time of social distancing, those holes might feel deeper and darker than ever before. Check in with your people – no matter what situation they are in.

Social distancing is hard for everyone– I'm not trying to say anyone's situation is worse than others. I just think it's important to acknowledge that for some people, social distance and avoiding "unnecessary trips out of the home" does end up meaning social isolation.

goodbye, my love

— CHAPTER 22 —

Coconut Shrimp

Okay, so back to the coconut emoji.

Narrator: Yes, we are back on the original timeline after a multi-chapter diversion.

JT (Justin Trudeau, not Timberlake) announced we were shutting down the country for "two weeks to flatten the curve." I was *freaking jazzed* at the idea of not going back to the classroom, and Dave had just landed for his week-long visit.

Back then, sharing unpopular opinions online wasn't exactly new to me, but it was still scary. I was someone who said what felt true, even if it wasn't cool or trendy or socially easy – and in doing so, I built deeper connections with the people in my community who felt the same, but were either too scared to say it or too ashamed they felt that way at all. It's how I developed a reputation as a safe space. Where teachers didn't need to pretend everything was great. Where it was okay to use worksheets, to take mental health days, and to not be thrilled about the teacher strike.

As much as I didn't want it to be a controversy, I knew how my relationship looked from the outside. So, I used the lull in education content to share bits and pieces of my relationship with Dave but still kept it pretty close to my chest. I fudged the timeline (Just "December" sounded better than December 26th), pretended the long distance was easy, and played it cool when inside I felt all-consuming intensity.

Dave and I spent the week making the most of our time together and ignoring the chaos outside – even though it felt like the world was burning. Walks with Ollie to the dog park, watching movies, and meeting each other's parents (from six feet apart, as per new rules). We spent hours in my office, each of us on our laptops – Dave playing games, me making learning packets to send home with students. I created and uploaded every theme I could think of to my store. No one knew what was going on and I wanted to get as much support out as timely as possible. Plus, they were selling like hot cakes.

While we worked, we'd chat here and there. One afternoon, the topic of pet names came up. None of the ones my exes had used felt right coming from him. Babe. Gorgeous. Baby. *Pup*.

We started joking about what we should call each other, and then – out of nowhere – Dave declared, "I'm going to call you Shrimp since I'm *so* much taller than you."

"I don't even *like* shrimp," I shot back.

"Too late," he grinned. "That's your name. I'm putting a shrimp beside your name in my phone."

I had to think fast. "Well then, I'm calling you Coconut."

We both hated coconut.

The fact that coconut shrimp is an actual appetizer sealed the deal. We started ending all our messages with our first private joke, a shrimp or a coconut emoji – and sometimes both.

° ⁺★₀ °★

As the end of the week approached, so did our ability to pretend everything was fine. What had started as jokes about an extra-long March Break quickly turned into genuine fear about what the heck was going on. Saturday was my 29th birthday, and suddenly I was glued to the daily Covid updates at noon. Overnight, I'd become a news watcher.

Lines marked the grocery store floors, masks were mandatory, and Ottawa declared a state of emergency. Nova Scotia followed.

How could an invisible force be causing so much panic? How did something so obscure have so much control?

It felt unbelievable. It *was* unbelievable. I kept thinking I'd wake up soon...or someone would announce it was some kind of global prank.

Just a day after Dave learned the military was suspending all leave passes (aka permission to leave the general area of their base) indefinitely, Nova Scotia announced they were questioning, and turning away, non-Maritime residents at the provincial border.

Dave wasn't allowed out.

And I wasn't allowed in.

I had finally met *the* guy and now this "unprecedented event" was keeping us apart? As if distance hadn't already made things hard enough?

WTF, universe?

My brain went into full chaos mode.

Did I need to leave today to beat the lockdown? Could Ollie handle apartment life in Halifax? What about my house? My job?

It had taken me days to muster the courage to talk to my principal about a leave of absence to spend the following year in Halifax. I was so worried she'd say no – or that the board would – especially since there was a shortage of French teachers.

She reviewed my application and told me to start over, cautioning me against using the word "boyfriend." She didn't want me to be put in a position where I'd have to choose between quitting my job or staying. I didn't either—because I knew what I'd pick, and it wasn't job security.

I went back to my classroom, rewrote the application and sent it off. The very next day, my leave was approved. It was official. I was off, and unpaid, for the 2020–2021 school year.

But if I wasn't allowed into the province... what the hell was I taking a year unpaid for?

I already felt behind. The idea of putting my relationship on pause, and pushing any reasonable timeline for marriage and kids even fur-ther out made me want to scream. Or puke. Or pop Ollie into the car and drive 15 hours with nothing but a suitcase and a dream.

But I didn't.

Against all my natural instincts – and with Dave's calm, steady voice in my ear, reminding me it *would* work out, that we'd be back to-gether soon – I didn't pack up my life the second my flight response kicked in. Maybe for the first time... I stayed.

"Love you, Shrimp," he smirked before giving me one last kiss.

"Love you, too, Coconut."

My body was in turmoil as I waved goodbye to him at the airport, the weight of not knowing when we'd see each other again settling into my stomach like a pile of bricks.

It couldn't have felt more wrong.

I kept waiting for a sign I'd made the right choice. It didn't come.

Fuck. This.

locked up

— CHAPTER 23 —

Mirror, mirror

Lockdown solo sucked. The only thing worse than not being able to see Dave was who I *was* seeing: myself.

For years I'd mastered how to pay extremely close attention to my surroundings. I made note of how people were feeling and what they did next. I trained myself to anticipate reactions, so I could try to *always* make the choice that would make someone else happy – or at least just not mad at me. I started playing out entire conversations in my head before they happened – just to tweak my tone, my word choice, my energy – to best fit the person in front of me. I was an expert in the art of mirroring – matching someone's language, humour, judgments, and behaviours so seamlessly that I created close bonds with individuals (and killer first date impressions).

The strategy worked – until it didn't. Every so often, someone would accuse me of being manipulative. Normally, I was quick to absorb harsh criticism and take it as fact. But manipulation implies a motive. A plan. A hidden agenda you're executing to control someone else. And I never felt that was me. I wasn't trying to control anyone. I was just trying not to make people mad at me. I wasn't manipulating – I was surviving.

Over time, I developed multiple versions of myself without even realizing it. I could adapt to any setting. Blend in. Become whatever version of me would be the best fit. I could be the party girl or the girl who ran half marathons. The hyper-organized girl or the *let's just see what happens* girl. The one you wanted to take home to your parents or the one sending texts that made you blush.

This got a little complicated in groups when the individuals knew different versions of me. And in a group who was I supposed to be doubling anyways? Which personality was I supposed to use as a lighthouse for social acceptance?

So then the world shut down and I was alone. I didn't know who to be. Or what I liked. Or what I wanted.

Inner mean girl: What the fuck? That's literally so messed up. Who doesn't know who they are at basically 30 years old?

Naturally, I did what any woman would do in that situation.

Narrator: Spend time in therapy figuring out who you are and giving yourself the space to be her?

I avoided reality entirely and threw myself into my business instead – pouring every ounce of energy I had into the only all-consuming influence left in my life: Teachergram.

Narrator: Oh boy.

Enter: Mariah circa Grade Five – the slightly controlling group project leader who *insisted* on being the only one allowed to write on the chart paper. With nothing else on my plate, I started organizing collaborations with other teachers on *Instagram* like it was my freakin' job.

I mean, it kind of *was*. Virtual teaching was a joke at this point. I created lesson plans and activities for my kids, hopped online for an hour or two, and then... nothing. The rest of my day was wide open for catastrophizing, panicking about the state of the world, and spiraling about the fact that both the government and the military were forbidding me from seeing my boyfriend.

Clearly, not a great use of time. So instead, I channeled all that frantic energy into my business.

I grew my audience with funny challenges and collaborative posts. I hosted giveaways to boost morale. I cranked out new products, built online adaptations, and created tools and lessons specific to virtual teaching. I was ready for the "new normal" – and I was *fast*. My ability to hyperfocus, perform under pressure, and pump out high-quality work put me *way* ahead of the curve.

And yeah, my store took off. I had my first 10k month the same month I launched the first Teachergram group chat.

At first, it was buzzing. There were sixteen of us firing messages back-and-forth. I'd pulled in everyone I vaguely knew and pitched the idea of making a collage together. Each of us would hold up a word on a piece of paper, and I'd stitch the photos together into one big message to post on our feeds:

"One day we will look back and be proud of how we persevered and came together."

Inner mean girl: Barf.

But it wasn't always so serious or try-hard. We dressed up fancy and took pictures in our bathtubs. We ordered matching tie-dye sweat suits before sweatsuits were cool. We did a baby photo "guess who" challenge and pulled together a big gift card giveaway.

Eventually, daily conversation slowed down. That's when Audrey, Viv and I started our own chat. They had both stood out to me in the larger chat: always available, always down to brainstorm. We had similar work patterns, similar ambition, and similar *this-might-be-un-hinged-but-let's-go* energy.

We talked all day, every day. Part business, part personal. And fairly quickly, I genuinely felt like we were the best of friends.

Even though it was entirely online, Viv and Audrey were my go-to group for *everything*. We were, I thought, real and true friends.

arrival at our house

— CHAPTER 24 —

The Accident

I crept across the laminate floors, each step creaking as I reached the bed. Quietly, I stuttered, "Dave. I. I'm. Something's happened."

My whole body was shaking. Shocked. Breathless. It felt like there was an electric current running through me, short-circuiting my ability to form words. It was pitch-black in our room, the curtains swallowing every trace of light from the streetlamps outside. Our house was small, but at that moment, it felt enormous.

"What do you mean?"

We'd been living there for about five months. The house reminded me of the quirky apartment I loved on Second Avenue – all big windows and dated floors that caught the light just right. In June, I felt at home as soon as I walked in.

Narrator: A huge relief considering she bought it without ever stepping foot inside.

With plans to move firmly in place but the border closed, Dave went house-hunting for me. He called me from each property, failing miserably at maintaining neutrality at the walkthroughs. I was on team, "any house could be the *right* house" and I haaaated dragging out decisions. His excitement for this house was obvious and that was all I needed to see.

Sometimes, you just know. And sometimes, you just go with it.

"I... I just took a test," I said. "It says pregnant."

He couldn't be mad at me. I was just the messenger. The pregnancy test was the real villain here.

"Are you sure you did it right?"

Peeing on a stick and waiting two minutes for the screen to say *pregnant* or *not pregnant* was pretty hard to mess up.

"I mean... I think so?"

"Do you have another one?"

I nodded and backtracked to the bathroom. I reread the instructions in case I'd somehow missed a critical step before taking the second test but the result flashed almost instantly: *pregnant, 2–3 weeks.*

Dave appeared in the doorway and held up his phone. "I looked it up. It's more likely to get a false negative than a false positive. So... I guess you really are."

I nodded again and held up the second test. Like I was a celebrity in a PR crisis I took control of the narrative and sent a picture of the tests to my group chats:

1) The Core Group
2) Audrey + Viv

Waiting 12 weeks to spill the beans never even crossed my mind.

Viv confided to Audrey and I that she was trying for a baby. Her period was late, and she planned to take a pregnancy test the next morn-ing. According to Viv, that's the best time of day to take it.

"Wait. Should I do a pregnancy test?" I blurted out, confused.

When was my last period? It was usually clockwork – shouldn't it have started already?

The girls pushed me to take the test, and we joked Audrey should take one too - unlike Viv, Audrey was actively working on *never* getting pregnant again.

Much like the Boy Scouts, an anxious girl is *always* prepared and I had pregnancy tests stashed in my bathroom drawer. I decided I'd take one in the morning, just to ease my mind.

Mom, Dad, please skip the next paragraph.

I couldn't remember exactly when it happened – but definitely sometime in the last couple of weeks. Maybe three. We were a little tipsy and a lot in love when Dave told me he'd never had sex without a condom before. I laughed because I thought he was joking.

He wasn't.

I knew we were going to get married someday, and he did too. So... we did it. *For science.*

One time.

One. Time.

ONE TIME?!

That's all it took? I guess my Catholic school education – complete with its constant, looming warnings about teen pregnancy – hadn't been *that* dramatic after all.

"What are you going to do?" he asked.

I shrugged. "Get ready for work, I guess."

A few minutes later, I stood frozen in the kitchen, coffee pod in hand, when it hit me: I couldn't drink coffee anymore. I was pregnant. What *else* was off limits?

My mind raced back to the weekend before, when we'd gone out for drinks with friends. I'd taken maybe two sips before someone made a joke about me being pregnant. At that moment, something inside me stirred – just a flicker – but we all laughed it off.

I didn't drink for the rest of the night. Actually... I never drank again.

I heard Dave coming down the stairs. His footsteps pulled me back into the moment, and I quickly tucked the coffee pod back into the cupboard. He rounded the corner in uniform and wrapped me in a hug. I whispered into his shoulder, "Are you happy?"

"Yes."

Of course he was. Any other answer wouldn't have made sense. On our very first date, he told me he wanted six kids. Was the timing perfect? No.

But I knew our baby would be. I was happy too.

"Do you still want to go out for dinner tonight?" he asked as he filled his blue Nalgene at the sink.

"Yeah, of course. Right. What should I wear?"

I'd forgotten all about our date.

"Let's dress up," he said. "Make a night of it."

He was going to propose.

*° *★°★

I'm an *excellent* surprise ruiner.

One winter, when I was about eight, it dawned on me – out of nowhere – that I hadn't seen a specific light pink cardigan with a little grey cat and a tiny taffeta bow in a while.

I hated that sweater. It felt so uncool. So babyish. I was embarrassed every time I wore it – especially at family functions with my cool, older cousins. My mom, on the other hand, loved it, and it was part of my official *wear this to look nice for Grandma* outfit.

For a reason we'll never know, I realized it was gone and suddenly *had* to find it. Nothing else mattered. My brain tunneled in on one goal: find the pink cardigan. I tore apart my closet and dug through the laundry. Nothing. But I wasn't giving up that easily. I wandered into my parents' room and spotted a laundry basket on the bed, covered with a beach towel. Odd, but okay. I lifted the towel – and there it was. Nestled in with my shorts and bathing suits was the pink sweater.

Mission accomplished.

I proudly skipped down the stairs, calling out, "Mom! MOM! Are we going somewhere?"

She was furious. Not *yelling* furious – but crushed. That specific cocktail of disappointment and exhaustion I didn't understand at eight years old.

I didn't get that she'd probably been planning this for months. That the pay-off to all that effort was supposed to be our surprised faces on Christmas morning when we found out we were going on vacation. Looking back, I see I robbed her of the *only part that was for her*. I didn't understand the mental load of motherhood. Or what it meant to be touched out. Or how working through your own traumas as a parent shaped every single reaction you had. I didn't know what decision fatigue was. I didn't know how close to the edge she might've already been.

All I knew was that she was mad – and it was all my fault. I had *literally* ruined Christmas.

It was raining that day, even though it was December. I dumped the contents of my piggy bank onto the counter with a note that said *I hoped this makes up for ruining the surprise*, grabbed an umbrella, and walked down the street. I kept looking over my shoulder – surely she'd see the gesture. Tell me to come home. That it was okay. That she wasn't mad anymore.

Inner mean girl: They don't care. They're not going to put up with your dramatics.

I genuinely thought running away would be better for everyone. If I wasn't there, I couldn't ruin anything. I couldn't make anyone mad. But I also really wanted someone – my mom, my dad, my brother – to notice I was gone and to see how sorry I was. I wanted the anger to be replaced with understanding and I hoped my willingness to run away would be enough to earn forgiveness.

Eventually, my mom opened the front door.

"Mariah. What are you doing? Get back inside."

She was still mad. Maybe she hadn't seen the money I left? I walked up the steps and saw the coins in her hand. She gave them back to me.

"What is this supposed to do?" she asked. "This doesn't help anything."

That wasn't the first – or the last – time I'd ruin a surprise. Nowadays, I'm *especially* bad for blurting out "you're pregnant!" the second someone says "I have something to tell you." (Don't worry – I have a 100% accuracy record.)

But that rainy day was when I first felt the shame of not keeping my mouth shut.

I closed the door behind me, went up to my room, and waited for the storm to pass. Like I always did. You know in superhero movies when they say, "Use your powers for good, not evil"? I felt like the villain. The one using her powers for evil. I didn't *want* to be one of the bad guys. So I learned how to channel my "powers" – my intuition, my gut, my lucky guesses, my hypervigilance, into tools that minimized my effect on others.

And most of the time, it worked.

° +⋆ₒ °⋆

The day before the proposal, I stood in front of my closet, trying on dresses and sending options to Viv and Audrey. Dave didn't know I knew he was going to propose, and I'd already learned my lesson – *repeatedly* – about ruining surprises.

I wanted to look good but not *too* good. Just good enough to be effortlessly cute in a way that would photograph well and not scream, *"I KNOW WHAT YOU'RE DOING."*

I couldn't wait to wear my ring.

In April, about a week before I sold my townhouse, and less than four months after our first date, Dave bought it – but before you freak out, I knew the proposal was a ways off.

I was leaving my job. Selling my house. Taking leap after leap for us. The ring was his way of saying, *I'm in this too.*

I'd just finished telling him about the surprise trips I'd ruined as a kid (yes, plural, it may or may not have happened three times) when he casually said:

"Well, what kind of ring *would* you want? If I get it now and just hold on to it, you'll never see it coming when I do propose."

I said I'd send him some pictures. He said that sounded good.

Truthfully, I hadn't ever thought about what kind of ring I wanted. I didn't want to jinx it – or get ahead of myself. But I started looking and the same one kept catching my eye.

A beautiful oval diamond, nestled between a cluster of three smaller diamonds on each side – two round, one ellipse. It was the perfect mix of unique and classic.

I sent him the link, heart pounding.

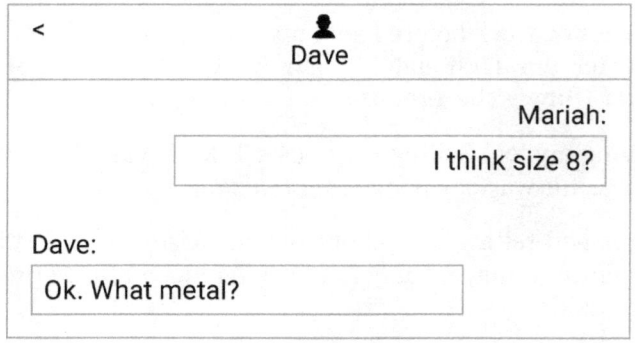

Dave:

Nice. What size?

What size? I had no idea.

We were weeks deep into "essential services only," and popping into a store to get measured wasn't an option, so I printed a couple versions of ring sizers, placed my existing rings on top, and studied them from all angles to figure out the closest match.

< Dave

Mariah:

I think size 8?

Dave:

Ok. What metal?

Another question. I started sweating. My first instinct was yellow gold. Lately, I'd been wearing more gold accessories and loved how warm they felt. But... my mom had always told me we were white gold girls. Not yellow. After all, white gold was classier. More beautiful. A classic. I loved my mom's ring, and since I'd never really questioned my own tastes, I went with what had stood the test of time: white gold.

But the second I hit send, I felt... off.

Not about the ring, or Dave. The *metal*.

I spent the next few hours poring over photos of the ring in all three settings, trying to convince myself I liked the white gold best. It *was* beautiful. Of course it was. But something about the contrast of the diamonds against the yellow gold settings made the details stand out more. It sparkled differently.

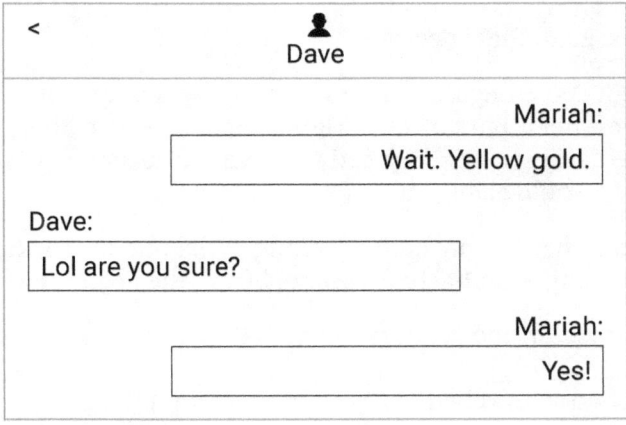

Narrator: She wasn't.

Whatever I want. Okay. What *did* I want? Ah.

Swipe. Swipe. Swipe.

I called him.

"Okay, rose gold. Final decision."

He paused. Asked again if I was *sure* – especially since rose gold hadn't even been part of the original debate – and then said he'd email the designer. He'd already placed the order and he wasn't sure if they would change it.

So I waited. Chewing my nails. Looking at the photos. Kicking myself for not knowing what I actually wanted from the beginning.

A few hours later, the reply came: the change was no problem at all.

I almost cried with relied and joy. I was *so* happy.

Turns out, *whatever I wanted...* was indeed rose gold.

engaged in our spot

— CHAPTER 25 —

Taken

The week before Dave was supposed to propose, the border finally loosened. My parents were finally allowed to visit us, and I was so excited to host them for Thanksgiving in our cute little house.

As "outsiders," they weren't allowed to leave our property, other than to return to the airport at the end of the weekend, but we made the most of it. Playing with Ollie in the backyard, cornhole in the front. Watching movies, playing games, and talking. Leading up to their visit was the longest I'd ever gone without seeing them in my entire life, and the visit itself was the longest time they had ever spent with Dave.

I felt so much peace that weekend. The pandemic had taken a lot from us – from everyone – and it finally felt like everything was clicking into place. There wasn't any drama, any awkwardness. In a time where everyone was pulling apart, it was comforting to spend so much time simply together.

The night before they left, I whispered to my mom and asked if she wanted to see the ring. I knew the proposal would be happening soon, and with all the restrictions changing on a daily basis, I wasn't sure when we'd be together in person again to show it to her.

She said yes, obviously – her excitement bubbling up into a big smile – and I led her upstairs to my office. There, in the emergency bag we kept packed and ready to go, was a side pocket with a small green velvet box inside. She put her hand to her mouth and whispered,

"It's so beautiful. I'm so happy for you."

I had found the ring a few weeks earlier, after months of searching.

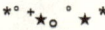

Now before you get salty and roll your eyes (like, why doesn't this girl ever learn her lesson about ruining surprises?), the reason I was looking for the ring at all was because Dave kept taunting me about it. For a while, I resisted. But there's only so many times a girl can hear, *"You'll never find it anyway"*, before she needs to rip the house apart and search behind every grate, in every drawer, and even in the attic.

So yeah, eventually I found it (take *that*, Dave), and it was even more sparkly and beautiful than I imagined it would be. But I never put it on. I saved that for when it was meant for me.

The next day, Dave drove my parents to the airport while I was back in the classroom after the long weekend. I got a tongue-in-cheek text from my dad while he was at the gate waiting to board:

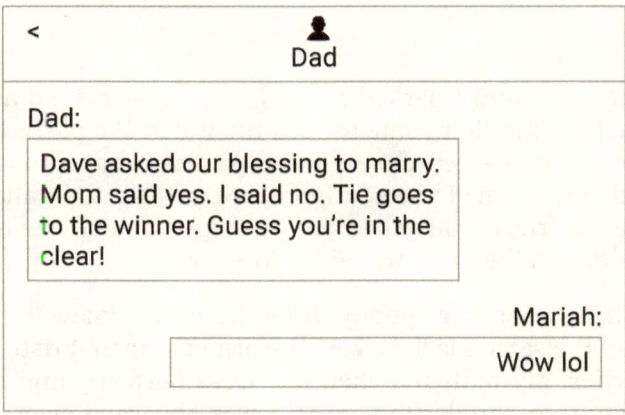

Dad:

> Dave asked our blessing to marry. Mom said yes. I said no. Tie goes to the winner. Guess you're in the clear!

Mariah:

> Wow lol

My dad and I have always had a relationship rooted in mirrored senses of humour so my instant reaction was to laugh. It was happening. I was excited, and surprised, to see the message. Shouldn't this have been kept a secret? Was bad secret keeping hereditary? Who cares – I was getting engaged.

° ⁺★ₒ °★

So much had changed since they had left four days earlier.

I knew my parents liked Dave and thought we were a good match. But what would they think of me being pregnant before we were married? Before we were even engaged? Though not an active member of any churches, my dad was raised very religious, and his traditional values seemed to pop up at random. I didn't know if this would be one of those times.

I glanced at my watch – I was running late. I gave Dave a kiss and jumped into my car, driving on autopilot. I couldn't get the smile off my face. I couldn't shake that full-body buzz. I didn't know what was going to happen, or what my parents would say, but I knew one thing without a fraction of a doubt in my mind.

I was completely in love with my baby.

*° +*ₒ °*

That night, Dave and I parked at the garage near his old apartment and walked the familiar route toward the water. We passed the little café where we had eaten cheese-filled pastries shaped like fish the first – and only – time I visited him before moving. We walked by the hill where his friend had yelled out his approval, and the bar where Icona Pop played the night we said "I love you."

I was wearing a long, burgundy dress, because I knew he loved the colour, and the same black jacket I'd worn on our first date less than a year earlier. My nails matched my dress perfectly and somehow weren't bitten to shreds (for once). I was shivering even though it wasn't *that* cold. Maybe I was nervous? Excited?

Inner mean girl: No. You're cold. Why are you so dramatic all the time?

I should have worn tights.

We held hands and walked the uneven cobblestones toward the water. The lights draped across the alley, lighting our path, our spot. I knew this was the place. The place where we had our photo taken for the first time, and then again to celebrate me moving there. This was it. Romantic, quiet, understated.

Well. If you ignored the family of tourists taking pictures and chatting loudly to each other. I could tell Dave was rattled. We had walked this path dozens of times and it was rare to see anyone else there. Dave was processing, unsure of what to do.

We reached the end of the cobblestones, the boardwalk stretching out in both directions. We should've turned toward the restaurant, but Dave was flustered. His plan was unravelling.

Okay, I was on it. I tugged on his hand a little and said, "Let's head back up that way – I'm a little too cold to walk by the water."

We turned around and walked back to our spot, finally alone. The lights seemed brighter, the night quieter, and my pace slower. Dave stopped and let go of my hand. He knelt down while saying, "Hold on a second," and pulled out the little green velvet box from inside his jacket.

My breath caught.

He opened the box, and there it was – *my* ring – sparkling under the string of lights above us, like it had been waiting for this moment too. I felt the air shift around us. Suddenly still. Like the night itself was holding its breath.

I looked at him. His cheeks were flushed, not from the cold. His hands were shaking just a little. He was blinking fast, like maybe this wasn't going exactly the way he'd planned – but maybe that didn't matter anymore.

My heart was thudding so loudly I was sure he could hear it.

A second went by. Then another. We looked at each other – two seconds feeling like two hours.

Another second passed. We each blinked. His brow furrowed slightly. Still, silence.

"...Well, are you going to ask me?"

He let out a breathy laugh. "Oh, right, yes. Mariah, will you marry me?"

"Of course I will."

Ring on my finger, kiss on my lips, fiancé at my side – I was on top of the world.

I couldn't wait to tell everyone.

My parents' faces filled my laptop screen, an impromptu Zoom call underway. It was a few weeks after the proposal, and my parents, so excited, were sending ideas for venues, guests we'd need to invite, and pitching wedding dates left, right, and centre.

I loved it and was down to talk about wedding stuff all day, every day – but it was hard to plan a wedding around a baby that no one knew about yet.

Now that we'd paid for a private scan, seen the little bean with our own eyes, and were confident I was actually pregnant, it was time to spill said beans.

"So, we actually won't be getting married next summer. We'll just be too busy."

My mom shifted from side to side and my dad nodded his head. "Oh okay, we understand. So when are you thinking?"

"Well. It's just... summer will be so busy because, well, we'll have a baby."

My mom's hand flew to her mouth as she gasped, and my dad's face was serious for a moment.

"No way," my mom said through her hand.

"Yep. We found out a few weeks ago. I'm due at the end of June." Dave was still silent beside me, waiting for whatever reaction was coming. He squeezed my leg reassuringly.

"That is wonderful news! I am so happy for you! A baby! A summer baby!" My mom was essentially cheering, her enthusiasm apparent.

Dad was a little more stoic, reserved. He nodded his head seriously and said, "Well, it's not like you guys aren't going to get married anyway. Who cares if the timeline is just a little out of order these days?"

I had been nervous about my dad's reaction to the news – unsure of his stance on babies out of wedlock – but more so, I was nervous about my mom's reaction. I couldn't help but think back to when I told them I was moving, and how badly that had gone.

When I went to their condo in April, having been officially dubbed someone in their "Covid bubble," and told them the news about tak-ing a leave of absence from work and moving to Nova Scotia to be with Dave, they both lost their minds, to put it lightly.

"No. Absolutely not. You are making a huge mistake. You don't just leave your teaching job. You don't risk your benefits, pension, pay-check – this is – " I stopped listening to my dad and dialed into my mom, who was crying and angrily wiping down the counters.

"I knew this was going to happen. I *knew* it. You're leaving us. For him. You're taking away my grandchildren from me. I can't believe you're doing this to us after all we've done for you."

I wasn't even pregnant. The logic made no sense. There would be no grandchildren to take away if I didn't move, anyway. It takes two to tango.

I let them be mad. I tried to calmly explain my perspective, my view of the risks, but they were too mad to hear me. After a few more minutes, they paused and I said I would talk to them later, and that I hoped they understood my position. I said I loved them, got in my car, and drove home.

Narrator: She handled it very well, to be honest. Good job. Tens across the board.

It had gone way worse than I expected. Like – way, way worse. I knew they'd be sad, but I didn't think they'd be furious. I hated the thought of letting them down. But I had to do it. It really didn't feel like a choice. Just the next step.

Months later, when we told them we'd be moving the wedding up to December – just three months away – and that I was pregnant, I was worried my mom would double down and be angry all over again. Especially since I had indeed "taken" her grandchild away in the end.

But they weren't mad. They were elated. And they leapt into joyful let's-get-down-to-it mode immediately. Suggesting venues. Helping read through the social distancing rules. Picking my dress with me over FaceTime. They were completely on the same page as us.

I was in love, pregnant, and running a thriving business.

I thought everything was falling into place. But really, I was just building a taller tower to fall from.

And no, that's not over dramatic.

the little girl with glasses

— CHAPTER 26 —

Unedited: FOB Speech

December 23, 2021

Aquatopia Conservatory

Speaking: Father-of-the-Bride

Testing, one, two, one, two. Check. Hello, everyone. I'm Bart, and according to the agenda, FOB, or father of the bride. This is Alanna, Mariah's mother. MOB. I'm doing the speech, but she was asked to join me so you could see both of us at the same time.

A big thank you to all of you for helping us celebrate this event amidst these difficult times. Many of you have travelled a great distance to help celebrate with us, and we are truly thankful. Mariah, my first child, what a wonder she was to us new parents. Let me tell you, bringing a precious life into this world is both a wondrous and incredibly scary thing.

I could regale you endlessly with stories about Mariah, but how, when I was a young father, finally had my first chance to take care of Mariah on my own while her mom was in the hospital for the birth of her brother Michael, all I got was a crying girl screaming at the top of her lungs, I want my mommy!

Or more little anecdotes, like all the little things I did to accommodate a little girl wearing glasses, like putting Vaseline on her cheeks where her glasses touched, where otherwise frostbite would occur when we went skating. Chaperoning a school ski trip and turning around a disastrous ski adventure with a girl who couldn't see 3D into a father-daughter downhill fun tubing adventure. These are some of my fond memories and minor examples of moments I was able to contribute to the growth and development of that person that is Mariah. However, in totality, all that we contributed in these moments are but a trifle compared to her own accomplishments. An honour science degree from a university in a town that felt as far away as, well, Nova Scotia. But believe me, it's not that far. With a postgraduate Bachelor of Education, *magna cum laude.*

She's already a leader in her field, in a successful teaching career and an arguably even more successful side business to boot. All indicators of nothing but continued success for her in the future. And of this, we're very proud to be sure. But for some time now, there was one piece of the puzzle missing. One aspect of her life that remained unfulfilled for what she felt was far too long. Today, we celebrate closing the loop. Putting in that last piece of the puzzle. We are im-mensely happy that Mariah and Dave have found each other and are demonstrating their commitment to each other in front of friends and family here today.

By all accounts, Dave is proving to be a most deserving and complementary partner for Mariah. But most of all, we're extremely pleased because Mariah and Dave are so pleased. And in the end, that's all that really matters to us.

In passing, I'd also like to mention what an incredible coincidence it is that Mariah is a teacher who moved from Ontario to Nova Scotia to be with a man who's in the Air Force, since my mother, Mariah's Oma, was also a teacher who moved from Ontario to Nova Scotia to be with a man who was in the Air Force. My mother's firstborn, me, has a birth certificate from the province of Nova Scotia, and so will Mariah's firstborn. What a small world.

Mariah and Dave, Alanna and I extend to you the warmest of heartfelt congratulations and best wishes for your future together. We're super proud and look forward to being a part of your lives in the next exciting stages, one of which is coming very soon.

about to ruin everything

— CHAPTER 27 —

Blocked

By Friday afternoon, I always ended up on the floor of my classroom. Literally.

I taught Grade Six English and dreaded it every single week. The drama. The sass. The inappropriate jokes. The ability to know better and the complete lack of giving a fuck.

Grade Six was not my vibe. I missed my kindergarten job. Setting up play centres, spending most of the day outside, reading stories with pictures and having dance parties just because. Sure, behaviour in Ontario had been bad, and yeah, I was potentially going to go on stress leave, but at least I liked it. *This* was torture.

I was pregnant and getting more uncomfortable (and irritable) by the day. I was constantly fielding comments about how big my belly was (spoiler: the baby was just under ten pounds), on pelvic rest just a few millimeters shy of placenta previa, and experiencing every weird symptom you could think of.

> Change in vision so my glasses didn't work? You bet.

> Weird bright rash around my mouth and nose? Of course.

> Morning sickness that lasted all day for 9 months? Sign me up.

> Insomnia that hit as soon as my head touched the pillow? Every night.

I was a mess and even more sensitive than normal. My ability – and quite frankly willingness – to filter myself to fit into whatever situation I was in was becoming increasingly small. It required a level of energy I just didn't have in me.

Lying on my side on the floor of my classroom, it felt like my insides were going to explode. I had so much stomach pain that I was debating calling my doctor.

Was this normal? Was the baby okay? Was I actually fine and just looking for an excuse to leave early so I could avoid teaching the Grade Sixes?

I was still riled up about how badly the Wednesday class had gone. I was beyond disappointed. I had given them so much time and support and reminders to complete what should have been a super fun project. I had let them pick whatever they wanted as their topic and taught them how to research using their Chromebooks. They could work with a partner, in a group, or on their own. I walked them through each step, breaking it into class-by-class chunks.

But still, there was a group that just would *not* get it done. They goofed off, made presentations with rude jokes in them, and were more focused on being perceived as cool than getting a single thing done in class. I had given them extra time, written home to their parents, asked them if they wanted to change their topics or their group. I got help from their homeroom teacher, who was experiencing similar problems. I pulled them aside, one-by-one, to talk about how it would affect their final grade.

Nothing worked and I was fed up. Still on my side on the floor under my desk, I sent a message to the group chat with Viv and Audrey, saying I was going to keep them in from recess until they got their work done.

It was a behaviour management strategy I had never tried before, and was way more "old-school" than a lot of admin and parents liked – more than I liked – but at this point they needed to get the projects done or they would be getting a zero.

I don't have the receipts for this one. But it went something like this:

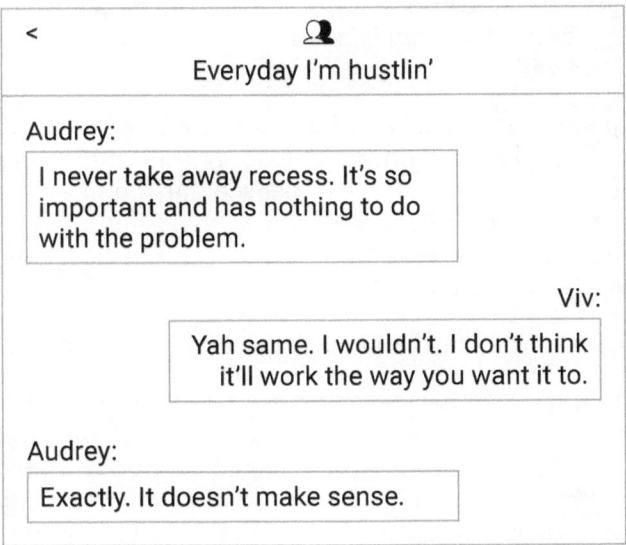

Inner mean girl: No one sees the issue here...

The messages continued between the two of them and I watched them pop up one by one, feeling more and more misunderstood and upset with every passing second. Agreeing with each other. Driving home the fact that they were on the same page, and I was on the outs. Othered. In the wrong.

Maybe I'm remembering wrong. Maybe they only sent one or two messages. Maybe they meant well.

Whatever the intention was, the impact on me was to feel embarrassed, judged, and ganged up on.

I was so frustrated, so tired, and just so done. I wasn't looking for feedback, and I wasn't expecting any pushback. I thought they'd send some heart emojis, or wish me luck. So their response really threw me off and put a bad taste in my mouth.

Look, I am the first to admit I am not great at getting feedback and find myself deep breathing, repeating, *Feedback is a gift* over and over again — trying to remind myself that someone's opinion doesn't mean they hate me and I suck. That line has stuck with me for more than twenty years, ever since my first performance review at the community centre when my boss said it to me (and that it was up to me what I did with it.)

But they just didn't get it. I had already tried everything they were spouting off as better options. I had put in the work to build relationships, break down the project into manageable steps, given extensions, and talked to their parents. I felt I had gone above and beyond already — especially given my low level of patience and capacity at that time.

I wanted to cry. Or a hug. Or at least a freakin' ice cream cone.

I also didn't want to have the same thing that seemed to *always happen* happen again. I didn't want to overreact. I didn't want to lose that closeness with the girls I talked to all day, every day. So I did the only thing I felt reasonable at that moment. I don't have the exact message – but it was as close to this as I can remember:

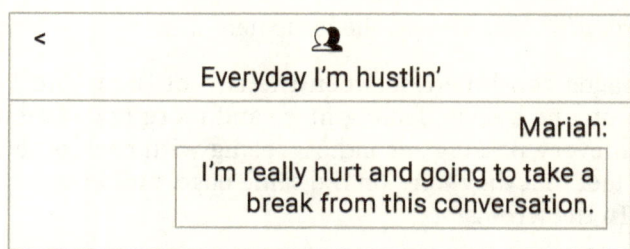

I thought I was being proactive. That by taking a step back when I knew I was running hot, I would prevent myself from reacting explosively and causing damage. I could tell I was extremely overwhelmed, overstimulated, and likely overdramatic. History had taught me this was a disastrous mix, so I thought that if I took a break, slept on it, and didn't react, I would avoid any drama.

I couldn't have been more wrong.

Just a few weeks earlier, Viv and I had gotten closer than ever.

While scouring for receipts for this book, I was slapped in the face by my still-very-much-alive habit of deleting anything that embarrasses me. Removing any evidence of hurt and shame from my phone so I can't re-read and obsess or send another message. Listen, I'm not here to lie to you or make myself look good — I think I look pretttttty yikes in a lot of these stories.

What I did find was this conversation with my mom from that time. And it reminds me this wasn't just a work chat gone wrong.

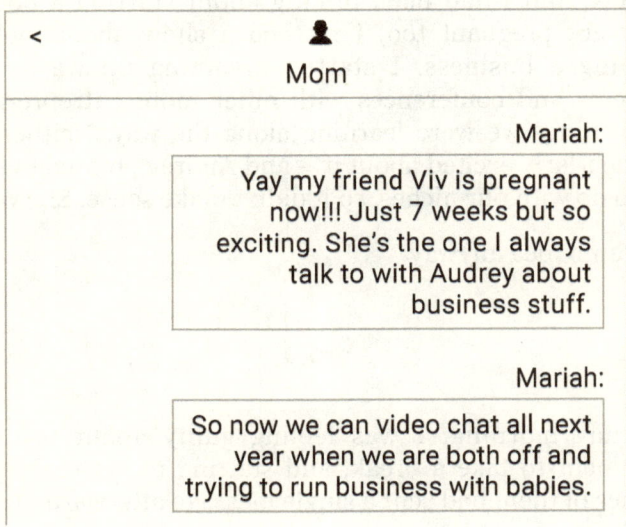

I was there when she spiraled about her HCG levels, telling her everything I knew and recommending resources to her. I sent her some of the maternity clothes I thought she'd look better in than me, and a book that had really helped me through some of my pregnancy anxieties. I felt a special connection to her, and honestly, I felt... cool for the first time in my life. She was without a doubt one of the popular girls on Teachergram – with her downtown condo, super aesthetic brand, perfect visuals, and love of trendy coffee combos.

To this day, I second-guess my clothing in social settings, judging myself and questioning why I always miss the mark. Other than my wedding, I've never once arrived somewhere and felt like I was dressed the part. But Viv was so effortlessly cool. In her fashion. Her posts. Her products.

She had picked me to be her friend. And we were having babies together.

Audrey, Viv, and I had been talking about starting a podcast. So when Viv got pregnant too, I pitched a show about motherhood and running a business. I started dreaming up ways we could run re-treats and conferences with other mom entrepreneurs and share the things we were learning along the way. Neither of them were particu-larly excited about it – and Audrey pointed out this had nothing to do with our niches, so it didn't make sense. She was right.

It was a dumb idea anyway.

*° + ⋆○⋆

On Saturday morning, I was feeling guilty about my dramatic announcement to take a break, and starting to get really paranoid that neither of them had sent a single message afterward.

I was lying on the couch and – for the first time – I saw my baby kick. I was so excited. I recorded a video to send to Dave and my family chat, and Audrey and Viv. I thought this would be a good, joyful icebreaker. Besides, I was pretty used to relationships in which some-thing happened, and then you just never talked about it again and moved on.

But... they didn't reply. A thumbs up on the video.

I was hurt and confused all over again – had my message really been that bad? I thought I was being mature. Proactive. I went back to read it again.

"I'm really hurt and going to take a break from this conversation."

That was it. I didn't think I had done anything wrong. Definitely not enough to warrant ignoring the importance of this moment in my life. So, I called them out. I don't remember the specifics, and again, no receipts survived the shame spiral that followed.

Inner mean girl: Convenient.

It was something along the lines of: "What? No response to the first ever video of my baby kicking?"

Not my best work.

Viv replied saying she was at a cottage and not spending much time on her phone. Okay, fine. But I couldn't help but notice she replied to *that* – and still said nothing about the baby.

Then Audrey's novel-length message landed. I had to tap to expand it. She said it was unreasonable to blow up at the group and then expect things back to normal. She said she'd never felt like a bad friend before, but clearly she triggered me over nothing, so maybe we shouldn't be friends. That it wasn't working for either of us.

I'm sure they had their own lists and reasons about why the friend-ship wasn't worth maintaining anymore – and I'm not claiming to be totally innocent here – but at that moment, all my walls went up. I was livid. Embarrassed. I re-read everything – what was I missing?

This message felt over the top – not the one I sent about needing a break.

I was overwhelmed. Pregnant. And now I was the only friend she'd ever had issues with? This, from the self-proclaimed "guy's girl" who'd had plenty of falling outs? And she was saying all of this in front of Viv?

I replied to Audrey, letting her know that the message felt "inappropriate to send in a group setting and would have been better off sent privately, especially considering Viv had shared she was at a cottage and trying to relax."

Super pissed off and overly formal HR Mariah: activated.

Audrey was out. Just like that. But, I hoped things with Viv were fine. I messaged her privately and she said she wasn't mad, she understood, she wasn't picking sides. I believed her. I wanted it to be true because I didn't want to lose Viv. I thought our babies would be friends. I thought we were peas in a pod. Looking back, I was probably just an easy pea – until I wasn't. She had a whole pod of peas waiting to slide in when I didn't fit.

But at the time, I clung to her words. But, it just didn't feel fine. It felt *different*. Forced. One-sided. And that was the thing I feared most: being more invested than the other person. Disposable. Unappreciated.

When I finally told June about this – years later– it still hurt. She said it made sense why I kept people at a distance. Why I pulled them in with a false closeness but never let myself be fully close. Out of fear that being my real self would mean rejection. She told me I didn't have to filter myself to be lovable. That I could trust I was worthy just as I am.

Sounds like a load of baloney to me.

(*Kidding. Please don't ire me, June – we have much more to discuss.*)

With Viv, I *had* let my walls down. And now I felt like everything was crumbling around me.

I messaged her, asking if she was sure we were okay because I'd noticed a change in her tone and didn't know if I was imagining it. I was hoping she'd reassure me that we were fine, and that I'd realize I was just being sensitive because of what happened with Audrey.

Instead, I was met with hostility and another friendship breakup.

This time, it really hurt.

*° +*₀ °*

Viv told me she didn't want a friendship with expectations around texting frequency or tone. That she had real life and real friends and didn't want pressure. I panicked and backpedaled (classic Blake breakup energy). I told her I didn't have expectations, I knew she was busy, I just wanted to be sure we were okay. I don't remember the exact end, only that one of us said it wasn't productive anymore.

The next day I sent a desperate, cringe-worthy email.

Inner mean girl: Thank goodness you included the whole thing in the next chapter for everyone to judge.

She never replied. She just cancelled her membership to my site, blocked me, and disappeared. I wish I had more evidence, but this is how I remember it and how I experienced it. And every screenshot I did keep, every conversation I had at the time, reassures me that I'm not making the whole thing up.

Within days, I was out of the Teachergram community. Instantly, a new group chat spun up without me.

And I knew, because I was close enough to the girls inside: close enough to hear how annoying the chat was, close enough to be sent screenshots, close enough to get pity DMs. Just not close enough for anyone to risk their own place in the circle.

It stung. It was Grade Seven all over again. But I couldn't fault them for protecting their own businesses. Because the right group chat could make or break you. These weren't just friendships. They were collaborations, audience sharing, referrals, launches, podcast invites. Visibility. Credibility. And mine was evaporating overnight—while I was seven months pregnant, fighting to turn my business into something I could live on.

The timing couldn't have been worse. Eventually, I stopped fighting to be *in* the group and fought to scale *without* it.

My baby was coming, and going back to the classroom wasn't an option. My business had to work.

Listen. If all this doesn't quite make sense to you, just know it doesn't make sense to me either. I've tried piecing it together, but the panic-purge reflex leaves holes. As far as I know, this is what happened. And my stomach still knots thinking about it. But hey, at least it couldn't get any worse.

Inner mean girl: lol

the scene of the crime

— CHAPTER 28 —

Unedited: The Cringiest Email

Sent Message

Wednesday, March 17, 2021
3:45 PM

From: Mariah
To: Viv

Subject: Apology & Kindness

Hey Viv,

I am super over texting these days but wanted to leave things on a better note than you. Snail mail seemed too slow, so an e-mail will have to suffice (although it is a bit odd- personal emails are very early 2000s).

I am super over texting these days but wanted to leave things on a better note than you. Snail mail seemed too slow, so an e-mail will have to suffice (although it is a bit odd- personal emails are very early 2000s).

I have nothing but nice things to say about you and want to reach out and apologize for how I came across last night in our texting conversation. I was trying very hard to communicate my feelings in a non-confrontational and rational way and thought I was doing that but Dave read my messages and disagreed. So, I apologize for my tone. I definitely didn't mean to start something and was really just trying to manage my anxiety by seeking some clear answers.

I don't think any of us have the capacity for dramatic friendships and certainly don't want to be the cause of one. I also know my pregnancy hormones are making me highly sensitive and reactive, which is why I am constantly over analyzing and reacting to situations. I am not sure if you are there yet with your hormones but I hope you never join me in this hot mess express.

All this to say, I think you are wonderful and will always be here for you if you have any questions about pregnancy, babies, business or otherwise.

Pregnancy and motherhood can be very isolating and overwhelming and I want you to know I will always be on your team and in your support network.

Mariah

Andrew's nursery

— CHAPTER 29 —

Nothing to lose

I couldn't believe it was happening again. By spring 2021, Nova Scotia schools closed again. The province was officially back in lockdown. Part of me was happy. I could barely walk, and being able to teach from home was going to be much easier on my body.

But it also meant that for the fourth time, I couldn't properly celebrate once-in-a-lifetime milestones. I didn't have an engagement party, my bachelorette was virtual, our wedding capped at 30 guests, and now my baby shower would be online. After years of celebrating everyone else's milestones, it stung knowing I'd never get the cheesy classics—like a toilet paper dress or dancing in a feather boa with drag queens.

And don't get me wrong I was grateful to have the reason to celebrate in the first place. Finally, I was getting everything I ever wanted: an amazing husband, a healthy baby on the way. I was trying not to be ungrateful. Or that girl who's always complaining about something.

But, yeah. That kind of sucked.

The silver lining was it made it possible for everyone I loved to attend – and it's not like I could have filled a room locally. I'd been in Nova Scotia for a year, but between lockdowns and some light social anxiety, the guest list would have been mighty small.

Marissa took the responsibility of virtual baby shower hostess extremely seriously. She planned games, handled the invites, and themed the whole thing with the cutest little foxes. It ran so incred-ibly smoothly, but what I was most grateful for was the message she sent me in April while she was deep in planning mode.

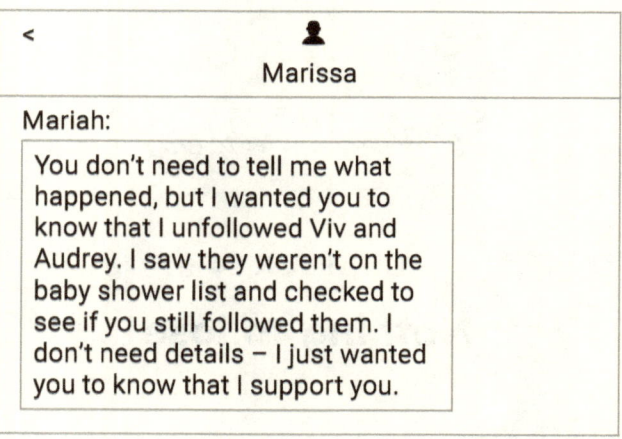

This was the first time, maybe ever, that a friend simply picked me. Without explanation, justification, proof, or even any insight at all into what was going on. I, alone, was enough.

I didn't know what to say.

After the fallout with Viv and Audrey, I was so embarrassed and filled with self-judgment that I kept the whole situation locked inside. The only person I confided in was Dave. I showed him the messages and cried on his shoulder countless times. Remember that cloudy glass of water I talked about my brain becoming? By then, it was spilling over – too murky for Dave's logic to cut through.

My go-to strategy of sharing as much as I could (good, bad, ugly) wasn't possible with water this murky. Besides, the glass was way too full. Any sudden movements risked a tidal wave – and not because I wanted to make myself look good. In fact, I regularly positioned myself subconsciously as the villain in my re-tells. The more I talked about it, the more I processed what happened and the more I could ensure people knew I was self-aware, sorry, and working on it.

A few months into writing this book and seeing June multiple times a month, she stopped me and asked, "Okay, can I stop you for a minute? You start a lot of your stories setting yourself up as a bad person with these huge missteps. I spend the entire time waiting for the bomb to drop – but it never comes. Why do you think that is?"

Idk June isn't that your job????

When Marissa messaged me, I cried. I cried out of gratitude for her friendship, her silent observations and inferences – and for the girl in me who had never felt picked. Whose ex-boyfriends stayed "followed" and "liked" on *Instagram*. Whose girl drama constantly ended with not picking sides. Whose wedding was missing faces that had been on the guest list before the groom.

Not even my inner mean girl could make light of how much that text meant to me.

Marissa's message inspired me to call Chloe, after years of silence, and apologize.

When I saw her on *Instagram* — pregnant in overalls — I realized I had nothing to lose, and I wondered if the message would mean as much to her as Marissa's had to me. Ever since we stopped talking, I missed Chloe. Losing her had left an angry hole I couldn't patch and I felt a sudden willingness to try.

Plus, I was experiencing a brand-new perspective shift as my due date approached. I saw people differently and needed people differently, too.

She took me up on my offer.

For over an hour I sat rocking in the nursery glider, phone pressed to my ear, finally talking about the hurt. We'd missed a lot of each other's lives. She missed my wedding and admitted to being deeply hurt when she saw pictures of Katie in the wedding party, feeling like she should've been up there too. She got a dog. And her son – who I'd held all over Disney World during the half-marathon trip – was now a full-blown kid.

I wasn't sure if we'd be friends again (don't worry, we are), but it felt good to clear the air. I'd been carrying that weight, just under the surface, for years, and right then, the healing started.

The abrupt end of my friendship with Viv and Audrey – okay, really just Viv – had shattered my already fragile sense of security in friendships and that conversation with Chloe started the very slow process of building myself back up. Of playing with the idea that maybe I deserved some grace.

Maybe I *was* worth being friends with – even though I wasn't perfect.

Buuuut I didn't trust it. The idea that I could mess up, be forgiven, and still have a place in someone's life? That seemed unrealistic. The concept of being safe to be myself in relationships was something I only started to "try on," as June would say, years later. And I wasn't sure I could pull off the look.

At this point, I needed evidence. Proof.

And most pressingly, I needed to replace the time in my day I used to spend in that freaking group chat. I had way too much extra time that was filled with anxieties about baby kicks, birth, and my growing self-hatred over my body while the pounds crept up.

This baby was *huge*, every step hurt, and with a low-lying placenta I literally wasn't allowed to exercise. I couldn't even walk Ollie – especially given how those walks had been going.

saying goodbye

— CHAPTER 30 —

I love you, I'm sorry.

Ollie had saved my life. And Dave knew it. He didn't question the thousands of dollars we were spending on training sessions, daily medications, and the dozens of special treats we would try – in vain – to use as rewards. He was involved, but passive, in Ollie's training. Dave came to dog training sessions with me, did the occasional exercise with him at home, and used the clicker without complaint. Eventually, he'd come to love Ollie as I did, but for a long time, Ollie was *my* dog. My baby.

As my bump grew, so did Ollie's reactivity. We wondered if it was rooted in protective instincts for me and a general response to changes in hormones, routines, and his environment. The stroller, for example, was a horrible and terrifying beast whose very existence made him cower.

But still, we had hope. We got him a ThunderShirt – a tight vest meant to calm anxious dogs in storms – upped his medication, got him a puzzle for his food to keep his brain busy, and Dave started walking him twice a day.

Ollie would come home from his walks charged up: eyes wild, panting, fluffy tail wagging vigorously. The walks seemed to stimulate him more than tire him out, and he spent the entire time hyperfocused on the noises around him, seeking out dogs and bikes.

Eventually, after drinking some water and getting some ear scratches, he would settle back into the house. Then, he'd cuddle up with me and fall asleep, completely at peace.

One day, he came in more frantic than usual. I was lying down and could barely see him come through the door over my enormous belly stretched out in front of me.

Dave was upset. "He bit me."

"What? No, he didn't."

Dave pulled down his jeans and showed me the mark. There it was. Teeth marks.

"We were at the mailbox and the dogs in the yard started barking. He went nuts and bit me."

I refused to believe it. "No, there's no way. He'd never bite us. You must have been pulling him back and your leg got in the way – and he was barking and closed his mouth on your leg."

Dave looked at me like I had two heads. Like I was insane. But he didn't get it. *What was insane* was the idea that Ollie would bite him. Bite another dog? Yes. He snapped often toward other dogs and – as much as I hated to admit it – he had bitten the trainer's dog during one of our sessions.

But bite a human? Let alone one of *us*? I couldn't believe it.

Dave was frustrated. "I don't know what to tell you. He bit me."

I knelt down to Ollie and hugged him. There was no way he bit Dave. He licked me while I pet him, burying my face into his body. He would never bite *us*.

I scratched his ears. Kissed his head. He'd never bite *me*.

*° *⋆ₒ °⋆*

Andrew, my five month old baby, was getting more and more mobile by the day. Ever since he was born, he hated sleeping. He resisted naps like it was his life calling.

Narrator: At four years old, Andrew still hates sleeping.

Andrew had a "false start" every single night — he'd fall asleep for about an hour, then wake up furious, overtired, and ready to start the cycle all over again.

So, I'd put him to bed and have an hour, max, to scarf down dinner, brush my teeth, maybe watch a show – before he was howling for snuggles. Then I'd be trapped for the night, simultaneously loving the baby snuggles and hating that I'd failed, co-sleeping against all the pre-baby opinions I had no business having.

During the day, if I was lucky, he'd nap while I bounced on an exercise ball in his pitch-black room, or if I cranked the portable white noise machine and walked up and down the gravel path with the stroller.

It was an unseasonably warm day at the end of November and Andrew was resisting his nap, again. So, I popped him in the stroller, turned on the white noise, and unlocked the side door. Ollie heard the click and jumped off the couch to run toward me.

Tail wagging, ears perked, head cocked innocently to the side. His eyes were without a doubt saying, "Ah mom! Are we going for a walk? Let's go! I'm ready!"

I checked my watch: 10 a.m. Most people would be at work already, their morning dog walks long over. We'd been doing lots of training sessions on the path lately, and I knew exactly where we could veer off to hide from approaching dogs.

I grabbed the leash, treats, and the prong collar I hated but our trainer wanted us to try. Ollie spun in circles, bursting with excitement.

He was so freakin' cute.

I laughed, got him set up, and walked out the door.

Ollie trotted beside us: tail wagging, feet prancing, occasionally wincing when the stroller shifted. We rounded the corner and bumped onto the trail entrance. It was so quiet I could hear the hum of the power lines above us, the birds, and Ollie's heavy panting.

I tightened the leash and praised him over and over, trying to keep him calm. The one obstacle between us and the open path was ahead. I tried not to let my nerves "travel down the leash," like we'd practiced. I hugged the opposite side of the wide path, stroller blocking his view of the overgrown yard with dogs.

Please don't be outside. Please don't be outside. Please don't be outside.

An unmistakable clang of the chainlink fence sent a chill through my body as two huge paws slammed against it. Barking. Growling. Another clang of metal. A second set of paws. More barking.

Immediately, Ollie lunged. The leash jerked my arm as he tried to squeeze between me and the stroller. He was snarling, barking, oblivious to my attempts to redirect him.

Two dogs off leash. One dog on leash. Puppy school imbalance all over again. He couldn't flee. He had to fight. I didn't blame him, but I couldn't believe it. The unthinkable had happened.

He bit me.

° +₊°✿

It fucking hurt.

Shocked, eyes brimming with tears, I turned the stroller around, pulling on Ollie's leash and dragging him back toward the house. We rounded the corner and as if someone had flipped a switch he stopped barking and started prancing again. He was revved up, but otherwise fine. Back to normal.

But I wasn't. In the kitchen, Ollie bolted to the couch while I bumped the stroller inside. Andrew lay in it, blissfully unaware. I gingerly pulled down my pants.

I was bleeding. A dark blue bruise spread across my thigh already. I didn't know it yet, but it would last two months. A daily reminder of what happened.

Crying, I quickly washed the open wound at the kitchen sink before pulling my pants back up. Shit. Andrew *needed* to go for his nap. It was a miracle he wasn't fussing in the bassinet of the stroller already. I grabbed my phone and went back to the path, leaving Ollie at home this time. Then, I called Chloe.

Tell everyone. Take control.

"No matter what you decide, I won't judge you," she said.

I still couldn't believe he bit me. Maybe my leg had gotten in his way while I was walking. Maybe it wasn't intentional. Chloe reminded me: intent didn't matter. The impact was the same. The exact words I'd become all too familiar with in therapy years later.

I looked down at Andrew, finally asleep, his tiny body just inches away from where my leg was bitten. I thought of the blood dripping down my leg, the size of the bruise already there.

What if he had bitten Andrew? His entire body was the size of my thigh.

Tell everyone. Take control.

I calmed myself down and hung up with Chloe before I lost my window of coherence. I could feel the walls closing in on my brain and I needed to talk to the vet about increasing the dose of his medication. I told the receptionist what happened and she booked me an appointment to come in later that day.

Tell everyone. Take control.

Next, I called Jordyn, the woman who lived beside me growing up and whose son I babysat for years. She had experience with rescue dogs like Ollie, and one had bitten her. We talked about what was going on, and she listened without giving any advice, any judgment. When we hung up she sent me a link to MangoDogs, the only trainers within a two-hour radius of us who would work with dogs with a bite history.

Their lowest package was $6500.

I noticed a link that said "Do you have children in your home?" It took me a minute to register that we *did* have a child in our home. *Our* child. I clicked it.

> *If there is a child under the age of 18 living in your home, and your dog is growling, nipping, resource guarding, or biting ANY humans (ones they live with or do not), we can't extend training to your family.*
>
> *We wish you the best in your dog training journey.*

Fuck.

*° +*₀ °*

As usual, Ollie and I entered the vet clinic through the side door - an accommodation made for us so he wouldn't be around other animals, or the shelving out front scared him.

The vet came in and sat down on the floor beside me, neither of us opting for the comfort of the couch. Ollie, though not a small dog, was curled up in a tiny ball in my lap, head resting on my leg.

My leg that still hurt.

She smiled kindly, tilting her head to one side, "So, what brings you in today?"

I started to cry. I told her everything. The bite of the trainer's dog, Dave, and now me. I told her about the four different trainers we had worked with and outlined the training techniques we tried. I told her about the medication, the tools, the environment and routines we tried to set up for him. I told her about Halloween, and how hard it had been with trick-or-treaters at the door and

Ollie freaking out all evening. I told her about our 5-month-old baby who was starting to move around more and loved the dog's tail. I told her about the line I'd read on MangoDogs and how I didn't know what else I could do.

I told her I needed help.

She was quiet. Stroking Ollie's head and processing the information that was pouring from my mouth.

She told me about her own kids and pets. She explained that her animals meant *everything* to her – until you compared them to her kids. I interrupted and said I didn't want to rehome him – he was *my* dog. I couldn't imagine him being with anyone else, wondering where I was. I told her I knew that was selfish.

She was gentle and looked me in the eye as she spoke. It didn't matter. With his bite history we couldn't re-home him anyway. Okay, so we could increase his meds again.

She agreed it was possible but couldn't promise results. She pet Ollie's head again, her hands gentle but her voice clear: the risk of wait-ing for a dose to potentially work was very high with a baby at home. She was uncomfortable with that treatment plan.

She told me she knew that what she was about to say was going to hurt me and she was sorry. She said we had run out of options. That we had done everything we could and more than most people would. That yes, he was young, so very young, but we had already prolonged his life by rescuing him from the streets and giving him so many chances.

Inner mean girl: You never should have adopted him. Another person would have trained him correctly. This is *your* fault.

She was still looking at me, choosing her words carefully, "Mariah, I don't say this lightly, and I'm so sorry, but, if I were in your position, I would opt for voluntary euthanasia."

I cried harder, hugging Ollie to my chest. She said we could do it right then and there, or I could think about it and come back. There was no pressure. She was here to support me.

Tell everyone. Take control.

I told her I needed to call my husband and my mom. She said to take my time.

So, I did. They told me it was a horrible decision and they were so sorry I had to make it. They reminded me to think about Andrew and to focus on the beautiful times Ollie and I had together. Both of them said that he was such a good boy.

They asked if I wanted to wait, and come back another day with one of them there with me. They didn't want me to be alone. But I couldn't do it. I couldn't bring him home, knowing that meant I'd have to bring him back to kill him.

I signed the papers. Paid the bill. It was the most fucked up feel-ing I had ever experienced. I sat beside him, soaking his back with my tears.

"I love you, I'm sorry."

The vet knocked twice and opened the door, a tech behind her. They were quiet, sensitive. The tech dimmed the lights and held out a muzzle.

"We just have to be careful."

They administered the sedative, but he was already calm. It was like he knew. He lay down on the couch and put his head down. His ner-vous and ever vigilant gaze softened as the tech pet his head. Within a few minutes, the vet said he was no longer conscious, and that it was common for animals to leave their eyes open at this point, but that he was essentially asleep.

They asked me if I wanted to stay until he was gone or leave.

"I love you, I'm sorry."

I left. Making one final mistake of looking back as I opened the door and seeing his little brown eyes staring at me. They said he was unconscious. Could he see me? Leaving him? Was this his last memory of me? Scared, alone and about to die. Watching the one person he trusted above all else walking away?

I sat in my car and sobbed. Every time I sit down to work on this chapter, I sob.

He was gone. My dog. My Ollie.

I killed the very reason I hadn't killed myself.

"I love you, I'm sorry."

Somehow, I drove home. The dog bowls, his bed, his toys - they were all gone. Tucked away by Dave to try and reduce visual triggers when I walked through the door. But, it didn't matter. I didn't need visuals to remind me of what I'd done.

"I didn't think you'd really be coming home alone," he said.

I thought back to my phone call with him, sitting in the vet office. Ever logical, ever calm, he listened and gently told me it wasn't his call to make. He loved Ollie, but he was my dog and he would never feel comfortable making this decision about him. It was up to me.

It was my decision. My fault. And I still don't know how to forgive myself.

Sitting on the edge of our bed, head in his hands, I saw Dave cry for the first time.

"I love you, I'm sorry."

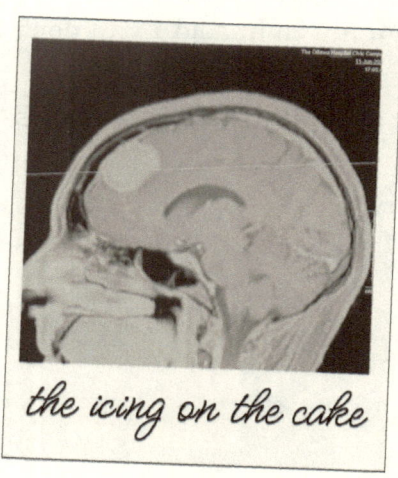

the icing on the cake

CHAPTER 31

Unedited: Trauma Dump

[Slide 1: A flatlay image of a white plastic scoop resting on top of a pile of rainbow-coloured sensory rice. Overlaid bold text reads: "An honest RECAP of 2021."]

[Slide 2: A collage of six photos:

1. Top left: A woman wearing a medical mask, eyes wide and red-rimmed.

2. Top centre: Closeup of her cheek and chin with red, inflamed skin from a rash.

3. Top right: She sits beside a hospital bed, gently holding the hand of an older woman hooked up to monitors.

4. Bottom left: A man in a chair in an ER, arms crossed as a woman's legs stretch out in a hospital gown.

5. Bottom centre: The woman sits at home, cradling a newborn on her chest.

6. Bottom right: A fluffy brown dog stands in a dry, grassy field, blue leash taut, staring into the distance.]

[Slide 3: Another collage of six photos:

1. Top left: The woman lays skin-to-skin with her newborn immediately after birth.

2. Top centre: A mirror selfie of her pregnant, hands on her belly, in a striped dress and denim jacket.

3. Top right: A man cradles the baby tightly, cheek resting on the baby's head.

4. Bottom left: The woman, man, and baby smile in toques, the baby in a knit hat with a pom-pom.

5. Bottom centre: The woman grins, holding a clear bin filled with educational materials labeled "A Playful Purpose."

6. Bottom right: A close-up of the baby peacefully sleeping on a white blanket, wearing a navy striped onesie.]

♡ 259   💬 71

December 31, 2021

aplayfulpurpose Just here to break up the highlight reels (including my latest reel) with an honest recap of 2021 so that if you too experienced the highest highs and the lowest lows of your life this year that you know you aren't alone.

I will always keep it real, but also try to keep it positive.

So today I'm taking the time to honour my lows and highs of the year and if any of these memories resonate with you then my vulnerability will be worth it.

These aren't pictures I've shared very openly because the stories they represent hurt.

I started 2021 off with a traumatic fall down the stairs and visit to the ER to make sure little bb was okay. I still, one year later, cry when I think about this experience and do not say it lightly when I share I have PTSD from this.

My pregnancy was filled with happy moments, but also many side effects and complications including a low lying placenta and a skin condition. It was a long 41+1 weeks filled with pain and anxiety. I felt like my body couldn't handle being pregnant and the constant comments of how large my belly was hurt just as much as the belly itself.

Little bb's birth was another experience of trauma for me. With over 30 hours of labour, 2 hours of pushing, an emergency episiotomy and being so sick I was almost hospitalized with sepsis, this was not what I imagined for my first time bringing a child into the world. It tainted my first moments and I'm horrified to say I wasn't able to feel love for him until the day after he was born.

Right before he was born, my mom was diagnosed out of the blue with a brain tumour. This was one of the worst phone calls I have ever received. Thankfully she had a successful surgery and is recovering well.

I struggled with severe PPA and PPD that were directly related to my lack of sleep and little bb's struggles with sleep. It caused me to be reactionary and even lose some friends. I'm not ready to talk more about this pain yet.

And finally, but most heavily, we had to make the impossible decision to put our dog down after years of working with him and trying our best. We had to put our son's safety first and I am riddled with guilt and sadness to this day.

Continued in the comments...

aplayfulpurpose But, as much as there were massive lows that I felt were breaking me, I experienced the greatest joys in my life as well.

The greatest of all was becoming a mother.

Something I have waited my entire life for and worried so much would never happen.

I loved having a bump (most of the time) and feeling the kicks and hiccups. It is an indescribable feeling and one I will never forget or take for granted.

I have loved growing as a person, mother and wife and settling into our new life as a family. We have experienced growing pains and it has been very difficult at times on our new marriage, but our love for little bb is an incredibly strong connector.

Watching Dave become a dad is something that brings tears to my eyes. He loves Andrew so fiercely and while we might not always agree on what this means, I know he'll do everything he can for the rest of his life to make sure little bb will thrive.

I'm incredibly proud of where APP has gone this year and how many dreams I have accomplished with a newborn. I didn't take maternity leave and I feel so inspired, clear and ready on where to take my business next.

Healthy_girl_101 I love your page for the realness of it!!!

MmeL I honestly don't know what to say except that I have so much respect for you Mariah and applaud your vulnerability on this platform. I'm so sorry that you had to experience so many hardships this year.

TheTeachingCart The highlights and the low points are what make us who we are. Love your honesty and openness

MegBB Thank you for your openness in sharing this- so glad we've been able to bond again in motherhood.

MmeBana Thank you for sharing your story. It's honest and real and you can see your strength and love come through.

JWells Thank you for your honesty. I love following you for this very reason (and for all your amazing teaching ideas too, of course!)

TheseTeacherMoments Thank you for sharing yourself with us on these tiny squares. Love you!!!

MommyCrafts Thank you for sharing such honest and candid moments.

Teacher4 You're so honest and brave. Your post was relatable in so many ways. Sending you so much love and hugs. Remember on your hardest days, that it's just a season in your story. It too shall pass and there will be sun again!

ThatGirlOverThere Oh Mariah, what a year it has been indeed. Thank you so much for your honesty. Motherhood is so raw and traumatizing and I'm thankful you and others and talking more about it. Wishing you a less "turbulent" 2022 filled with love and more memory making!

DeQueen Your honesty...I am teary. Thank you for being so relatable and real

HeidiB teary reading this. So honest and relatable in so many ways

the "surprise"

— CHAPTER 32 —

Baby Boy

It was just after one am. 1:07 to be exact. Day 1 of Camp Kinder was done and I was completely exhausted – but still, I couldn't sleep. I'd been tossing for hours, obsessively checking my phone for updates. Gillian had been admitted to the hospital earlier, and I hadn't heard from her since.

Gillian:

> He didn't make it.

Mariah:

> I'm so sorry. I love you.

She was alive. But what she wrote didn't make sense. I read the words again. As if maybe the letters would rearrange themselves into something else. Something survivable.

Fuck.

It was the first year of my virtual kindergarten teacher conference. The dream I'd carried since the cancelled PD day in 2020 was finally coming to life and the timing was perfect because I could feel myself leaving A Playful Purpose behind and craving something bigger. Something with more reach. More impact. I was energized at the thought of moving out of the spotlight as host and into an organizer role – lifting other women up, making space, keeping the experience grounded and relevant no matter how long I'd been out of the class-room.

And I thrived at Camp. Leading virtual sessions for hundreds of educators felt easy and electric. It felt *real* – for me, and the 400 attendees whose names covered the walls of my office, each one on their own sticky note.

No one at Camp had any idea of what was going on behind the scenes. Hundreds of glowing comments flooded in. Half of attendees signed up for the next event before the weekend ended. I had become an expert at masking. At delivering. At putting on a show. But my heart was broken. So between hosting duties and troubleshooting issues I collapsed to the floor, consumed in grief.

*° *⋆ₒ °⋆*

This was supposed to be our second time having babies together.

Inner mean girl: YOU get two babies when Gillian has none? When she is the nicest, kindest person on the planet? This should have happened to you, not her.

I met Gillian at prenatal yoga when I was pregnant with Andrew. She was magnetic – talking to every single person in the room, instantly breaking down barriers of discomfort and awkwardness. After the first class, I knew I wanted to be her friend. But I couldn't just, like, walk up to her and say that. I wasn't a psychopath. At the end of the second class, she walked up to me and asked if I was in the *Facebook* group for moms having babies in 2021. I said no so she asked for my number to send the link.

She put me in her phone as "Mariah Yoga Yoga," the second *Yoga*, a typo she kept for years.

Gillian was the most social, open person I'd ever met. She was friends with everyone. A true extrovert. I was amazed by her ability to be fully herself in any setting, how she seemed to navigate relationships with grace and ease.

She brought me into her mom group when I was just two weeks post-partum, the fog thick around me. She always made sure I was comfortable and appreciated. She made sure *everyone* was comfortable and appreciated.

It didn't surprise me to hear how affected the medical staff had been by her tragedy. Or that the doctor who delivered Baby Boy later came over for coffee. Gillian is, at her core, a connector. Someone you want to be around. Always thinking of others. Always making things better.

When Gillian got sick earlier that week, she ignored all my attempts to persuade her to get help. She wanted to stay home with her son, who was the same age as mine, and rest. Going to the hospital felt like a luxury she couldn't afford. Something most moms can relate to. But it got bad, fast. Thankfully she finally agreed to go in, unaware how many of us – including the nurses and doctors – were scared for her life.

Listeria.

IVs were placed anywhere they could go, trying to get her body under control. She was being monitored closely. Eventually, they decided to deliver. The baby was doing well. The NICU could handle this. He might be there for a bit, but he'd be fine. Delivering was safer for both of them.

Gillian went into surgery optimistic, excited to meet her baby. She was feverish and shaking, but focused on her son at home and the baby she was about to meet.

When I saw her name pop up on my home screen in the middle of the night, my first reaction was full-body relief. She was alive. But that relief twisted into an anguish I'd never known.

Day 2 of Camp Kinder was a performative blur. I turned it on for the camera, smiling and laughing in front of more than 700 teachers. But when my hosting responsibilities weren't scheduled, I collapsed off screen. Dave didn't understand why I was taking it so hard. He didn't understand how much it hurt that I had two babies safely inside me. And Gillian had none.

As a mom, you find yourself connected to other moms without much history or justification – especially when your babies are close in age. That was the case for Gillian and me. I felt her loss in my bones.

Gillian was a shell of herself. When she returned home from the hospital I brought groceries to her doorstep, trying to stay out of sight – afraid my belly would hurt her even more. But she came to the door, wincing in pain and cradling her now empty abdomen. I held her and whispered I was sorry into her hair. We cried together on the front steps and she tried to walk me, and herself, through it.

She had been fine. He had been fine.

Then suddenly, she wasn't.

Suddenly, he wasn't.

Suddenly, he died.

It made no sense.

° ⁺★₀ °★

For weeks, I was consumed by grief for Baby Boy and Dave was more confused than ever, often walking in on me crying, "I don't understand. He's not your baby. Being sad doesn't help Gillian – you need to be strong for her."

I couldn't. I wasn't strong. I was one of three in Gillian's inner circle, holding space for her darkest thoughts and hardest hours. I never wavered. Day or night – it didn't matter. We'd go over the same things again and again: food choices, medical details, what the doctors said. Anything she needed, I was there. Nothing else mattered.

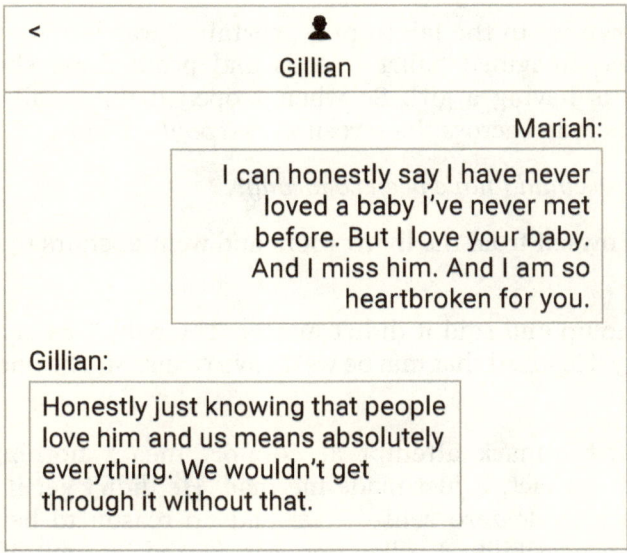

This was our new normal. Just weeks earlier we'd been debating boy-boy vs. boy-girl twins, my biggest pregnancy drama being unexpected gender disappointment.

Finding out I was having a boy brought massive feelings of shame and sadness that surprised me – but Gillian never judged me.

My parents, brother, and sister-in-law had flown into Halifax for Andrew's first birthday. I was only a few weeks pregnant but already showing and eating like a high school linebacker. Dave and I had planned a big reveal: Andrew would open a gift with a "Big Brother" book the next morning. But that plan imploded when we sat around the dinner table and my brother said, "So – we have something to tell you."

I gasped and turned to my sister-in-law, "You're pregnant!" She laughed nervously and nodded. I was thrilled – this was the dream my brother and I had always talked about.

"Me too!" I blurted. The table went silent. My cheeks burned. I should've waited. Should've let her have her moment. Why did I always do this? Everyone recovered, congratulations were exchanged and the next day, my early sex-detection blood work results landed in my inbox.

I had shown up to the lab in pink, certain I was having a girl. I'd named her, imagined ballet lessons and prom dress shopping. I *knew* I was having a girl. So when I opened the email and blue confetti exploded across the screen – *It's a boy!* – I froze.

What? How could I have been so wrong?

I excused myself from the living room and went upstairs to lie in bed and cry.

Dave came up and said it didn't matter. The baby was healthy. We were lucky. He joked that maybe we'd have twins. Maybe one was still a girl.

Dave's off-the-mark attempt at comfort meant nothing to me that night. In fact, it just made me mad. He didn't get it. And his twin theory made zero sense – we had no reason to believe that was even a possibility. I rolled my eyes, kicked him out of my sad-girls-only bed to let myself wallow.

Inner mean girl: Wallow is generous. She was acting like she was in mourning, which is soooo over the top.

I know it sounds silly – especially in the context of this chapter – but in that moment, it truly felt like I had lost my daughter and the life I had imagined with her.

Tell everyone. Take control.

After I dropped my family off at the airport, I called Marissa and un-enthusiastically told her I was pregnant – with another boy. I knew she'd get it. She had two boys before having her daughter.

Sure enough, she completely understood. She reassured me that having two boys was wonderful. That as soon as my baby was born, I wouldn't be able to imagine him being anyone else. But she also affirmed that having her daughter had felt different – and the relief when she found out her third was a girl was *real*. My feelings were valid.

As soon as I got home I messaged Amy (yes, *the* Amy from the fore-word), who you'll hear more about soon – I promise – but for now you need to know she was an acquaintance for years turned friend and business confidante who had two boys. Her words echoed Marissa's. She completely understood, my feelings were super normal, but as soon as he was born, I wouldn't be able to imagine my life any oth-er way. Both of them said, mostly joking, I could always have a third.

But I didn't want to try for a third kid on the off chance I *might* get a daughter. Three kids felt like way too many. This was supposed to be our second and final addition.

The reality was hard to stomach: I would never have a daughter.

A few days after the "It's a boy" email, we booked a private ultra-sound to confirm the pregnancy and see the baby. So far, I only had a couple pee-covered sticks to go on and I wanted a visual. Something to make this baby feel *real*.

The tech put the wand on my belly, pressed the cold gel into my skin, and abruptly pulled it back.

"Ope."

Dave and I looked at each other. And just like that – we knew. His dumb little jokes on the drive over had been right. My wild appetite made sense. My body already looking super pregnant at eight weeks checked out. Right then and there, my childhood dream – acted out with dolls for the first ten years of my life – was coming true. I was having twins.

My hands were shaking. I couldn't stop laughing. They'd be born just before Andrew's second birthday. We'd have three under two. I texted a picture to Chloe, Gillian, and Marissa. All three immediately replied: "Wait – is this a joke?"

Nope. No joke. There were two babies in there. I wouldn't find out the sex of the second twin for a while, but when I did – I learned I had been right all along. I *was* having a girl.

I just didn't realize I was having a boy, too.

— CHAPTER 33 —

Google History: I'm scared I

🔍 I'm scared I am going to drop my baby walking down the stairs

Intrusive Thoughts

Intrusive thoughts are unwanted, involuntary mental images, ideas, or urges that repeatedly enter the mind. While often associated with conditions like OCD or PTSD, research shows they can also occur in ADHD due to differences in attention regulation, impulse control, and working memory. In ADHD, intrusive thoughts may be intensified by emotional dysregulation, making them harder to dismiss. They can range from distressing "worst-case scenario" images to socially anxious replay loops and are not necessarily reflective of a person's desires or intentions. [23]

Sensory overwhelm

A state in which the brain receives more sensory input than it can effectively process, leading to discomfort, irritability, or shutdown. Sensory overwhelm can be triggered by environmental factors such as noise, light, texture, or smell, and is common among people with ADHD, autism, and sensory processing differences. Symptoms may include difficulty concentrating, emotional outbursts, or the need to withdraw to a calmer environment.[26]

almost dead

— CHAPTER 34 —

Go Get your Daughter

I threw up the entire drive to the hospital. I was 33 weeks pregnant with twins and had been filling mixing bowls since 4am.

TMI? I feel like we are at this level now. Hope you agree!

In classic Mariah fashion, I had already posted on *Instagram* stories about how sick I was. Lotty, who I'd grown closer to as a member of Gillian's inner support circle, saw it and checked in. I took the opportunity to freak the fuck out.

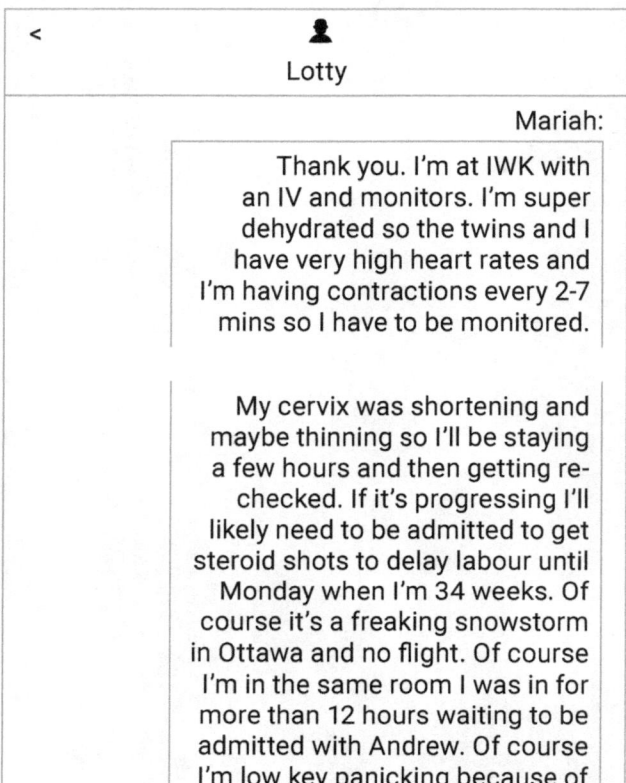

Mariah:

> Thank you. I'm at IWK with an IV and monitors. I'm super dehydrated so the twins and I have very high heart rates and I'm having contractions every 2-7 mins so I have to be monitored.

> My cervix was shortening and maybe thinning so I'll be staying a few hours and then getting re-checked. If it's progressing I'll likely need to be admitted to get steroid shots to delay labour until Monday when I'm 34 weeks. Of course it's a freaking snowstorm in Ottawa and no flight. Of course I'm in the same room I was in for more than 12 hours waiting to be admitted with Andrew. Of course I'm low key panicking because of what happened to Gillian.

Also in classic Mariah fashion, I was more worried about ruining Andrew's Christmas by being in the hospital or delivering the twins early, than I was about my actual health.

I had a bad stomach bug and needed seven bags of fluid to rehydrate me and bring the twins' heart rates back down. By this point, Gillian's loss consumed so much of my anxiety that *her* story was on *my* medical chart. No matter who I was talking to at the hospital, I simply couldn't *not* bring it up. Everyone needed to know. Everyone needed to be vigilant. I was at the hospital every week for some sort of check up on the twins and after the fourth person said, 'Yes, I see that here,' I realized I could stop telling people... they already knew.

Narrator: She didn't stop.

Tell everyone. Take control.

The nurse who administered my weekly iron infusions knew after she asked why my heart rate always spiked drastically when I entered the hospital compared to my doctor's office readings.

The ultrasound technician who checked the twins' positions weekly knew after I broke down sobbing, devastated at week 36 that the twins flipped and I was told I'd have to have a c-section.

The anesthesiologist at my c-section knew when he innocently asked how I was feeling about the procedure that day.

Nurse Rachel, the one person in the room of 21 medical professionals who was solely assigned to me during the twins' delivery, knew – and stroked my hair, telling me everything would be okay.

I was a mess, but we were, in the end, "fine." The twins were born by scheduled c-section at 37.5 weeks. They basically "birthed themselves," alongside the largest placenta the staff had ever seen (my favourite claim to fame and fun fact to overshare).

Ready for some more vomit? Perfect, because I threw up the entire procedure – something that feels extremely alarming when your abdominals are cut open and you need those muscles to vomit, by the way.

Daisy came first, just over 6lbs at 8:26am, then James, just over 7lbs at 8:28am. Before I was stable enough to hold her – and without so much as an explanation – Daisy was whisked away and held in the NICU all day long on idiotic technicalities like shift changes that pre-vented her from being discharged to us even though she was, in their own words, fine.

Daisy was all on her own, after being with her twin and her mom her entire existence to that point.

If I hadn't already been vomiting, this fact alone would have been enough to make me sick.

*° +*o*

Dave and I forced ourselves to speak respectfully to the medical staff in the NICU – and it was hard. We knew they were doing incredible work. We knew they worked hard. And we knew we had a very low collective trust and tolerance level for medical professionals. I had a laundry list of bad experiences involving pregnancy and birth by this point, and my current stay wasn't shaping up to be any better.

Minutes after her birth, Daisy was whisked away to the NICU. I hadn't even gotten a chance to touch her. To see her for more than a second between bouts of throwing up. We couldn't get any clear answers on how she was doing, or why she was there. She *could* have been discharged — she was, in their own words, fine, but Daisy spent her first day in the outside world separated from me and her twin for the first time, all because of technicalities that made our blood boil — like shift changes delaying her sign-off.

Excuse me? This was a newborn baby, not a prescription the pharmacist hadn't had time to fill yet.

The hours crawled by. No one gave us a clear answer. Every time we asked when she could be released, they just shrugged. And I couldn't even go to her. I tried, but always ended up throwing up so much I couldn't leave the room.

I imagined her crying. Alone. Cold. Surrounded by strangers. She'd been with her brother and me *every second* until now. And now – nothing.

Dave went marching back to the NICU, demanding answers and telling them he wasn't leaving until he had his daughter in his arms – and finally, almost 12 hours after she had been born, I was able to hold her for the first time. Finally, we were all together.

I just wanted to get home. I just wanted to clock out of the hospital and never go back. But seven days later, I was back. Same halls. Same hospital. Same fear.

Only this time, I was the one dying.

*° *⋆ₒ ⋆*

Throughout my pregnancy I was consumed by fear and guilt about bringing siblings into Andrew's life. He was my everything and as a new mom I couldn't stomach being away from him – or having others look after him. I cried daily while putting him to bed, my tears soaking into his blonde hair as he lay on my growing belly, convinced I was ruining his life bit by bit.

Narrator: Her doctor upped her depression meds at this point.

I was obsessed with making sure my decision to have more kids wouldn't negatively affect anyone – especially him. So, it wasn't surprising to anyone that I ignored my recovery instructions and still lifted him up. Or that I hobbled outside with him six days postpar-tum, determined to play in the fresh snow.

Rest felt like a luxury I couldn't afford. Guilt had the louder voice. Besides, it was my mom's birthday and the next day was Dave's. It wasn't the time to slow down. My body tried to tell me that I was pushing too hard. I wasn't okay. I needed help. But I was trying so hard to prove everything was fine that I ignored every signal it sent me. The irony was not lost on me.

I had begged Gillian to go to the hospital, desperate to protect her from the worst-case scenario. And now here I was, doing the *exact* same thing. Refusing to go. Refusing to rest. Refusing to acknowledge how bad it was.

Listen. I had gotten better at accepting help (out of inescapable necessity) compared to Andrew's early days, when my postpartum depression was completely unchecked. Back then, my intrusive thoughts had a starring role.

Going on a walk meant I was overcome by visions of a rogue tire flying down the hill and smashing into the stroller. Heading down the stairs meant imagining my arms giving out and the baby tumbling all the way down. Giving him a bath came with a full-on internal battle. What if I suddenly forgot he was there? What if I walked away and he drowned?

Inner mean girl: Could happen.

There was a constant tug of war between "I can't do this and he'd be better off without me" and "No, I don't want help. This is *my* baby."

I wasn't alone, though. Gillian had walked that road with me. We texted through sleepless nights, tracked wake windows, obsessed over sleepy cues, and hired the same high ticket sleep consultant. Eventually, the boys started sleeping. We made it through. And just like that, it was time to get back into the trenches and do it all again – with two babies this time.

*° +*₀ °*

It was midnight after our snowy playdate. Dave and I were sitting in the dark, each holding a six-day-old baby. I was shaking uncontrollably. He took James from me, concerned I was going to drop him and then, without warning – I threw up into the first thing I could grab: an empty gift bag.

Narrator: I promise there is *almost* no more talk of vomit after this chapter.

Dave wanted me to go to the hospital. I wanted to go to bed.

Every breath felt like a knife stabbing my lower back, but his suggestion still made no sense. I had brand new babies who needed me and a toddler who wasn't even two, waking up from nightmares every night. I couldn't leave. They *needed* me. I told him I wasn't that sick and that it would pass. I just needed some sleep.

I lay in bed, shaking and throwing up, while Dave called the nurse line. She barely let him finish before saying I needed to get to the hospital *immediately*. I didn't want to go. But I knew I had to.

I was clear: if I had to go, Dave and my mom had to stay with the babies. If I couldn't be there, they needed their dad. Dave taking me wasn't an option. So, he went downstairs to wake my parents, who were staying with us for a few weeks, and asked my dad to bring me to the ER.

My mom helped me get dressed while Dave brushed off the car but the snowstorm underway erased his effort within minutes.

My dad could hardly see the road in front of him, but I was in so much pain, I barely registered the drive. My lower back was screaming in pain. I was somehow freezing and boiling at the same time. It reminded me of the blood infection I'd had after Andrew was born – the one that came just shy of sepsis.

Only this was worse. *Way* worse.

The triage nurse hardly looked at me and barely said a word to me or my dad. It was obvious she thought I shouldn't be there. Maybe she was having a bad day, maybe I was masking too well, but whatever the reason was my dad and I were shocked by her bedside manner, especially when she looked at me in disgust when I took my mask off – because I needed to throw up.

I already felt guilty for being there – I didn't need her judgment about the decision to come in.

But then...Nurse Rachel walked in. The same Nurse Rachel who held my hair and my vomit bag during the c-section just a week earlier. She stopped in the doorway and cocked her head to the side, "Hey! I know you. What are you doing back here?"

What was I doing there? What was she doing there?

Rachel didn't work in triage. She had told me she was always in surgery. When I asked, she told me it was a complete one-off that she was in the ER. She was just helping to cover someone's break. I burst into tears. She sat beside me on the gurney and touched my leg. Immediately, Rachel jumped up to take my temperature. It was "dangerously high." She radioed for the on-call doctor, who rushed in and, after only a few minutes, confirmed what I had tried to ignore: it was a *really good thing* I went in.

I brushed her off and asked to go home. I rambled about leaving my 6-day-old babies and my not-yet-two-year-old. And then she said it. The thing that snapped me out of my denial.

"If you hadn't left them tonight... you would have left them for good."

Wait. What?

It took over an hour and three nurses to get the IV into my arm. Once I was stable enough, I was finally admitted, and around 3am on Dave's birthday my dad went home to rest.

The nurses could hear my sobs from down the hall.

One after the other, different women came into the room to tell me I was lucky to be alive and should "enjoy the break."

I was livid. This wasn't a break. This wasn't even my choice.

The results were surprising: I had E. coli in my bloodstream. I Googled it on my phone — big mistake.

E.Coli in the bloodstream is a life-threatening medical emergency that requires rapid diagnosis and treatment. It can lead to organ failure, kidney failure, or even death if not addressed quickly.

I clicked another link, this one on the Government of Canada website.

There is no medical treatment for E. coli infections.

Oh good.

A few hours, and many bags of antibiotics and fluids later, Dave arrived with the twins. They would all stay with me until I was allowed to leave. It helped. A little. But I still ached for Andrew.

Gillian stepped in – checking on Andrew and texting me updates. Our roles had completely switched. Now *she* was the one worried about *my* life. She was the one reassuring me it wasn't my fault. I recognized that if I believed it when I said the same to her that I should believe it when she said it to me. But still, I hated it. And I hated myself for being in that position in the first place.

I just wanted to *go home*.

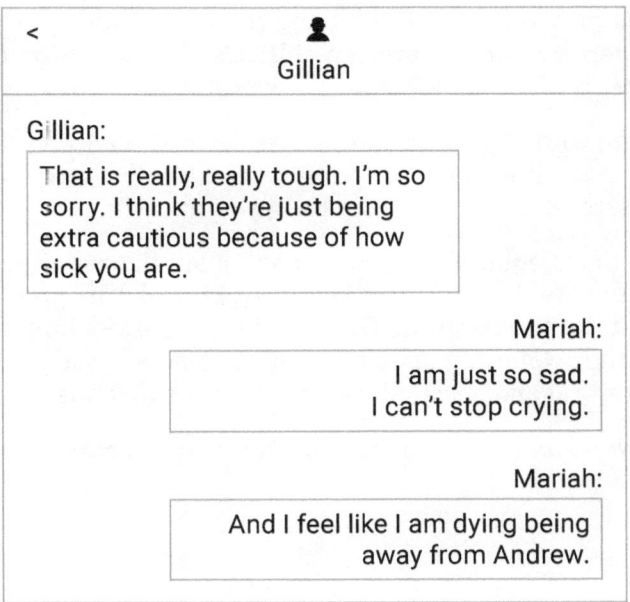

Gillian:

> That is really, really tough. I'm so sorry. I think they're just being extra cautious because of how sick you are.

Mariah:

> I am just so sad. I can't stop crying.

Mariah:

> And I feel like I am dying being away from Andrew.

Inner mean girl: You...literally were dying... and somehow *still* managed to make it even more dramatic.

Less than a week later, two babies asleep on my chest while I lay on the single bed set up in their nursery. I got to work on the third year of Camp Kinder. Organizing speakers. Setting up the website. Posting on *Instagram*.

As if I hadn't just almost died.

But I loved it. Working on something big while snuggling my babies close — those moments were when I felt the most like me. It kept me sane in those early days when it's so easy to disappear into motherhood, to become everything for everyone and forget who you are. Quietly, slowly, a problem emerged. It wasn't the nap windows. Or motivation. Or money. Or even time.

It was the growing weight of having three kids under two, a near-death experience, the grief from Gillian's baby and now, our move back across the country for Dave's new posting.

Lying there with Daisy and James in my arms I realized I didn't give a shit about the drama that came with the education world. I had way more important things to put my energy into.

It wasn't that I couldn't continue making six figures and scaling A Playful Purpose. In fact, I was confident I could. The problem was I didn't want to. Teachergram. Curriculum changes. Staffing shortages. Funding cuts. None of it mattered to me anymore. I had stepped back from that world and it scared me how much I *didn't* miss it.

But that world *was* my business – and my business paid half our bills.

signature pose

— CHAPTER 35 —

Not a Coach

A loud ping interrupted the music blaring from my car speakers. I looked out the window at the darkening sky and briefly considered turning around.

⚠ EMERGENCY ALERT / ALERTE D'URGENCE ⚠

July 13, 2023 | 12:17pm

Environment Canada has issued a tornado warning for this mobile coverage area. Take cover immediately if threatening weather approaches.

A tornado was *not* on the packing list for this mid-week adventure.

I scanned the horizon and figured it was probably fine. Before the music could start up again it was interrupted by my phone ringing. I clicked the button on my steering wheel to answer the call.

"Hello?"

"Hey – did you get that alert? What the fuck?"

It was Alana, the photographer I was on my way to meet for my first brand photoshoot.

We agreed we were probably fine – besides, we were already halfway there. After a few more seconds I hung up, cranked *Speak Now (Taylor's Version)*, released *just* in time for the long drive, and blasted "Enchanted" as loud as humanly possible.

Child-free for the first time in years, I felt free. And guilty for feeling that way.

° +★₀ °★

Just two and a half years earlier, I'd walked down the aisle to that song – timing my entrance *perfectly* to that moment at 1:36 when Taylor sings *this night is sparkling, don't you let it go* for the first time.

I had dreamt of that moment since 2010, fantasizing about my one-day wedding while walking the dirt "cow path" between my apartment and the University of Guelph, hot pink iPod Nano in hand, the original version of *Enchanted* on a loop.

Literal cow path, by the way. Just mooing away. Every day.

When Dave and I picked our wedding music, I didn't hesitate: I was walking down the aisle to *Enchanted*. I had waited over a decade for my *Speak Now* moment.

I freaking loved our wedding, by the way. No chaos. No drama. Just joy. Just us. Lauren, our photographer, and the videographers – Marc and Tiffany – said we were the most relaxed couple they'd ever worked with, which honestly felt comforting given we were marrying less than a year into knowing each other, expecting a baby, and doing it in the middle of a pandemic with a smaller guest list than planned.

And listen, we knew it was a big ask. We were just a few days out from Christmas at a time when gatherings came with inherent risk. The Core Group sat out, worried about missing their family holidays.

Every one of us in The Core Group is now married. But I'm the only one without a group photo in the collection – bride in the middle, Core Group girls gathered around as bridesmaids and guests of honour.

It's not like I had perfect attendance, by the way. I missed Marie's wedding with strep throat, Hannah's in Egypt because of money, and later, I'd miss Jessica's in South Africa because I couldn't imagine leaving my kids. We all had our misses and our reasons. But none of that logic landed at the time. My inner mean girl kept reminding me that my wedding was local to three of the girls, that the rest were in town anyway, and that everyone else had at least one Core Group member in their bridal party. The fact that I never made the cut – while not surprising – was major inner mean girl fuel. But let's try to tune her out, okay?

Just days later – after I'd already flown back to Nova Scotia – they met up for a socially distanced hangout. Hurt, I reacted by "jokingly" writing something along the lines of, "so you're getting togeth-er for this but not my wedding?" but unlike what happened with Audrey and Viv – where one emotionally-charged message ended everything – the chat didn't freeze me out after my outburst. Marie, ever the most direct, asked if that comment was really necessary. I have to admit to distancing myself even more after that. But eventually, my hackles lowered and it was back to business as usual.

June loves this story. She says it's proof you can have *"despites"* in friendship and that real friendship isn't about never hurting each other – it's about what happens after. She told me once, "They loved you despite the outbursts. Despite the spirals. They loved you while you were still figuring out how to love yourself."

She might be right, but don't tell her I said that.

*° +*ₒ✦

As it turns out, everything ended up exactly how it was meant to.

The "no's" from The Core Group opened spots on our Covid-limited guest list, and I invited Marissa and her husband – who said yes immediately – and family friends, Stephanie (from all the way back in Chapter One) and her husband. All four of them played pivotal roles in my career and personal life, offering support and guidance without judgement ever. In the end, having them there was exactly what I needed.

Yes, our wedding was small, but every key element of my girlhood dreams were there. A beautiful, slightly pink ballgown. Stunning, generous florals everywhere. My brother, his wife and, of course, Katie standing beside me at the altar of the most beautiful venue I ever imagined. I'd even booked Laura, the wedding photographer I'd bookmarked and fangirled since 2014. I basically wallpapered our house with her photos from our day, reliving in the moments she captured so perfectly every time I passed a frame.

Clicking through our wedding gallery unlocked a new obsession and investing in photography became part of our family life. I was quick to book maternity photos, newborn sessions, and even a shoot for Andrew's first birthday with my brother, sister-in-law, and parents as special guests.

Scrolling through professional photo galleries is something I've come to realize I absolutely cherish. I've always known I was a visual learner, but seeing their faces, capturing their personalities fills me with so much peace that I've learned I'm a visual ground-er too. The pictures root me in reality when memory alone feels slippery, and I revisit them regularly, coffee in hand during quiet early mornings.

Still, I kept waiting for the "right time" to book brand photos. Cost wasn't the issue. It was me. It took years to finally believe it wasn't performative or cringey to show up in that way — to treat photos as an investment in my business and myself. Just like family galleries gave me the visual proof of moments I never wanted to forget, brand photos could give me the same kind of evidence: that my work was real, that it mattered, and that I belonged in the frame.

In May, with four-month-old twins and an almost two-year-old in tow, I joined an "accountability" group chat on *Instagram*, organized by Danielle, a teacher I'd known online for a few years. The timing was perfect. I needed a kick in the butt to start moving again, wanted to support this new branch of her business, and, honestly, was craving connection of any kind with the Teachergram community. Maybe this would bring me back into the fold.

Being in that group changed my life – but not for health reasons.

I introduced myself in the group and forced myself to sit back as an observer. I knew I had the potential to overwhelm or overtake the chat and was getting tired of hating who I was socially. It was better to avoid putting myself in a situation I'd regret.

Alana, another member of the group, introduced herself next as a former teacher who burned out, quit and became a family photographer. She mentioned she took Danielle's family photos – including the one she had as her profile picture.

Wait. Was this a sign?

I couldn't stop thinking about how brand photos might change my marketing. All intentions of sitting back evaporated, as I blurted that brand photos were a business bucket list item for me and that we should talk.

A few days later, I booked my first shoot with her. I was surprised how low her prices were and happily paid for the Airbnb she recommended – a funky, girly, bright space that perfectly captured the A Playful Purpose brand. The shoot was set for early July, just a week after our move back to Ontario, and what would be my first time away from the kids that wasn't an emergency "you might die so you have to go to the hospital" situation.

The plan was to capture photos to market Kinder Planned – my flagship program that already had more than 500 teachers using it – and my yet-to-be-launched offer: a virtual support group for teachers struggling with burnout called the Dream Team. The idea came from how magical Camp Kinder had felt for the hundreds of participants and for me as the moderator and someone who had spent a lifetime looking to belong.

Helping teachers with their planning and report cards in Kinder Planned made a difference, but I was hungry for more. More impact. More connection. I was determined to create a welcoming, online "staff room" where teachers could speak candidly, swap ideas, and make friends. I knew the photoshoot would bring fresh energy and credibility to this new direction.

I was *so* excited. I prepped for weeks scrolling Pinterest for inspiration and scouring thrift shops for vintage Polly Pockets – the perfect metaphor for Dream Team: a community in your pocket, whenever you needed support. It felt like my future. Exactly what I wished I'd had as a teacher. Exactly what I hoped others needed too.

Narrator: It wasn't.

*° ⁺*ₒ °⁺*

Walking into the Airbnb was surreal. I fumbled with the lock and stepped into Alana's outstretched arms. I always loved meeting another hugger.

We'd never met before – but you never would've guessed it.

Our nervous energy and awkward jokes clicked instantly, and, like me, Alana was dialed into subtle expressions and gestures. Uncomfortable in my post-twin body, she noticed when I crossed my arms looking at the preview in her camera, surprised at my reaction and leaping into action. Saving me from having to say I didn't like the way my stomach looked, she simply smiled and said we'd try it again. She took extra care to position my body in a way that felt more comfortable, and her sensitivity without judgment is something I'd come to love about her over the next few years.

She stayed *way* longer than she was supposed to, an issue we'd later work on in coaching, don't worry, and yet the conversation never lulled. We talked about marketing, sales strategy - everything business that I loved to talk about. She was hungry to learn, and I was happy to teach – flexing muscles I'd earned as a teacher but in a new, and much more stimulating context. I was amazed by her skills and approach and eagerly offered up every hard-won lesson from my scrappy start, immediately invested in growing her business.

As we wrapped the shoot, Alana asked if I'd consider coaching her. I laughed and shook my head. I was a teacher (okay, fine – an ex-teacher by this point.) – not a coach.

I didn't realize I had already slipped into the role.

Just a year earlier, Amy (told you we'd get to her) and I had been venting about how often business owners pivoted from B2C to B2B just to make more money. It was *so* annoying. There was no way I could sell out like that and become a business coach – the industry overall gave me the ick.

Amy and I had met in teacher's college. We were in the same small cohort of 30 or so aspiring educators and though we weren't close then, we connected years later after realizing we'd both turned our education degrees into thriving businesses.

On a whim, I signed up for an online mentorship program on passive income for course creators and convinced her to join me.

The content blew our baby business owner's minds. We learned about *real* business strategy – terms like funnels, tripwires, buyer psychology, copywriting – it was like learning a brand new language. Busy with kids and businesses, we still found time to talk every day. Without so much as a discussion, we organically split the courseload, each of us focusing on different things at a time and filling each other in on missed calls and big takeaways that were relevant to our businesses.

We transformed during that program – but honestly, without Amy, it's hard to imagine I would've seen the same results.

That program was also where we learned the stark difference between B2C (business-to-consumer) and B2B (business-to-business) businesses.

Amy and I were two of the few people out of hundreds in the program who served non-entrepreneurs. From where we sat, the B2B business owners implemented the course strategies faster – and more easily. They had income claims. Financial ROI promises. Stuff we couldn't leverage in our marketing at all. It was frustrating, honestly. We felt stuck, and unseen – like our business models were the problem.

Spoiler: they weren't. I know now we were wrong. It wasn't the *nature* of our businesses that was the problem. It was the *strategy* – one that wasn't built for our market. ROI is subjective, and value doesn't always mean dollars, but we didn't know how to leverage that at the time.

Strategy is fixable. Fluid. Personal. Once we fixed that, our businesses exploded.

One of my favourite flexes is that in 2025, Amy joined my coaching program and made over $13,000 in three days – more than she'd made the entire previous quarter as a B2C business.

But back in 2021, Amy and I believed B2C business owners who "pivoted" to B2B lost touch with what B2C founders actually needed – and what actually worked. All of this spun through my head as I sat in the AirBnB after my photoshoot with Alana, trying to focus on writing emails and blog posts. Eventually, I gave up and put on *Vanderpump Rules.*

I couldn't be a coach. I was flattered she had asked, but it just didn't make sense.

The next day, I loaded the car and got ready to go back to real life. As I awkwardly fumbled with the lock, the plastic Polly Pocket cases clinked together in my bag and I decided to stretch my freedom just a little longer.

I felt guilty for not rushing home to my family – or using every second of my time away to be hyper-productive. But I also knew this was it. My one shot at true freedom for a while, and I took it.

I got a coffee at a local café. Made a bouquet of dried flowers at a tiny floral shop. Explored boutiques and ate a blueberry scone. All the while anticipating all of the good on the horizon.

When I got home, I hugged my babies and dropped right back into my routine of 5am work sessions and naptime hustling. I ran an incredible round of Camp Kinder. I prepped for The Dream Team launch and invited some long-time customers to join early, for free, as community leaders to help get it off the ground.

Just over a month later, I sent the email announcing the Dream Team was open. Certain this was it. My next big move. Finally, the clarity and calm I'd been craving.

And then Teachergram took me down.

program inspo

— CHAPTER 36 —

Unedited: Jealous of Teachergram?

Sent Message
Monday, August 14, 2023 8:32 PM From: Mariah To: A Playful Purpose Email List Subject: Jealous of teachergram? Preview: Same. But not for long.

Hey there, @NAME!

Sometimes, we feel alone *even when we are surrounded by other people.* That feeling of discomfort in the teacher's lounge, not seeing eye to eye with your teaching partners, feeling new whether you are or not- you aren't alone in these feelings.

Maybe you see "teacher squads" on instagram and feel a pang of longing. Of feeling left out. Of wishing you had a group of your own.

Picture this: a vibrant community of like-minded educators who've got your back and will be there to lift you up every step of the way. Whether you've had a long day, want to co-plan, need to celebrate a win with people who just "get it" and everything else along the way, you know your crew will be there for you.

If you could indulge me with a drumroll, please...

Allow me to introduce you to The Dream Team! A life-changing journey where camaraderie meets classroom magic where everyone is welcome, your seat in the staffroom is always comfortable and your interactions leave you feeling energized and heard.

Here's a bird's eye view of The Dream Team:

→ **A Strong Support Network:** Connect, collaborate, and grow with educators who share your passion and dedication in a dedicated space off of social media. Free from distractions, comparison and ads, our community space on TAPP is an oasis.

→ **A Safe Space to Share to be Yourself:** Let your hair down and share your challenges and triumphs in a judgment-free zone. We are all on the same team and want to lift each other up and support each other. All educators are welcome regardless of assignment, teaching philosophy, language of instructions and any other differentiator. All conversations will be kept confidential within the group.

→ **Achieve Work Life Balance:** Get ready to thrive with strong boundaries and strategies that will completely change the game. From our exclusive mindset workbook to our guest coaches and weekly challenges, you will flourish inside the Dream Team.

I'll pop into your inbox again on Wednesday to share all the info so you are ready to jump in when the doors open on Friday night.

For now, if you're curious (I hope you are!!), then click here to explore the Dream Team site and let me know what you think!

Can't wait to see you inside,

Mariah

emotional support double double

— CHAPTER 37 —

Unedited: Intentions vs. Impact

[A quick-cut reel of five short clips, each about one second long, showing shifting moods and simple, everyday moments. It opens with rain falling on reddish leaves. Then, sunlight filters through bright green foliage. A woman in glasses and a yellow shirt smiles into the camera holding a coffee mug that reads "Good Morning Beautiful." In the next clip, she's in a flannel shirt, eyes closed and hand on her forehead, clearly stressed or overwhelmed. The final moment shows her smiling on a porch, surrounded by floating bubbles, with the words "We'll be there" on screen. Each clip is overlaid with text: "Rain." "Shine." "Good." "Bad." "We'll be there."]

♡ 30   💬 5

August 15, 2023

aplayfulpurpose ✖ NO DRAMA ✖

Staff room awkwardness and cliques aren't welcome in our space.

We are committed to being the support network you can always turn to. To celebrate, troubleshoot, plan and laugh with. To vent, cry and confide to. The Dream Team door is always unlocked and inside you'll be greeted with friends, colleagues and true understanding.

The doors to our private community open on Friday.

Get ready for:

🫶 Community
🧠 Mindset challenges
🔥 Guest coaches
🔐 Wallpaper vault
✨ Mindset Magic Workbook
🧠 @theteacherapp membership
📅 Exclusive live events
🎁 Prizes and giveaways

Doors open Friday. Comment Dream Team for more info 🏎️

TheFrenchFriend: After your last e-mail talking about "teachergram groups", I'm wondering how this "private community" is any different? I don't think it's fair to send a mass e-mail suggesting teachers might feel excluded from certain groups when all the teachers or groups I know on instagram have been nothing but welcoming and inclusive. Perhaps a little clarity in the e-mail would avoid any assumptions people were going to make about these groups. To top it off, you're now turning this into a source of income. I don't see how this is any better.

> **APlayfulPurpose:** @TheFrenchFriend sent you a message but I'll share here too. Other than the subject line designed to peak interest, my email wasn't actually about teachergram groups specifically. It was for everyone out there who, like me, has struggled to find a group that really gets them and makes them feel welcome. We are creating a space of support, friendship and growth outside of the distractions and pressures of social media. I do have a free Facebook group (currently has an epic BINGO game going on!!) but this space is going to be dedicated and focused to well-being and hosted on @TheTeacherApp

August 15, 2023

APlayfulPurpose:

Hey! Happy Tuesday! I'm just looking for a little clarification on your comment on my post. I think I've upset you two and definitely didn't mean to so I'm a little confused and apologize for any miscommunication in my email newsletter. I didn't mean to offend or hurt anyone, so please let me know so I can avoid doing anything in the future. Definitely not my intention nor was I referencing any group at all. This is an email based on feedback from my direct audience.

TheFrenchFriend:

Thanks for reaching out. When I read that email and see words like "Or you feel left out", teachers can take that and understand it to mean that those "groups of teachers" are not inclusive. I would hope that most wouldn't but some people interpret things differently. It almost plants the idea in their head that they were left out or excluded when that's never been the case. The subject line "Jealous of teachergram groups" just didn't sound very positive. So it felt like the groups were used to raise a point and then bring people into this private community. I don't know what it includes but I feel like a free Facebook group could accomplish many of those things.

APlayfulPurpose:

I can see that! I actually already have a Facebook group with 2.5k members and with their feedback we are moving to a paid platform that is off social media and free from ads / easier to find specific content compared to things that get lost on Facebook. Payment also increases investment and engagement and goes toward our live events, guest coaches etc.

Again, everything is based on community feedback and well intentioned. I didn't mean to say anyone was actively excluding-more on the line of "regular" non-influencers feeling that sense of wanting to be in their own group.

CraftsForTeachers:

I agree with the above comment. And I will add that many people have reached out to me because they felt personally attacked or that this is actually creating drama that wasn't there before.

CraftsForTeachers:

I personally don't have an issue with creating any type of group to support educators) paid, or not, on Instagram or elsewhere). But that message you sent out last night really felt like you were targeting specific groups of friends on Instagram.

APlayfulPurpose:

Okay! Thanks for the honest and open feedback. I'm still unclear why it was felt that way but I'll keep it in mind.

TheFrenchFriend:

Thanks for explaining. You said "I can see that!" so I assumed this meant you understood why it was upsetting. I'm not sure there's much more to add if you don't see how it was upsetting. There's no issue with the platform you want to create, but to do it at the expense of other teacher groups isn't really fair.

APlayfulPurpose:

I understand my language choice for sure! Just not why you felt your group was targeted.

CraftsForTeachers:

I don't feel the need to continue this conversation.

CraftsForTeachers has left the group

August 15, 2023

SpecialtyZone:

When I read this Mariah I was sincerely shocked. After reading between those lines and reading the remarks circled it really looks to me like you are implying that quote "teacher squads" on social media are not inclusive therefore feeling alone or left out therefore leaving teachers feeling alone and or left out and then trying to turn a profit from teachers feeling excluded. This did not sit right to me. I understand business and truly this isn't the way to do it.

I sincerely hope that you reflect on this and think about the implications of making these kinds of comments. I don't want to drag this conversation on but I do urge you to reframe because what this implies is simply not true and I think many would agree.

APlayfulPurpose:

I am truly sorry you feel that way. To be honest, that's not what my email meant to imply at all, and my inbox is flooded with educators who feel alone and seeking a group. All content I create is based on my own experiences in real life and online. I am so happy you have had such great experiences and hope that continues!

I am creating a wonderful community for every educator - but honestly, my audience are not influencers and this project has been extremely well received.

SpecialtyZone:

To be honest it's the wording... and I think you know what it implied...

Obviously it's not doable to form close friends with everyone but I think to say "feeling pangs of loneliness" or feeling left out is quite direct. Also asking people who you think feel any type of way to pay for a subscription under the guise of "being jealous of teacher groups" as you said in your tagline is not right.

I appreciate your apology but I think we will have to agree to disagree on this one. I thought I would let you know how this might impact some of the teachers that you are sending this too. Anyhow, I thought I would let you know how I felt about that. Take care.

"Man I'm thrown
and I don't know
what to do."

USHER
CONFESSIONS PART II

small but mighty

— CHAPTER 38 —

Rebrand

I read the email I'd sent over and over, analyzing the lines circled in red. I sent screenshots to anyone who might have context — I didn't have the bandwidth to bring anyone up to speed.

This was bad. Like, *really* fucking bad.

My launch was gaining traction – but not the kind you want. Between outright DMs and passive aggressive *Instagram* stories, the voice of the few was loud and persistent.

You know when one person says they don't like your outfit and suddenly you're self-conscious even though you loved it and a dozen people said you looked cute? Logically, you know it's just not their style, or maybe they're projecting. Logically, you know your opinion should matter most. But logic doesn't stop it from sucking.

That. But for my livelihood.

For once, I didn't feel like I was being too sensitive. I kept HR Mariah in the driver's seat and stayed private, breathing through each message. Slowly, encouragement trickled in from followers, fellow business owners, and teachers: *"Is this about you? Are you okay?" "The bullying in the teacher community is WILD rn."* Amy, especially, let me rehash every nuance. She agreed: it wasn't in my head.

But those private messages felt quiet compared to the noise against me. No one used their platform to stand beside me the way some had used theirs to drag me down. I understood why — fear of conflict, fear of losing business — but I also knew I wouldn't have stayed silent if the roles were reversed.

June often calls me brave for that. She says most people stay "neutral" rather than risk open conflict, even if it means keeping relationships that don't feel real. To me, that kind of silence feels heavier than the fallout of speaking up.

My VA, Stacey, was my shield. She muted, unfollowed, and blocked accounts that seemed to only lurk to judge. We never deleted public comments — transparency mattered — but I didn't want those people in my space, especially near anything about my kids.

I didn't handle it perfectly. But I did what I could, and I offer that version of me more grace now than I ever did then. I hadn't done anything wrong — but I felt like if I'd been more popular, it wouldn't have been an issue. The irony wasn't lost on me: being told there weren't cliques online while a group collectively ganged up on me.

I can see now my words struck a nerve. They triggered something. And I'm not here to argue who was right. The truth is this launch changed the entire trajectory of my business. The program was never for them anyway. The people outraged already had support systems. I was trying to create something for the ones who didn't.

*° + *₀ °*

My enthusiasm for The Dream Team died that day.

Instead of showing off the stunning photos Alana had taken or indulging in extra Canva time to play with the Polly Pocket branding, I winced every time my scheduled content went out. Was something in this one offensive? Would more screenshots be passed around, my words and intentions picked apart?

Still, a small but mighty group joined the Dream Team. They said it was *exactly* what they needed and I tried to focus on them – the ones who *got* it. The ones it was for. But it was impossible to stop the spiral.

Why was I always the one on the outs? The one whose apologies didn't matter? The one who never got picked? The common denominator.

I was the problem, again.

Inner mean girl: I've been saying this for years.

I thought back to Olivia deciding to cut ties in Grade Seven. I re-analyzed the fallout with Audrey and Viv. Maybe they *had* been real friends. Maybe I *was* the bad one. I spiralled about my wedding, wondering whether the Core Group actually *could* have come but chose not to.

If someone else had made these choices, reacted this way, said these things would they have responded the same outrage? I pushed it down and told people I didn't care. I moved forward. I pressed on. Inside, my brain was screaming: Retreat. Hide. Burn it all down.

And that's exactly what I did. I just wouldn't realize it until November.

I couldn't just sit still and wait for a miracle to happen. So, I rebranded. *A new logo and colour palette fixes everything, right?*

Uncomfortable in my digital skin, I tried a new niche on for size. I changed my handle to *Teach Well Live Better* and shifted my content to talk more about teacher wellness than teaching strategies. I shared my burnout story and resources to support teachers on the brink. I collaborated with experts – body image specialists, nutritionists, mental health professionals. I started working on a teacher wellness journal and launched a dopamine-boosting sticker club. I was determined to make my business fun again.

Basically, I cut my own bangs after a breakup.

I pretended everything was fine, but I couldn't get comfortable – everything felt like resistance. And there was another thing: Alana's words were still in my head. So quietly I started a brand new *Instagram* account. The little "o" at the top of the profile felt refreshing, safe and a little surreal. There, I could post without fear. There, I was anonymous. Untainted by my past. There, I was starting fresh. Alana became my first follower (and my first coaching client and slowly my audience grew. Slowly, I found my voice again.

And if you think it was a smooth transition because I had years of experience under my belt, think again. It was messy. I was figuring out who I was without an established brand to default to. I was discovering what I truly wanted to do, who I wanted to work with, and what starting from zero meant.

I wanted to completely give up my old account right then and there (with like 137 followers and a $20 digital product) but Dave, ever logical, reminded me that A Playful Purpose Inc. had paid me steadily for over two years, and we couldn't risk halving our income. He said not loving your job but getting it done was normal.

We lived in our dream house, nestled on two acres in a rural town. We watched *Survivor* every Friday night and occasionally splurged on charcuterie boards for at-home date nights. We shared inside jokes about our kids' funny habits and genuinely loved spending time together as a family. The kids were growing up fast, and we were settling into routines that felt very much like us. Was I really going to jeopardize that?

Plus, there was the tiny matter of those hundred or so pre-sold tickets for another year of Camp Kinder, and speaker agreements already underway. Dave, trying to be helpful, said it was normal to not love your job – and still suck it up, get the job done, and collect a paycheck.

I was stuck.

I knew I couldn't fake it. To this day I wear my heart on my sleeve, react impulsively and struggle to make myself do the things I don't want to do. I leave my sweet, sweet accountant's emails – with very basic questions inside – unread for six days, for goodness' sake.

How on earth could I run a business I didn't even want?

My heart wasn't in it. But I had to try.

Fight?

Flight?

Freeze?

I was retreating, ready to burn it all down, but also fighting to see if that *was* the only option. I wondered if I could run it completely passively. I talked to a serious buyer about selling. I was still putting in effort and still showing up. I just wasn't pulling it off the way I thought I was.

I outsourced everything I could: resource creation, social media, even more admin to Stacey. I blamed my years out of the classroom, the tightening purse strings of teachers and the saturation of the market. I was frustrated that no matter what I tried, no matter what new ideas I had, nothing seemed to land.

In yet another voice note spiral – completely deflated about how stuck I felt in A Playful Purpose – Amy finally saw her opening.

She had noticed the change. She called me out on my reluctance to share anything personal and generic content. She wondered if my messaging wasn't landing because I wasn't really there anymore. She, ever so gently, asked if maybe the situation during the Dream Team launch had impacted me more than I realized.

I felt the familiar walls start to rise up, my defenses lifting. But for some reason, without warning, in the middle of the grocery store parking lot, I stopped pushing it down. Maybe it was the kindness in her delivery, maybe it was because I deeply trusted her insights, maybe it was because I was tired of pretending. In any case there was no denying it: she was right.

Amy encouraged me to open up to the community I'd spent years building and supporting. She reminded me how many people genuinely cared about me and would want to know what was going on. She said I deserved to feel safe in the space I had made safe for so many others.

She told me I didn't need to decide anything right away and nudged me to just think about it.

So I did.

For the seven whole minutes it took me to drive home.

Kids napping, house quiet, Dave working in the garage, I propped my phone up in front of the sliding glass door (natural light still a priority, even mid-breakdown), and hit record.

I knew they had their version and I had mine. It's just that I wasn't interested in keeping my story inside any longer. And yeah, I hoped someone – or a few someones – would see my truth and tell me I wasn't crazy.

No rehearsal. No notes. No real plan for where I was going or what I wanted to come from it.

After eight minutes, I was done and I uploaded it to my feed before I could talk myself out of it.

The relief was *instant*.

*°+ ⋆° ° ⋆ *

I'd been carrying a secret load I didn't even realize was there – fear. Of what people would say if I let them in. Of the original commenters doubling down or accusing me of lying. Of the fact I was upset about being targeted online – could I even talk about that without *doing the same thing* and targeting them back?

But the support that followed calmed my nerves about any potential backlash. The next day, I made another reel – and it didn't take bribing myself or outsourcing to post it. It felt like a celebration.

Narrator: A cheeky celebration set to Karma by Taylor Swift.

I was so grateful to have been heard by the people still in my corner. Many reached out to say they'd seen the posts but hadn't realized the impact they'd had on me. Strangers were apologizing – validating that they'd seen the smear campaign but hadn't known what to do about it.

I messaged Amy and thanked her for pushing back. She was relieved I had taken it so well, "Honestly, I feel like something needed to be done. If I helped in any way to push you toward feeling better about this, I'm glad."

*° +★₀♟

I still felt like I was looking over my shoulder – checking story views, dissecting every share, bracing to be screenshotted into another group chat. But it was also when I started to trust myself again. When I started to believe that I wasn't overdramatic.

And maybe it looks confusing from the outside – a series of small but hurtful things that shouldn't matter *that* much. But impact matters more than intention, right?

And then – out of nowhere – my life fell apart in a way that made all of *this* feel unimportant. In an instant my attitude shifted from *pretending* I didn't care…to *actually* not giving a fuck.

video still

— CHAPTER 39 —

Unedited: Public Breakdown

November 8th, 2023

A Playful Purpose Instagram Feed

Duration: 8 minutes, 32 seconds

Speaker: Mariah

Caption: Please watch

This video is a long time coming. Buckle up. It is going to be a long one, but I really need to talk to you. And I need to talk to you as my community that I have spent years and years and years building and some of the things that have been going on lately, some of the choices that I've made, some of the things that have been going on behind the scenes. And I need your help.

Basically, it all comes down to bullying.

Pretty much this started back in September. And in September I was launching Dream Team and I had a really exciting launch plan set out and I was really excited about the offer and I still am excited about it. We've got a really nice group of teachers in our online space but something happened during that launch and truthfully I have not been the same since.

During that launch I actually started getting an onslaught of really, really hurtful, hateful messages from other people on Instagram, from other public figures on Instagram in the teacher community. And it got to the point where I was just not only being bombarded with messages, but there were also stories going up left, right and centre that I knew were passively aggressively targeting me.

And I was getting messages saying I was preying on teachers and that my business practices were disgusting and that I had no place creating a community for teachers and that I was painting teacher-gram in a bad light and that everyone was always welcoming and able to be friends with everyone.

I ended up actually having to block about 20 accounts because I just could not handle the volume of hatred that was coming my way over a project that was really important to me. Dream Team was something that would have changed my life when I was a teacher in the classroom and having it just be torn down like was really hard.

[Speaker pauses and appears to be holding back tears]

Anyways, at the same time, I started getting a bunch of messages from people because they had noticed a slight change in my account, talking a little bit more about wellness. I started getting messages from people about how I was a fraud and how they didn't want to learn from me because I wasn't in the classroom anymore, just really preying on my imposter syndrome.

It wasn't a lot. It's just those voices are so much louder than all of the wonderful, amazing community members. And it really affected me. It really silenced me.

I think it just brings me back to that vulnerable 16-year-old version of me who just has always wanted to fit in and has always wanted to be accepted. And this larger community of cool people just tearing me down really affected me.

I know I no longer felt safe posting in my own community because I didn't know who was reporting back to them. I didn't know all of their accounts. I didn't know their personal handles and I just felt really unsafe posting anything about my life because I didn't want it to be attacked.

So that's why I went quiet.

At the end of the day, I love sharing. There's a reason I started on social media at all - I love sharing about my mundane day-to-day life. And I... and I got away from it because of fear and because of rejection and because of being embarrassed.

So at the end of the day, I want to go back to A Playful Purpose at its core because I don't want bullies to decide my course of action. I will need your help. And therefore, I want to bring you in on making the plan.

If you've watched this video, I'm looking at the clock notes over eight minutes. Shout out to you. You're the best.

10 minutes before

— CHAPTER 40 —

Get Home Now

It started like any other day. I worked from 5am to 7am at my desk in the corner of our living room before switching hats and settling into mom mode. Dave was at work at the military base about 20 minutes away, with limited phone access. This was normal, and I'd catch him up on the kids and everything we'd done when he got home around 4 p.m.

I noticed that Andrew, two and a half years old at the time, was acting a little...off. He was calm and half-heartedly playing – his baseline level was high-energy, high activity level. The twins were asleep in their cribs and we were playing with the marble run when he suddenly turned to me and said he was tired.

Andrew – while ahead in every gross motor function and in the 99th percentile – had a speech delay. He was quiet for such a wild kid and hated sleeping, so when he used *words* to tell me he was tired, it made the hairs on the back of my neck stand up.

The thermometer flashed red: 100.4. Not ideal, but not overly concerning. The twins were rousing from their sleep, so I asked him if he wanted to lie down in my bed, which is right off the main liv-ing space, to watch *Paw Patrol*. He nodded yes – but I noticed he didn't smile.

He snuggled into our bed – the California king enormous compared to his tiny body nestled in the middle – and I kissed his forehead.

I was concerned.

One twin on each hip, I walked quickly back to the main room. I didn't even change their diapers. I wanted eyes back on Andrew, fast – I thought he might throw up and he *hated* throwing up. Ten month old twins settled into their activity centres, I walked the few steps back into my bedroom. Andrew heard me and rolled over.

As I reached down toward his forehead, wondering if the fever had spiked, his eyes rolled backward. His mouth fell open. His little body started convulsing.

He was having a seizure.

"Oh my god, oh my god, oh my god."

I scooped him up into my arms, carrying him on his side as I raced to the kitchen to call for help.

"Mummy's here. I got you. Mummy's here. I got you."

I dialed 911.

"Mummy's here. I got you. Mummy's here. I got you."

Why was no one answering?

"SOMEBODY HELP ME!"

More ringing.

"Mummy's here. I got you. Mummy's here. I got you."

Andrew was still shaking. His eyes glazed. His lips turned blue. I felt like the floor had fallen out from under me.

Don't die.

"PICK UP THE PHONE!"

I somehow held Andrew with just one arm and freed up a hand to text Dave, my hands quivering. It was nearly impossible to type:

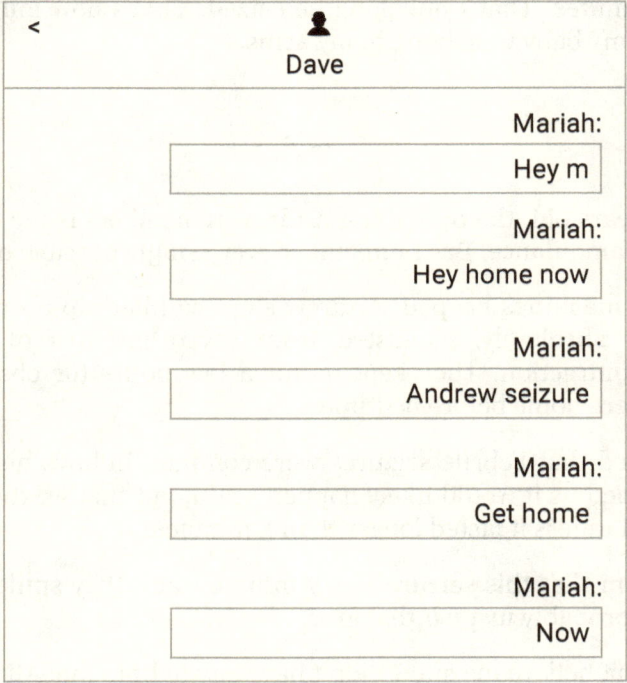

The messages didn't deliver.

Finally, the operator answered. I told her what was happening, desperation thick in my voice. I told her his lips were blue. I begged them to hurry. I kept yelling for someone to help me. She told me to put him on the floor, on his side.

I sent a message to my dad, telling him he needed to leave work and drive to Petawawa immediately– and to get ahold of Dave somehow. He wouldn't get my messages. He wasn't allowed his phone at work.

I walked over to the playroom – the twins staring at us in silence – and sat cross-legged on the floor, Andrew in fetal position in front of me, still seizing. His little noises haunt me, even now.

Finally, he stopped shaking. I kept my hands on him, he was breathing heavily as he lay, asleep on the floor. He slept until the paramedics walked through the door a few minutes later.

Seven minutes. That's how long he seized. That's how long I spent thinking my baby was dying in my arms.

At four years old, the only thing Andrew remembers is me throwing up in the ambulance. But I remember every single horrible moment.

Hospital machines beeped. Andrew slept cuddled up on my chest, his body absolutely exhausted from seven minutes of nonstop muscle contraction. They kept us for a few hours for observation, but we were home before bedtime.

We learned that Febrile seizures were common in boys his age and they warned us it would likely happen again, but that we didn't need to call 911 unless it lasted longer than 5 minutes.

I told them that this seizure was 7 minutes, and they smiled gently, saying it probably just *felt* that long.

They didn't believe me and I didn't have any fight in me. All that mattered was that Andrew was okay, and we were going home.

It took me days to break down.

I was in shock and putting every ounce of energy I had into making sure Andrew was okay. When anyone asked how I was doing, I replied automatically, "Thank God I was home and right there when it happened" – a sentence that I now recognize completely avoids the question altogether.

Listen, I *was* grateful. And completely resolved to never return to the classroom – or any job that took me away from my children. But I admit I was completely avoiding the need to process why that certainty now existed.

Andrew's trauma from the experience was, on the other hand, unavoidable. He was terrified of the change table where he broke down in tears, and recoiled from touching it. We took it out of his room and put a single bed in its place. I slept there until his fever was gone, unable to shake the fear of him seizing during the night – a distinct possibility the hospital staff told us about nonchalantly.

On day four, Stacey told me to have a shower once the kids were down for a nap. And not just any shower. *The* shower. The one where you finally let yourself cry.

So I did. The warm water cascaded down my body. The steam holding me tight. I let myself go there – reliving what had happened, what I had seen, what I had felt. Before I knew it, I was in my heartbreak position, curled up on the floor of the shower, sobbing.

The next day I sat down at my desk at 5am, frozen. The thought of dealing with any of the online bullshit that took so much of my energy, patience, and happiness no longer made any sense to me.

I didn't have it in me to filter myself. To play the game. I knew without a shadow of a damn doubt what *really* mattered to me. I was done, and I was prepared to burn it all down.

I glanced at the monitor on my bedside table as it cycled through Andrew, Daisy, and James sleeping in their beds.

Mummy's here. I got you.

goodbye forever

— CHAPTER 41 —

Unedited: The Goodbye Post

[Slide one: black text on a white background]

I don't even know what to say. But I couldn't say... nothing.

Over the years you have listened and read and supported me, and my family. You have watched me transform from a girl making some resources and burning out, scared she'd never have the life she dreamed of, to living that life to the fullest.

Through cross country moves and wedding bells and pregnancy announcements, you've been here.

Through new offers and new ideas and new ways to connect, you've been here.

[Slide two: black text on a white background]

From idea to full blown business making 6-figures a year, you've been here.

Thank you.

Now, it's time to turn over a new leaf.

I want to leave you with the reminder that you are so much more than just a teacher.

[Slide three: black text on a white background]

And you don't have to stay one just because you were trained as one and have job security.

If you want to, I am so happy for you.

But if you don't, please know there is happiness and freedom on the other side. And you can ignore the haters telling you that you're crazy to even consider it.

♡ 183   💬 11

July 25, 2024
aplayfulpurpose @mariahmakesithappen 🖤

Madameb Thank you for all that you've done and continue to do for educators!!

MagicBecca Wishing you all the best! So proud of you for choosing what you love!

JessieB Thank you for your inspiration to see beyond the stability and to do what we love

Frannie54 Thank you for everything! Your resources and even just learning about you and your growing family has been incredible.

Heidiii So grateful to have found you years ago, to have been in the trenches of postpartum with you, and to see you moving on to follow your next wonderful dream.

"Hush, just stop.
There's nothing you
can do or say, baby.

I've had enough. I'm
not your property as
from today, baby."

BRITNEY SPEARS
STRONGER

leaving the airport

— CHAPTER 42 —

Justin and Selena

I plopped my bag on the passenger seat and heard the crinkle as it landed. Oops. I needed to be more careful now that it had a bag of *All Dressed* chips inside – packed for my American business coach. They were her favourite and only available in Canada, so I grabbed some at the gas station.

I was spending the night at my parents' condo near the airport before catching my early morning flight to Montana. I called my mom from the car as I pulled out of the gas station and asked her to pick me up socks and sandals – two things I hadn't had time to grab before the trip. I felt disorganized. Unprepared. Like someone playing mom-business-retreat-dress-up and waiting to get found out. I had read through the itinerary over and over, trying to visualize myself there, but I just couldn't.

When I joined the coaching program a few months earlier the retreat was the part I was most excited for. It was, I thought, exactly what I needed – a break from my regular life, the chance to connect and decompress, to be around other women. But as the date approached, my excitement disappeared.

I blamed it on being busy. There was a lot going on with work, the twins starting daycare twice a week or the first time. That's why I rationalized not realizing I didn't have socks or sandals to pack until I was on the way.

At the condo, my mom asked if I was excited to be getting time away. I wanted to share her enthusiasm, it felt important to her, like something she never got. But... I didn't.

"Don't worry," she said. "You just need to get to the airport and then it will feel real."

The airport was only about ten minutes from their house, so, at 4:07am, I did what any thirty-something millennial mom would do in my position: blasted *All Too Well (10 Minute Version)*. As the last few notes played I pulled into long-term parking and stretched across the centre console, reaching for my fanny pack. Huh. I couldn't see it. I lited up my bag, my jean jacket. Nothing. I elt along the floor and under the seat. Not there.

Suddenly, like I was watching a movie in my brain, I saw it: sitting on the dining room table at my parents' place.

I'd left it there. That meant I didn't have my wallet or my passport. I looked at the time: 4:17am. Could I even get out of the parking lot without a credit card? Was this a sign I wasn't supposed to go? I called my mom, hoping she hadn't fallen back asleep yet, and asked her to meet me on the curb with my bag.

*Cue *All Too Well* round two*

4:27am: I waved to my mom and listened to it for the third time as I turned back to the airport.

4:37am: I walked into the airport and cleared customs and security on autopilot. There weren't any lines to slow me down until I got to Tim Hortons, just a few gates away from mine. I'd been looking forward to getting a large double-double and a sour cream glaze (the ultimate pairing) since I got up that morning, but all of a sudden I started to feel sick. The ceiling vent was blasting hot air onto me while I stood there, and the one woman working was doing her best – but, for the first time that morning, there was a wildly long line that wasn't moving. At all.

4:51am: I left the line to go sit down and messaged Dave.

Dave:

What don't you know?

Mariah:

If I should go.

Mariah:

I'm so sweaty I feel like I have a fever and I feel nauseous.

Mariah:

No one around me seems hot. Everyone is in sweats and sweatshirts.

Dave:

First time away, my love.

Mariah:

I just feel so hot. I don't want to be sick on the plane. I think I could throw up.

Mariah:

The only reason I basically want to go is I feel I'll be judged if I don't go. I'm sure it'll have fun moments. I signed up because I thought I wanted to go.

Mariah:

In theory, it's cool and fun. Getting together with them. Seeing a new place.

He called me.

I didn't talk much – I didn't have much to say, and I didn't want people around me to hear I was sick and feeling uncomfortable. I walked to the bathroom, Dave's calm, logical voice in my ear.

"I feel like you want me to tell you not to go, but I'm not going to do that. I don't want you to regret not going... or blame me for not going."

I locked myself into a bathroom stall, listening to him reassure me that the kids would be fine. That I would be fine. I knew he was right.

The night before, while kissing the twins and Andrew goodnight, my intrusive thoughts hit me like a pile of bricks.

What if the plane crashed?

Blah blah, there are fewer plane crashes than paper cuts or whatever you're about to tell me about airline safety. My brain didn't want to go. That was clear. My body, fighting against my brain every step of the way, was going through the motions of what I was *supposed* to do. Muscle memory after countless trips throughout my life.

Jekyll and Hyde. Bonnie and Clyde. Justin and Selena. My brain and my body were on opposite missions and I had no idea which one was right.

Here's how I imagine it played out:

Body was in the lead. We were at the gate. We could see the plane. She smiled triumphantly and lifted her chin (not mine, I was in ma-jor low-chin mode). Take that, Brain!

Brain didn't like that. She was out here doing the most for Body. Try-ing to keep her safe. And this is how this bitch repays her? A smug chin lift? Brain was pissed.

Brain was like, *girl, you don't even know what I can do. I own you.*

So she turned up the heat. Body started sweating – why was it so hot in here?

Body went to the bathroom to splash water on her face.

Brain tunneled Body's vision so she could only see right in front of her – peripherals were a privilege, not a right.

Body walked out of the bathroom, removing her sweater and tying it around her waist.

Brain cued the intrusive thoughts like a conductor of the world's most passive-aggressive orchestra. And when that didn't work relied on her secret weapon: nausea.

Body caved. *Okay, Brain. I hear you. I don't know why you're so hell-bent on us not going, fine. Just call off the nausea, would ya?*

Brain agreed – once we were out of there.

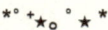

I walked over to the smiling woman at the currency exchange desk who asked how she could help me.

I said, "Hi. Umm. How do I leave this area?"

Wonderful currency exchange lady: "Like, other than on a plane?"

"Yeah. I don't think I can do it."

"Girl, I'm going to level with you... I don't know. No one leaves once they've gotten this far... they just get on the plane. What's goin' on? You okay?"

"I just don't want to go. I can't go."

She nodded, knowingly.

"Is this a girls' trip?"

"Yeah. Sort of. I've never met them. We're in an online group together."

"Mmmmm. Run, girl. I have only heard horror stories of drama and chaos on girls' trips lately. Trust your damn gut here."

"I'm sure they are nice. I feel bad. I just can't go. I can't leave my kids."

Announcement calling Mariah Scrivens to Gate 11 over the airport speakers.

"That you?"

I nodded.

"I mean, what if you *did* go, but you said you weren't going, and just stayed at a hotel near the airport and chilled for a few days?"

"I don't want to fly. I want to go home."

"I get it, girl. Do you. I can't help you, though. You'll need to go talk to the gate agent."

"Okay, thank you."

"You're good, girl."

I walked over to the gate, where a trio of neat flight attendants were clustered together. One woman leaned into her computer and asked, "Are you Mariah Scrivens?"

"Yes, but I'm not going to go. I can't go."

She looked up, her expression shifting from annoyance to confusion to concern as her eyes met my face. She didn't question me, didn't ask why. She looked back at her computer, her fingers clicking across the keyboard.

"No problem, sweetheart. I'll get an agent to escort you out through the back."

I trailed a young employee headed out on her break. She walked fast. When we got to the exit door, she wished me luck. As I stepped outside, the sun rising in the distance, the cool air hit my face. Instantly, I felt better.

6:27 a.m.

Nausea gone. Temperature normal. Knot in my stomach, released.

Brain and Body were on the same page. They probably high-fived.

That's when it finally dawned on me: I hadn't been sick. I had been having an anxiety attack.

Nice. I hadn't had one of those in a while. And hey, I didn't get lobster claws this time. Look at me go. *Growth.*

I opened up Slack and recorded a voice memo into the retreat channel.

"Okay, good morning. Hi. I'm supposed to be on the plane right now – and I'm not. I had an anxiety attack in the airport and just couldn't get on the plane. I've never been a nervous flyer, so I don't know i it's about the kids, or the twins just starting daycare, or what... but yeah, I didn't get on the plane. I'm sorry."

Driving back to my parents' condo, I didn't listen to anything. Just let myself sit, replay the morning in my head, and settle back into myself. When I arrived, my mom was sleeping, so I sat outside, enjoying the double double and sour cream glaze I'd picked up on the way (no line at that Tim's, for the record), scaring the crap out of her when she woke an hour later and saw a figure in her yard. While I waited, I booked myself a lash extension appointment at the spa in her building and called Dave and the kids to let them know about the change of plans.

I felt so peaceful and content. I had listened to my gut instead of forcing myself onto the plane like I would have before kids and I was so freaking proud of myself. What a queen.

I got a few messages back in the group saying they understood and that my kids were so young, it made sense. I thought that was that. I would join them at the March retreat and had months to prepare mentally for it.

But...that's not what happened. I *did* go on retreat in March. Just not that one, with them. A few weeks after my airport anxiety attack, I actually left the program all together, forfeiting the 20k paid-in-full investment with that decision.

And don't get me wrong: I learned a lot from the coach. Buyer psychology, sales mindset, offer stacking. She's sharp, and a lot of her feedback genuinely helped me.

But over time, the dynamic just stopped feeling good. I started to dread calls. I second-guessed myself constantly. The tone in the group shifted, and so did the experience for me. I began quietly clocking all the ways it no longer felt aligned: refusing to give feedback, cliquey energy, moments that felt more competitive than collaborative.

Like so many times before, it wasn't one big thing. It was a bunch of small moments that added up until I couldn't ignore them anymore.

And then there was the Slack message.

It started with a comment I left on one of her Threads. It was tongue-in-cheek, something like, *Wait, was I left out because I didn't go to Montana?*

I thought it was harmless. She didn't.

The next day, she sent me a multi-screen Slack message saying she was hurt and disappointed by my lack of professionalism, *and* that I had "waited until the last minute to cancel" going to Montana.

My guard was up, but HR Mariah, now a little more bold but still professional, was on it. I explained that her allegation wasn't fair because I hadn't planned to cancel *and* I apologized for the comment and how it came across. I told her I would be more mindful moving forward but the damage, it seemed, was done.

We moved on, sort of. I replayed the conversation over the next few weeks: the way I felt misunderstood, the way my anxiety was brushed off as bad timing. I started calculating my every word and reaction from that moment on. Self-preservation mode: activated.

Less than a month after the Montana-trip-that-didn't-happen, I spent the weekend at a hotel in Ottawa. Dave had the twins. Andrew was at my parents'. I felt ready for the time away – excited, even. Besides, I knew I could get home if I needed to and I knew the load was lighter on Dave this time.

It wasn't lost on me how different this trip felt. Maybe because I was within driving distance. Maybe because I would be with just one person– not five. Maybe because I had my own hotel room and could actually recharge. Or maybe... I was simply meant to do *this* and not that.

I was spending the day with Libby – one of my first clients, for in-person VIP coaching. Another ride-or-die who completely burned down one business while working with me. What can I say? One of my biggest flexes is sniffing out what my clients *actually* want – and giving them the strategy, self-trust, and gentle kick in the booty to go for it.

When Libby joined, she had just moved from Toronto to Ottawa with her husband and two young kids. She was burned out from her corporate project management job and had opened a boutique dayhome to be more present and less stressed. We built out a full lead gen and retention strategy that filled her roster and capped her income. But she was still overwhelmed. By the time she closed the dayhome door, she had nothing left for her own kids. So I asked her – point blank – "Do you actually want to run a dayhome? Or do you want to be an entrepreneur, and that was the fastest way in?"

She didn't even hesitate. She wanted to flex her project management muscles again, and she wanted to build something sustainable – without an income cap and set working hours.

So that's what we did. In her first month of her new business, she brought in just over $8,000. But more than that? She felt that inner exhale of, *Ohhh. This is what I'm meant to be doing.* And she was crushing it in her new role.

Anyway. Enough gushing about Libby. This is my book. *I'm* the star here.

Our VIP day was incredible. We met in person, ed off each other's energy, and got *so* much done. Afterward, we debriefed over fajitas and both passed out early – brains full, bellies fuller. Libby left with a mapped-out launch, emails written, and a whole new offer suite.

I left with big things too: The realization that, uh-oh, I might be obsessed with in-person coaching (but had no idea how to scale that in a 99.9% online business), and the deep unsettling certainty that I needed out of the contract with my coach.

Up until this point, I'd kept all my feelings about her to myself. I was embarrassed – embarrassed that I'd signed on so impulsively, that I paid in full ($20K USD... my Canadian girlies feel my pain here), and that I was more interested in impressing her than listening to my gut.

But when Libby, who was my client and my COO at this point, casually asked how my own coaching experience was going, the word vomit spilled. Everything came out. The contract that said I couldn't speak negatively about her, the tone of the messages, the pit in my stomach. I told her that I have a history of going cold on people on a dime, so I don't know i these were actual red flags or just me overreacting.

She listened. Eyebrows raised while she scanned the screenshots I showed her. She turned to me and said, "No. This is not okay. You need to get out."

That was what I needed to hear. Someone I respected telling me I wasn't being dramatic. That the program wasn't just expensive in the literal sense – it was *costing* me, in ways I could no longer ignore.

I didn't make a scene. I didn't ask for a refund on my investment. I just quietly stepped back, backed out of the program, and backed myself instead.

the suit shoot

— CHAPTER 43 —

Orange Power Suit

The next time I saw Libby in person, she was saving the day — showing up to my photoshoot with Alana, nail glue in hand after one of mine popped off right before we started shooting. Disaster narrowly avoided, she stayed for the afternoon, took B-roll, and hyped me up about the look that had finally made it off my Pinterest board.

Her jaw dropped when I walked out in the orange pantsuit. Exactly the boost I needed to keep it on.

Other than the one time at horseback riding camp when I wore a blazer for our "horse show" at the end of the week for our parents, I had never worn a suit jacket in my life. It felt silly. Performative, even.

It felt like too much.

But still, a bright blazer had been on every brand photoshoot inspo board I'd ever made — dating back to my A Playful Purpose days. It took me four photoshoots with Alana to finally wear the thing I'd loved all along. To finally believe I could show up in a suit — even if I spend most of my days in leggings, covered in snot from other people's noses (my kids, to be clear) — and *still* be showing up authentically.

They say a picture is worth 20,000 words (adjusted for inflation, obviously.) and for the first time, I saw a business that looked the way I felt about it.

These new photos were doing more than making my feed look cute. They were *marketing my business*. I was embodying the results, not the routine. Showing up as myself on my best day — not fading into my average one or trying to prove I was relatable and underselling what I'd built. Instead, I showed up embodying the business I actually wanted and was relatable by simply relating.

That shoot was the catalyst. (I know, I know — it's giving rocket emoji em dash AI vibes. But it's accurate, okay? Remember: I *was* a science girlie for a hot minute.)

I reimagined my services. Moved my office into its own room and painted it pink. Was asked to be a keynote speaker. Sold out my coaching spots. And started writing this book.

To recap:

In August, I officially shut down my long-established six-figure business.

In September, I had a panic attack at the airport.

In October, I wore an orange powersuit.

In November, I ran a Black Friday promo — with those photos — and made enough to pay off the credit card that still had $15K on it from a program I never should've joined.

And in December, my new friend Kat invited me to Phoenix.

— CHAPTER 44 —

Google History: is ADHD

> 🔍 Is ADHD bad?

ADHD

While ADHD is often defined by its challenges, many traits can be leveraged as strengths in the right environment. These include creativity, adaptability, intuitive problem-solving, high energy, and the ability to hyperfocus on meaningful tasks. When supported and aligned with personal values, these qualities can lead to excep-tional innovation, persistence, and connection. Harnessing ADHD strengths often means working *with* one's brain rather than against it, designing systems and environments that amplify natural motiva-tion and curiosity.[31-33]

🔍 Is ADHD overdiagnosed in women over 30?

ADHD Diagnosis in Adult Women

Current research suggests ADHD is still **under**diagnosed in adult women, not overdiagnosed. Many women go unidentified until adulthood due to gender bias in early diagnostic criteria, which were based primarily on studies of hyperactive boys. In women, ADHD symptoms often present as inattention, emotional dysregulation, and internalized struggles rather than overt hyperactivity, leading to years of mislabeling as anxiety, depression, or "personality" issues. Increased awareness and screening in recent years have led to more diagnoses – but this reflects a correction of historic underrecognition, not an inflation of cases.[34-36]

she did it

— CHAPTER 45 —

Permission Slip

I was on the plane.

I was *actually on* the plane. Less than six months after my epic airport failure, I boarded. And this time, I felt excited. At peace. Ready. Just one gate over from where a United agent had helped me flee during my anxiety attack, a text came through while I found my seat.

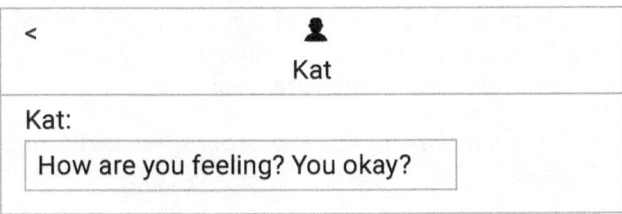

The text didn't surprise me, Kat had been checking on me for weeks. I'd never travelled with people who considered my mental health part of the travel plan, and this was the first time I'd be spending significant time with other neurodivergent women. I didn't have a diagnosis yet, but if the algorithm was to be trusted, I was starting to suspect I had ADHD.

Was I nervous? Sure. Two flights, a short connection, and five days in a house with people I'd never met in person are prime spiral conditions. But this time, Kat would be there.

*° ⁺★ₒ✹

In September 2023, building my new *Instagram* account from zero, every new follower gave my brain the opportunity to live out its alter ego as a flashlight wielding interrogator with a fresh round of questions: *Will this be the person who buys from me? Why are they here? Who even am I?*

Just girly things

Scrolling one day, following whatever trendy piece of growth hacking advice I'd seen that week about engaging with similar accounts, I found Kat. She caught my eye immediately. Pink branding, rural Ontario-based, candid humour.

Kat was a social media strategist and marketing pro who focused on local small businesses, and this girl was freaking *impressive.* Her feed, her knowledge, her business – *this* was someone I wanted to be around. I shared one of her posts to my stories, hoping it would get her attention without being too forward.

Now did I re-share her post and add some sort of normal, chill text like "Love this" alongside? *Of course not.* No, no, my friend. Instead I wrote the oh so subtle following sentences:

Obsessed with @socialkatmedia. My exact vibe and lowkey wanna be real life friends.

Years later, and officially friends, Kat told me when she saw my tag that her immediate thought was: *Is this spam? Is this girl for real?* But, nevertheless, she replied by asking me a question about rural life, and even followed me back. Cue inner "eek" of glee.

By November, we were swapping services. She gave me a social strategy session; I put her in one of the earliest iterations of my coaching programs.

A few months later, she started posting about an Arizona mastermind trip — where she'd meet up with fellow entrepreneurs and spend a week working, dreaming and setting up the next wave of business.

Ever awkward, ever impulsive, and encouraged by our regular candid conversations, I replied to one of her stories about the trip:

It was mostly a joke. (*Narrator*: it wasn't) That summer, she signed up for 1:1 coaching with me, and quickly extended our contract for a full year. By fall, I *was* invited to Phoenix.

In May, three months after that trip – and three weekends away with Kat later – she sent this message in our Slack coaching chat:

> *Just thinking about how impactful you've been on my business. The perfect mix of guidance and advice, with hands-on, I'll-help-you-do-it support. Thanks for getting into the trenches with me.*

But, I'm getting ahead of myself.

After Kat officially invited me along, I called the airline from the failed Montana trip. Turns out I could use my flight credit from the panic attack incident – and the agent gave me extra legroom "because you've been through it." I took it as a sign.

Prepping for Phoenix, I felt good about Kat. We'd worked together for months and I knew we'd get along in person. Arden was new to me and I couldn't read her vibe but I was *70% sure she would like me*.

This led to my first "uh oh" moment – when I asked Kat after a call if Arden, a data analyst from the west coast who hosted the getaway, was just... not into me. She laughed.

"She's literally the nicest person ever. You'll love her."

Turns out, she was right. When we arrived in Phoenix, Arden picked us up from the airport and brought us back to the house. I can't thank her enough for how comfortable, and welcome, she made me feel. She went out of her way to help me feel included. Also, she's brilliant – talking about data and automations with such passion that I bought her program on the spot.

The rest of the weekend was just... calm. We swam, walked, snacked, skipped surface-level conversation, and strategized in each other's businesses.

For my "hot seat" session, I walked through my offers and capacity. Dave would be away for months for training, and I needed to be realistic about what I could handle. I shared (somewhat shakily) what the fall had looked like:

- I may or may not run out of my anxiety medication, decided I was fine anyways and stopped taking them cold turkey.

- I may or may not have been suicidal and officially diagnosed with depression (which was pretty rude because until this point I had *only* had PPD but my kids were too old to claim this title anymore).
- I may or may not have deep regrets over how I handled solo parenting, and the rage that felt like a volcano in that time.

Dave was leaving again soon, and I needed to do things differently.

Kat sat on the couch, reminding me that I could shut down my membership – the one draining my evenings – and go all in on 1:1. That I was allowed to make it easier.

Arden asked the hard questions: who did I want to work with? What tangible results did I want clients to walk away with? How could I use metrics to eel confident scaling back?

And then Olive, the other entrepreneur on the trip – a copywriter with therapist energy and Arden's best friend – chimed in.

"What do you really need right now? Because you don't need us to make a plan or an offer stack. You can do that in your sleep. So, what do you really need?"

I was embarrassed to say it.

Permission.

I'd spent so much of my life scanning for how others felt about me. Making decisions to try to avoid conflict. Operating in fight-or-flight (okay, mostly flight). I needed a riend to say: it's okay to do less. It's okay not to be "on" all the time.

And they did.

Their words reminded me that I didn't need to bend over backwards to prove I care. I didn't need to carry the pressure of client results like a boulder on my back. I wasn't failing because I wasn't doing more – I was already doing too much.

*° *⋆₀ °⋆*

That night, while lying in our own rooms in the Phoenix house, Olive sent me a meme. It was a line drawing of a simple character and a big bowl of French fries structured like a comic strip. It said:

"I am a lot.

But a lot is not too much.

For example: A lot of potato

...is not too much potato.

With potato and with me,

A lot is perfect."

(@worry__lines)

She had no idea that I had already named my book Just A Bit Much. She had no idea how healing this simple grid of drawings about potatoes would be.

Or maybe, she did. And that's why she sent it.

*° ⁺★ₒ⚓

A new voice started talking that weekend.

One even my Inner Mean Girl was nice to:

Inner Child: Can we play on the weekends now? Like, actually rest and not get in trouble?

Inner Not-So-Mean Girl: You can even play during the week. You're safe now.

On the plane ride home I pulled out my iPad, wiped my thumb across the shiny new Phoenix sticker from the airport shop, and opened my tray table... and a blank Google doc.

I knew at that moment that this Phoenix weekend would be the final chapter of my book; it was the missing piece of the arc that had stopped me from even starting until I was 30,000 feet in the air that day.

Right then and there, above the clouds as the sun set in the distance, I typed "Chapter One."

Kat & Mariah

— CHAPTER 46 —

You're Not a Bad Person

Arriving home, the swapping of red sand for snow was made sweet by the hugs and kisses from my kids – and my husband. Side note: if you're a mom in the trenches and you can swing it, take a few days away. It's amazing how everyone's perspectives (and appreciations) change with just a little distance.

It made such an impact that these planned *workations* became part of my regular routine. In April, Kat and I met up at an Airbnb between our towns for an in-person VIP day and weekend work sprint. I returned to that same spot in June – printed manuscript in hand – to revise Draft One of this book.

But it was the weekend away in March, just one month after Phoenix, that had the biggest impact.

Spending time with the girls in Phoenix was the first time I'd been around women who openly talked about having ADHD. I'd already been referred for an assessment, and the algorithm had been feeding me late-diagnosis ADHD content or weeks. By the time I flew home, the seed that had been planted had become a full-on sprout.

Apparently, having three or more running narratives in your brain at the same time and at all times isn't normal. Neither is feeling extreme rejection and shame over fairly tame feedback. Or wiggling your toes and picking your fingers and twirling your hair and grinding your teeth because sitting still is boring. And interrupting, oversharing, anxiety, and hyperfixating are basically the ADHD starter kit, by the way.

Still, I figured I was probably making it up. That I just wanted to fit in. And my parents were skeptical too – like many are. They said there was no way. I'd gotten great grades, was quiet in class and was now a successful business owner.

My therapist, on the other hand, said I could save my money. June was confident – based on my childhood, present-day patterns, and what she saw in our sessions – that I had a pretty classic case of ADHD, masked by years of people-pleasing and being a good girl. She also told me that undiagnosed ADHD had likely taken a massive toll on my ability to build trust and sustain relationships.

Pretty rude, June.

There was only one way to be sure: pay over $2000 and spend eight hours in assessments so I couldn't gaslight myself into believing I was making the whole thing up.

(Spoiler: I still tried. I told the nurse I was probably manipulating the answers to get a diagnosis. She replied, "Yeah, that's not a thing." Again: rude.)

The assessment, if you're wondering, was *horrible*. At one point I burst into tears, and the nurse broke character – stepping out of her neutral, "The doctor will go over your results later" role – to reassure me, "Don't cry. I promise you're not a bad person. You just have ADHD."

Sitting for hours, answering questions that exposed every flaw and weakness in one sitting? Brutal. Between tests, I tried to laugh it off, "Wow. I'm either crushing this or totally failing."

I didn't know if having ADHD was the win or the fail.

The days after the assessment felt foggy. I went to therapy, a shell of myself, grieving the girl I used to be – the one who thought she was lazy, dramatic, or broken instead of simply wired differently. It's not that I believed an earlier diagnosis would've magically fixed everything – and Libby, who was diagnosed young, confirmed that. But I couldn't stop wondering how many relationships might have played out differently if I'd understood my brain sooner. How much compassion I could've given myself. How much self-hatred I could've avoided.

I told June I wouldn't change anything – not if it meant risking the life I have now. My kids, my husband, my business. I wouldn't undo any of it. But I still wished for a softer adolescence for my inner child.

Inner Child: Maybe it's not all my fault?

Inner Now-Not-So-Mean Girl: No. You're not the common denominator. You just didn't know.

No one did.

I'm learning that two things can be true at once:

You can be a good person and make bad choices.

You can fail and still be successful.

You can be happy with your life and still wish it had started differently.

I am, and I'm not, just a bit much.

Either way, I'm enough.

the moment

— Epilogue —

Unedited: Voice Memo Transcript

March 10, 2025, 8:47am

Retreat AirBnB in Ottawa

Speaker: Mariah

I am sitting in the Airbnb right now. Everyone has left. My first official retreat is over and this is a voice note on my phone. I really wanted to record this in this moment when it's super fresh and top of mind and something that I don't want to forget, honestly.

So we're going to do a retreat wrap-up, but also talk about being content — because I think that's something that a lot of entrepreneurs struggle with and also kind of feel like is out of reach.

And I am someone who has always been reaching for the next thing. My mom, my husband, they're always telling me, "You know, you're never happy. You always want more. You always want to be making more, doing more, changing up your offers, fixing your website, posting on socials." It's always more and more and more.

I think they were right. Don't tell anyone that I said that, but they definitely were right.

I have historically always been someone who is really hard on myself, who wants to achieve great things, and who is constantly pushing myself to be doing more and more and more — achieving more, working harder, getting more income, whatever it is.

And during the retreat this weekend — which was my first time hosting a retreat — I had all 10 of my upper program coaching clients come into Ottawa. Three of them flew in, a bunch of them were driving four, five, six hours to get here. And we all met up at this Airbnb in Ottawa and spent three nights together.

We watched the Eras Tour. We made bracelets and we just hung out and did some trauma dumping and all of the things that you love to do in a sleepover-type situation — balanced with focused work time and B-roll collection and a photo shoot and two incredible workshops and time to really talk about everyone's businesses.

I was not surprised but surprised that at least half the group is walking away with a brand new direction for their business — and not in a pivot, "I'm burning it down to the ground" way, but just in a "I didn't think that was possible and now I do and I'm going to go for it" kind of way.

One thing that was really, really apparent is that everyone is bringing community into their business in one way or another. There's a big emphasis on community, on gathering — and a lot of this is in person.

It is nice to have those experiences again. We were laughing that we all feel like we've known each other for a year, but I've never seen their bodies. You know? It's always been shoulders up on the Zoom call. So seeing them in person, seeing how they move, seeing how they interact together – it was truly just such a wonderful experience.

And just the experience of existing together as humans and business owners – without the distractions of home, without the obligations and the cleaning and all of that hovering over us – was so powerful.

And I reminded them of this all the time, but especially at the end of my workshop on identifying their true big dreams and getting below the surface of the things that are holding them back from those big dreams and saying them out loud, was to remember how they felt in this moment.

Because at this moment, there are no distractions. There are no kids calling your name. There are no drop-offs that you need to adhere to. There isn't cleaning that needs to be done.

When you're at retreat, you are you – a different version of you that you very, very rarely get to tap into.

During that workshop I was running about big dreams and picturing what you really wanted for your business and where you wanted to go – my mind was totally blank.

Totally blank.

I was coming off of a really intense week with my ADHD assessment. Everything felt top of mind, and this was a really big career milestone moment for me. I was really focused on facilitating and hosting.

So I thought, you know, I'm not thinking of big dreams in this workshop because I'm facilitating it.

Now, a couple hours later, it was Libby's turn to run a workshop. And her workshop was a follow-up, and it was about setting tangible action steps to make sure that these big dreams don't get left behind and that we take some steps forward to implementing them.

So I thought, okay, I want to participate in this. So I'm going to use some of the downtime to do my own workshop – figure out what my big goals are, my big dreams, so that I can sit down in this workshop and start doing it.

I start journaling a little bit. Nothing's really coming to mind.

I was looking around the room. There's 10 women riveted on her. Listening. Writing down notes.

And I just stopped. And I recorded the moment.

Because in that moment, I realized:

I don't want more.

I am living my big dream.

This is it. I've arrived.

And that is honestly a crazy feeling.

It still feels surreal to be feeling this way.

To feel so settled.

I just feel like my whole life, I've been climbing uphill and uphill and uphill. And now I'm like, I'm good.

And I might not be good forever. But I've been thinking now for a few months – you know, when my kids go to school and my days open up, I don't want to fill it with more work. I want to keep my work level the same and let the other parts of me expand into those time chunks that are opening up.

I love what I'm doing.

I love being so high touch with all of my clients and using my creative energy and my problem solving and my solutions and all of those things that I'm so good at – on their businesses.

Of course, my business is going to grow and my goals might change. But as of right now, I truly don't have a bigger goal that I'm aiming for.

I'm happy.

I love doing what I'm doing.

And it's all about refinement.

And making it work as easily and as best as possible.

I want to reassure you that you can get there. Because if you had told me this three months ago, six months ago, three years ago – I absolutely would never have believed you.

I thought that entrepreneurship was always striving for the next thing. Was always reaching for the stars and pivoting and never being satisfied and doing one thing.

But I'm content – a feeling I've truly never had.

And I just want to sit with it for a bit.

My whole life I've wanted to be a mom. And I'm here.

My whole lie I've wanted to have a ulfilled lie. And I'm here.

And I love my business.

I love my clients.

And I love the life that it allows me.

It's just such a great feeling.

And I am so grateful for everyone who came in for the retreat and was so vulnerable and was so open with everything that happened and all of the experiences that were shared and the laughs that were had and the tears that were shed and the dreams that were shared.

All of that allowed me to be super present in the moment and just acknowledge that this is enough – because it is so meaningful.

And I'm really excited for this next phase of business where my focus is not on expansion and more and more and more.

My focus is on refinement. My focus is on making sure the people that come into my programs are the right people for the program. That they're going to get the results. That they're going to have the experience and contribute to the experience that I'm looking to create – which is that energy and excitement and momentum and progress of expanding, pivoting, scaling the business that you truly love.

And I'm really excited to see that happen.

And to watch it unfold.

just in case

— Appendix A —

Trigger Warnings

This section is here for readers who need or want a full list of sensitive content included in this memoir. Please feel free to use this information to care for your mental health as you read. Some readers may prefer to skip chapters, read with support, or take breaks – all of those are valid.

You're the expert on your own boundaries.

Please take care as you read.

Your safety and wellbeing matter more than finishing every chapter. Skip what you need to. Close the book and come back later. Or not at all. You're allowed to protect your peace.

Suicidal Ideation and Depression

→ Chapter 11, 13, 44, 45

Child Medical Emergency

→ Chapter 39

Still Birth and NICU

→ Chapter 33

— Appendix B —

References

1 Rula Health. (2024). *ADHD and negative thoughts: Understanding and challenging your inner critic.* Retrieved from https://www.rula.com/blog/adhd-negative-thoughts

2 Relational Psych. (2023). *The emotional toll of ADHD: Exploring mental health impacts.* Retrieved from https://www.relationalpsych.group/articles/the-emotional-toll-of-adhd-exploring-mental-health-impacts

3 ADDitude Magazine. (2024). *What is executive function disorder?* Retrieved from https://www.additudemag.com/what-is-executive-function-disorder

4 Verywell Mind. (2024). *What is executive dysfunction in ADHD?* Retrieved from https://www.verywellmind.com/what-is-executive-dysfunction-in-adhd-5213034

5 Cleveland Clinic. (2023). *Executive dysfunction.* Retrieved from https://my.clevelandclinic.org/health/symptoms/23224-executive-dysfunction

6 Isaac, V. (2024). *Arousal dysregulation and executive dysfunction in ADHD. Frontiers in Psychiatry,* [online]. Retrieved from https://www.frontiersin.org/journals/psychiatry/articles/10.3389/fpsyt.2023.1336040

7 Turkoglu, C., Okyaz, F., & Arslan, E. (2025). *The relationship between ADHD and autonomic regulation: A pupillometry-based study. Springer.* Retrieved from https://link.springer.com/article/10.1007/s44411-025-00185-7

8 Cleveland Clinic. (2025). *Hyperarousal: What it is, causes, symptoms & treatment.* Retrieved from https://my.clevelandclinic.org/health/symptoms/hyperarousal

9 Healthline. (2024). *ADHD and limerence: What's the connection?* Retrieved from https://www.healthline.com/health/adhd/adhd-limerence

10 Attachment Project. (2024). *ADHD and limerence.* Retrieved from https://www.attachmentproject.com/love/limerence/adhd

11 ADDitude Magazine. (2023). *What is dyscalculia? Overview and symptom breakdown.* Retrieved from https://www.additudemag.com/what-is-dyscalculia-overview-and-symptom-breakdown

12 Wikipedia. (2024). *Dyscalculia.* Retrieved from https://en.wikipedia.org/wiki/Dyscalculia

13 Medical News Today. (2023). *Object permanence and ADHD.* Retrieved from https://www.medicalnewstoday.com/articles/object-permanence-adhd

14 NAPA Center. (2023). *ADHD and object permanence.* Retrieved from https://napacenter.org/object-permanence-adhd

15 The Mini ADHD Coach. (2023). *Object permanence in ADHD.* Retrieved from https://www.theminiadhdcoach.com/living-with-adhd/object-permanence-adhd

16 Meinzer, M. C., et al. (2019). *ADHD and depression in adulthood: Clinical implications. Psychiatry Research,* 270, 110–116. Retrieved from https://pmc.ncbi.nlm.nih.gov/articles/PMC6630926

17 American Psychological Association. (2024). *Managing emotional dysregulation in ADHD.* Retrieved from https://www.apa.org/monitor/2024/04/adhd-managing-emotion-dysregulation

18 ADDitude Magazine. (2024). *Rejection sensitive dysphoria and ADHD.* Retrieved from https://www.additudemag.com/rejection-sensitive-dysphoria-adhd-emotional-dysregulation

19 Relational Psych. (2023). *Understanding rejection sensitive dysphoria.* Retrieved from https://www.relationalpsych.group/articles/understanding-rejection-sensitive-dysphoria-and-its-connection-to-adhd

20 Verywell Health. (2024). *Rejection sensitive dysphoria.* Retrieved from https://www.verywellhealth.com/rejection-sensitive-dysphoria-8728800

21 Relational Psych. (2023). *ADHD and sensory processing*. Retrieved from https://www.relation-alpsych.group/articles/the-link-between-adhd-and-sensory-processing-how-to-manage-sensory-overload

22 Verywell Mind. (2024). *Hyperfixation in ADHD and autism*. Retrieved from https://www.very-wellmind.com/hyperfixation-in-adhd-and-autism-7693647

23 ADHD Advisor. (2023). *ADHD and hyperfixation*. Retrieved from https://www.adhdadvisor.org/learn/adhd-hyperfixation

24 Choosing Therapy. (2024). *ADHD hyperfixation*. Retrieved from https://www.choosingtherapy.com/adhd-hyperfixation

25 The Mini ADHD Coach. (2022). *How your ADHD brain is responsible for intrusive thoughts*. Retrieved from https://www.theminiadhdcoach.com/living-with-adhd/adhd-intrusive-thoughts

26 Lane, S. J. (2019). *Sensory over-responsivity as an added dimension in ADHD*. *Frontiers in Integrative Neuroscience*. Retrieved from https://www.frontiersin.org/articles/10.3389/fnint.2019.00040/full

27 Shaw, P. (2014). *Emotional dysregulation and attention-deficit/hyperactivity disorder*. Retrieved from https://www.ncbi.nlm.nih.gov/pmc/articles/PMC4282137/

28 FocusBear. (2024). *Harnessing co-regulation strategies for ADHD management*. Retrieved from https://www.focusbear.io/blog-post/harnessing-co-regulation-strategies-for-adhd-management

29 Child Mind Institute. (2025). *What is co-regulation?* Retrieved from https://childmind.org/article/what-is-co-regulation/

31 Sedgwick, J. A., Merwood, A., & Asherson, P. (2019). The positive aspects of attention deficit hyperactivity disorder: A qualitative investigation of successful adults with ADHD. *ADHD Attention Deficit and Hyperactivity Disorders*, 11, 241–253. https://doi.org/10.1007/s12402-018-0277-6

32 White, H. A., & Shah, P. (2016). Scope of divergent thinking in adults with attention-deficit/hyperactivity disorder. *Creativity Research Journal*, 28(3), 275–282. https://doi.org/10.1080/10400419.2016.1195655

33 Healio. (2022). *Creativity, flexibility among strengths in people with ADHD*. Retrieved from https://www.healio.com/news/psychiatry/20220517/creativity-flexibility-among-strengths-in-people-with-adhd

34 Quinn, P. O., & Madhoo, M. (2014). A review of attention-deficit/hyperactivity disorder in women and girls: Uncovering this hidden diagnosis. *The Primary Care Companion for CNS Disorders*, 16(3). https://doi.org/10.4088/PCC.13r01596

35 Nadeau, K. G., Littman, E., & Quinn, P. (2020). *Understanding women with ADHD*. Silver Spring, MD: Advantage Books.

36 ADDitude Magazine. (2023). *ADHD in women: Symptoms, diagnosis & treatment*. Retrieved from https://www.additudemag.com/adhd-in-women-symptoms-diagnosis-treatment

1994

— Thank You —

Acknowledgments

I don't even know where to start. So, in the great words of Maria von Trapp, "Let's go back to the very beginning."

Mom, Dad, I'd literally not be here if not for you, but I also wouldn't have written this book. Thank you for looking after my babies with so much love and care that I am at peace when I'm away from them at events and retreats that make my business so much more than a paycheck. Thank you for pushing me away from the original book concept. Thank you for always loving me "despite." I love you, Mom. I love you, Dad.

To my brother, and his family, thank you. You see me, you accept me, and you don't hold outbursts and emotions against me. I love you, Michael. I love you, Keeley. I love you, Z and L.

To the people in this book, thank you. Whether it was a reason or a season, I wouldn't be here without you. In this book I hope you feel reflected, and I hope you eel respected.

To the women who made this book happen: Ellen, my editor; Alana, my photographer; Samantha and Simar, my publishers. Thank you. For the safety to exist, for the permission to express.

To my therapist, "June." Thank you for listening to me. Thank you for teaching me. Thank you for saying the same things over and over until I start to believe them. Thank you for not "firing" me when I was masking and everything seemed fine. Thanks for seeing the good in me, and making me see it, too.

To my kids, who I pined for and would die for, thank you. You made me who I am. You are everything. I love you, Andrew. I love you, Daisy. I love you, James.

To my husband, who met me where I was, and stays with me as I grow, thank you. For being the rock, the voice of reason, the reality check. I said it in our vows, and I'll say it again: I promise to work every day to make you proud as a woman, wife, and mother. I love you, Coconut.

To you, the reader who picked up this book. Thank you for giving me this space in your brain and in your life. Thank you for spending this time in my memories. I hope you know you are spectacular. I hope you know you are exactly on track. I hope you know you are not too much. You are, and always will be, just enough.

Thank you.

xx Mariah

— Thank You (Again)—

JUST A FREE GIFT

Hello, it's me.

(Mariah, the author you've been hanging out with for the last 300ish pages).

While fiction books simply *need* to be a paperback in my world, I've been embracing the e-book life lately. So, I'm just gonna go ahead and give it to you! Scan the QR code for your copy and my robots will email it to you faster than you can pick a song in your car.

You rock, don't ever change.

Ps. Wanna do me a solid? I'd love a review. On Amazon, GoodReads, or even just a message on IG, I wrote this for you, and I'd love to know what you think... but more so, I'd love to know how you feel.

xx Mariah

— About the Author —

Mariah Scrivens

Mariah Scrivens is a marketing strategist, writer, and former teacher who built two multi—six figure businesses from her kitchen table with three kids under two and a brain that refused to rest. After a late-in-life ADHD diagnosis, she stopped trying to fix herself and started lis-tening instead – rebuilding her life and business around her energy, not her ego.

Known for her honest storytelling and sharp strategy, Mariah is also the founder of Sprinkle Toast. A boutique agency that gets marketing off your desk. When she's not working, writing, or chasing a quiet corner of the house, you can find her re-watching Love is Blind (season one) and ordering the same Starbucks drink she's had since 2012 (dirty chai tea latte).

Just a Bit Much is her first book – but not her last.

www.mariahscrivens.com

@mariahmakesithappen

mariah@mariahscrivens.com

www.ingramcontent.com/pod-product-compliance
Lightning Source LLC
Chambersburg PA
CBHW021216130626
46554CB00004B/1247